THE WAYFARER

ANDY KIND

Rowley Wise

The Wayfarer
By Andy Kind

ISBN: 9781068257100
First Published in Great Britain 2025
By Rowley Wise.

Cover by Amy Borrell

Find out more about Andy at his website: www.andykind.co.uk.

To Mum, Dad and Gemma,
who have been constant and faithful co-travellers
on the longest journey I've ever taken.

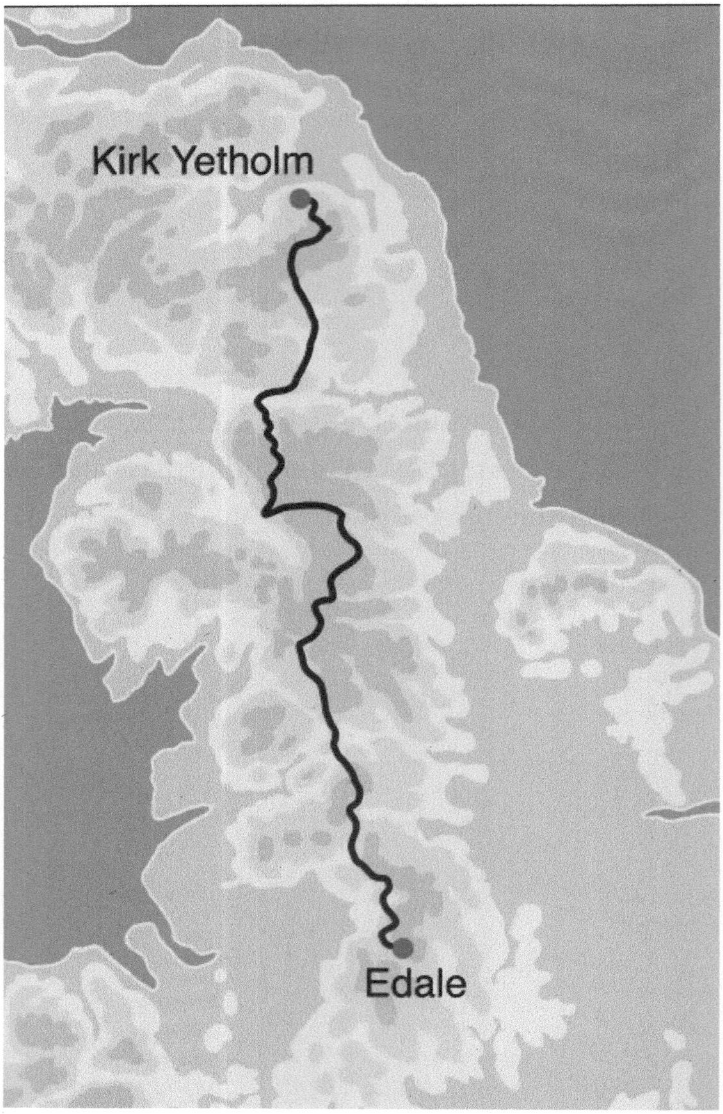
Kirk Yetholm
Edale

Come, birds of spring
And sing.
Sing your song;
Bang that gong
That tells frigid winter, 'move along'.
His icy grip is strong…
But ice melts at the sound of singing,
At the dawn of arm-swinging: that joy-bringing singing that sees us springing back into life.
Despair is winter's husband; Redemption, spring's wife.
So sing. From high in your nest, just do your best;
Your music has never left us unimpressed.
There's this thing called Hope to which we cling; that elusive thing that takes death and removes its sting.
Frozen grief's a bitter pill.
So if you will, Birds of Spring, come…
And sing.

The following things that happen actually happened.
That's what happens when you let things just happen.
Andy Kind

CHAPTER 1
DELUSIONS

It was today.

It always is today, of course, and isn't that just one of the more bittersweet facets to humanity: your tomorrow hasn't arrived yet and you certainly can't get back your yesterday. Still, you will always have today. And it was today.

The idea had been renting a room in my mind for the best part of two decades, but it had chosen a crisp pandemic January morning to finally come knocking. Desperate for company of any kind, and turning aside from my study of what I shall always count as a very promising moustache, I opened up and bade the thought enter.

I tell stories for a living. The joy of a good story is the seeing yourself in it; the problem with a pandemic is that everyone's story becomes the same, like a bag of Pick 'n' Mix left to warp into one coagulated and unappetising gloop. The hopefulness that usually came a-wassailing at New Year was in bed with the virus, the extended winter lockdown ensuring that Christmas 2020's most given gift had been cabin fever.

If I'm honest – and distance always makes honesty easier, doesn't it? – over the course of those interminable lockdowns I had slowly shut down. The forced retreat indoors from the creeping spectre of Covid-19 had starved me not only of my community but of my purpose. I was a comedian in a pandemic; a tree stripped of its leaves. By Lockdown 2 (the sequel is never as good) I was listing 'Get in/out of the bath' as two separate items on my daily to-do list, sometimes only completing one of them. Self-care had eroded, self-esteem crumbling helplessly after it, and both had been replaced by an uncomfortable, unwelcome culture of self-critique. Maybe it was the same for you?

Under that sort of reflexive microscope you start to feel your way around your being with a scrutiny that you hadn't really tried before: touching upon those places where your heart has become encrusted, your mind encysted, where even your soul is feverish. You walk inquisitively down the corridors of your mind because there's nothing else to do, and you find there a labyrinth of locked doors – locked from the outside, by you – in which are stuffed hidden shame and crushed hope, broken expectations and raw honesty. Instead of dusting off the keys to deep self-appraisal though, the urge is to simply build yourself a new corridor, a garish extension to your mind palace, which leads you away and further away from those self-sealed doors – anything, really, to prevent you stumbling into a dusty alcove and finding a mirror that reflects the very thing you're trying not to see: yourself as you actually are. As Friedrich Nietzsche says, "When you look into an abyss, the abyss also looks into you."

The whole book won't be like this, I promise.

Enough was enough! Something must be done! The naval-gazing hermit life was not for me and I desired to tell a new story. Actually, I already had a new story to tell but I needed another one to keep it company. It had want of a travelling companion, I decided – and don't we all?

'I'm going to walk the Pennine Way,' I declared from the comfort of my Chesterfield armchair. Nobody responded, but in fairness I do say this sort of thing quite a lot. Some people, blessed as they are with neurotypical brains, are natural finishers; others are eager beginners. For my part, I'm more of a conceiver: excitedly splashing about in the ideation of some epic dream or scheme, projecting and future-casting my undoubted success in the matter onto a silver screen somewhere, so that, by the time I finally come to set to work on the thing itself, I'm definitely exhausted and almost certainly bored. It's not that I never complete anything – if you're reading this then the book is either published or I'm dead and you're sorting tearfully through my possessions, in which case could you please finish this for me because I think it has a lot of potential. But I'm not known for crossing that many finish lines, and I was ready for that to change.

It was time to get fit and to get *out;* to binge once more on life and adrenaline, and to go looking for those old friends Joy and Hope who had been self-isolating along with the rest of us. Maybe they lived in the hills?

In his masterful book *A Philosophy of Walking,* Frederic Gros says: "Boredom is immobility of the body confronted with emptiness of the mind…with the body active, the mind is no longer affected by its lassitude."

That was settled then. The hermit needed to become a pilgrim – or, at the very least, a pedestrian! With life feeling like such a non-place, there would be something healthy about just going from place to place. More than that, in each person's life there must be a point at which loss stops winning and victory stops coming in second. Sick of being a beaten finalist in my own existence therefore, for only the third time in my life I would take the path of *most resistance,* and have a jolly good adventure along the way. The walking community has contained all sorts through the ages: the vagabond, the ranger, the travelling showmen, the witchfinders, the flaneur. I would add myself and my moustache to that merry band, and commit to climbing the equivalent of one and a half Everests in just over two weeks.

The January sky was flushed with crimson as I laced up my trainers, set my Strava app to 'Run' mode and started out towards Crow Lane, a steep secluded road that climbs from Chesterfield's centre up towards the outskirts of the old market town. I was raring to go, my mind captivated by thoughts of Yorkshire dales and Scottish peaks. Those thoughts were replaced by less germane ones when, less than 1km from my front door, I heard my right hamstring pop like a balloon signalling the end of a poorly-planned and really rubbish party. Peeling myself off the tarmac I limped back home, head hung, moustache inconsolable, wondering whether the person who invented the phrase 'Don't try to run before you can walk' had also suffered from curmudgeonly hamstrings and a complete lack of self-awareness.

What made it worse was that I didn't even need to run. All I needed to do was walk: one foot in front of another, one step at a time, right foot then left. Lesson learned. I would need some time to heal before I ventured out again, and the journey ahead would be painful and gruelling, but, when you think about it, all real progress is trapped behind discomfort.

That was January. But now it was today.

"I have traced a path which I will follow.
When my advance begins, nothing will be able to stop it."
Immanuel Kant.

January 31st 2009

I had brought her to Edale to propose. I had planned it carefully. We would walk into the hills along the start of the Pennine Way (the longest footpath in Britain, so if you're planning on starting a long journey together… are you with me?), admire the view, then wander back to the Norman church where I had arranged for a friend with a guitar to appear like the Shopkeeper in Mr Benn, and there I would propose. Romantic yet dignified and free from cliché – and above all, somewhere that, if she said no, I could escape into the hills to live as a wildman.

I parked the car in Edale village, we donned our walking boots and I packed a small rucksack with the only items I had that might be useful for hill walking: a small length of rope and an apple. I also had a whistle, in case we fell down a ravine or a herd of sheep needed me to step in as referee. *Be prepared*, as Lord Baden Powell would have said. I had disrupted not one but four football matches walking back with it from *The Great Outdoors*.

The chill in the air felt quintessentially English, exhibiting the chastising sternness of an Edwardian childminder. Off we went, passing The Old Nag's Head pub where, all being well, we would later eat lunch, and out towards Kinder Scout.

All was proceeding according to plan. We walked a couple of miles, stopped for a flask of tea, retched at the sight of a sheep carcass, continued. I was starting to relish the imminent drama, but then, when we reached the point at which I'd planned to about-turn and head back to Edale, I tried to text my guitar friend. I had no signal, and no way of confirming our arrival time.

I needed to move. Snatching a half-full beaker of hot tea from her hand and burning her mildly in the process, I packed away the flask, hurled the apple core at a live sheep and put the erroneous rope back in the bag. Then, trying to maintain some modicum of composure, I said, 'Shall we head back?' and started off down the track without waiting for a reply. She looked confused, bewildered and in pain from the scalding hot liquid I'd splashed on her. She got to her feet and started coming after me, with purpose rather than compliance.

'What are you doing? Why are we heading back? This is my day as well, you know. Why did you pour tea on me?'

I didn't possess the answers she sought.

'We'll be late for lunch!' I slung at her in an over-the-shoulder way as I galumphed off horizonwards.

'Andy!! Stop running away. We've come all this way and I was enjoying it, but all you seem to care about is yourself. This relationship won't work if it's just you in the centre of it.'

Oh no!

All I could do was keep on moving back towards the village, skimming placatory, half-mumbled sentences in her direction. But the closer we got to Ground Zero, the longer she went without an explanation for my waywardness, and the greater the chance therefore of me getting back to the church and proposing to a girlfriend I no longer had!

I strode onwards, recklessly trying to get back to the village, anxious not to get too far ahead of the woman I loved and upon whom I had inflicted third degree tea burns.

'Andy, I feel sick,' she moaned.

Edale village and its church spire were on the horizon, moving closer.

'A lovely pub lunch will cure what ails ya!' I responded, sounding like a mediaeval cretin.

Finally, finally, we re-entered the village and limped past The Nag's Head, totally dishevelled and out-of-breath. (I have cleverly edited the part where I failed to navigate a stile and fell painfully on my bottom, hurting both my pride and my bottom.)

'Ooh, I could do with a sit down,' I said. 'Could you do with a sit down, I know I could – let's sit down.'

'The pub's not even open yet, you weird man. What is wrong with you?' She shook her head ruefully, like she'd been cast in a shampoo advert but the fee wasn't great and her heart wasn't really in it.

'Well,' she said with a tired huff, 'we might as well go and sit on that bench by the church.'

'Yeah, OK, good idea, great!' I said excitedly. She hadn't broken up with me. Now she was offering to go and sit where I needed her to sit. This was happening.

As we slumped on to the church bench and I tried to throw her off any possible scent by talking a lot about scampi, I realised that I couldn't see my guitar friend. To make matters worse, the landlord of The Nag's Head unbolted the pub's front door and erected an A-board displaying the daily specials.

'Right, shall we go and have some lunch then?' she suggested.

'Erm… I'm not sure I'm that hungry.'

'What?! You've just spent 10 minutes straight talking about scampi. I've never known anyone talk about scampi uninterrupted for that period of time – I didn't even know it was possible.'

'Oh well, you know, you can talk yourself out of these things, can't you…'

'What is wrong with you?'

Then I heard a guitar.

'Ooh, what's that?'

A red-haired woman came strolling nonchalantly round the side of the church in full minstrel attire, strumming away and saving my scampi (bacon). I have never been more relieved to see someone with a lute. I could have married my friend at that moment – which would have been woefully counter-productive, I admit.

I got down on one knee.

'I'm sorry I scalded you with hot tea. And thanks for not laughing at me when I hurt my bottom. And will you marry me?'

I had taken the eloquence and poetry of a simple proposal by the hand, led it into an alley and kicked it brutally to death. In none of the reveries in which I'd imagined this going down had I ever conceived of prefacing 'Will you marry me?' with 'I hurt my bottom'.

But she said yes.

Day 1
Edale to Crowden
16.5 miles

"'Take the Adventure, heed the call, now ere the irrevocable moment passes!' 'Tis but a banging of the door behind you, a blithesome step forward, and you are out of the old life and into the new!"

Kenneth Grahame, Wind in the Willows

"The true adventurer goes forth uncalculating to meet and greet unknown fate."

O. Henry, The Green Door

CHAPTER 2

IN THE BEGINNING WAS THE ROAD

Monday 24th May 2021, 9:17am

It happened this way.

I was sitting on a bench in the Derbyshire village of Edale, looking up at the church of the *Holy and Undivided Trinity* and wincing. Above and beyond her spire the Pennines stood glowering, dwarfing the feeble steeple, as dogmatic and uncompromising as any caricatured religious figure. Worse still, they seemed to be glowering directly at me.

The air in the Hope Valley that morning had a strawberries-and-cream quaintness to it, a spring-infused breeze crossing lawns and hedgerows like the local parson making his rounds. The church gardener, cheerful and spindly, was negotiating with his petrol mower, plotting the decapitation of the spearwort and white clover populations that had settled so precociously on *his land.*

I smiled at the gardener and he nodded back, then I snapped a photo of the church and sent it shuttling out of the valley: 'Good morning, Mummy, Alice and Heidi! Here Daddy goes – nervous but excited!' I also sent a picture of my hefty rucksack, hanging from the rear pouch of which was Alan. Alan is my friend and, more pertinently, a novelty Christmas doorstop in the guise of a fox who cost me £12.99 from Dunelm Mill in 2019 – back on old earth. In practical terms he would prove as useful as the 'g' in lasagna on this walk, but I knew the plans I had for him. Here's his full backstory in case it's of interest to you.

When the first lockdown hit and my gigs and preaches shifted online with all human interaction obliterated, I searched for something – anything – to imbue my talks with the idea of connection and repartee. At the back of the store cupboard I found Alan, his small inscrutable face poking out of an Aldi bag-for-life, gold and silver festive streamers wrapped around him, making him look fabulous.

'I need you, Alan, in my darkest hour,' I told him. And so I started using him as a trope in my recorded talks, initially as quirky scenery for the viewers, but the rule of Chekhov's gun is that if there's a revolver on the table in Act 1 then it needs to be fired in Act 3, and so Alan's rise to prominence was as inexorable as it was a sign of me flirting with a nervous breakdown. Before long I was building his character, developing his skill-set, making him the star of little pre-recorded vignettes. When the 'Eat Out to Help Out' scheme came into force and I started to see people in the flesh again, 'How's Alan?' was usually the first thing I heard from the friends I hadn't seen in months, followed up quite quickly by, 'Do you think you might be having a nervous breakdown?'

'He's fine and quite possibly.'

Alan became so synonymous with my pandemic life that, as a symbol of the new freedom which lockdown easing was bringing, I had chosen to bring him with me on this long, long, long walk.

'Nice to get back to your roots I should think, Alan? Back into nature.'

My roots are a factory just outside Bedford, sire, I imagined him saying.

With that inscrutable face now poking from a rear rucksack pouch – minus the streamers because this was no time to celebrate – Alan and I sat together under a crystal blue sky, staring down the road towards the Nag's Head pub and, a long way beyond that, somewhere over a rainbow maybe, to Kirk Yetholm, a tiny village just inside the Scottish border where successful Pennine wayfarers reach their journey's glorious end.

I had started this journey to Scotland twice before. Due to atrocious foreplanning and undiagnosed ADHD, I had never got past Malham. "Desire without knowledge is not good," reads *Proverbs 19*, "how much more will hasty feet miss the way." This time would be different though, I repeated to myself. I had trained well, prepared properly and my footwear didn't read 'Made in Kafiristan' (which I'm pretty sure is the fictional country invented by Rudyard Kipling). I was also, however, about 40, which didn't seem fair and is the age at which people stop calling it tragic if you die. 'Hey ho, he had a good run,' they would say when my breathless corpse was found at the top of the first gentle climb.

'You're not old, Daddy,' Alice had told me the week before I left.

'That's kind of you, love, but I am. I'm the guy who lost the city of Atlantis in the first place.'

I was to be joined for the first half of this day of days by my good friends, Jon and Phil. Jon was a friend from church, who claimed he was acting on behalf of Derbyshire Council and ensuring I left the county without causing undue trouble. Phil is an ultra fell runner who just wanted to make me feel old and sloth-like. He would have no trouble there.

Jon met me under the spire of the church.

'Is it a bad sign that I've found you sitting in a graveyard, Andy?' He gave me a guileless smile and scratched his tightly trimmed, Nordic-coloured beard.

'That remains to be seen, doesn't it?' I replied, handing him a pair of waterproof trousers which had caused my rucksack to overflow.

'Thanks Andy, but I've actually brought my own trousers. Maria checked with me before I left the house that I was wearing some.'

I laughed detachedly, then flicked my head in the direction of the bench I'd just been sitting on.

'I proposed to my wife on that bench, Jon.'

'Did you really, Andy?'

'I did… Let's go for a walk.'

I hefted my rucksack, clumsily slipped my arms through the padded shoulder straps, readjusted the height of the lumbar pads, buckled it up at the sternum, tightened a cord or two – and I was ready.

'Oh, hello, Alan,' Jon said on noticing the bepouched fox. 'How is he?'

'He's fine, thank you.'

'Good, good. Do you think you might be…'

'Quite possibly, Jon, yes.'

'OK. Maria just wanted me to check.'

I halted under the archway to glance back at the church. At *that* bench. I wanted this to be the final time I looked back for the next fortnight. I smiled maybe, said something like a prayer perhaps. Then I walked out of the graveyard.

CHAPTER 3

OVER THE HILLS AND FAR AWAY

We ambled through Edale village, up the lane past gritstone cottages towards the Nag's Head, the clanking and clunking and swishing of my gear providing a stylised musical score to the opening scene of what I hoped would be an epic adventure-quest for the modern age – whilst fearing it may end up more like the Coen Brother's *No Country For Old Men,* where the main character dies off-screen before the end of Act 2.

The official start line of the Pennine Way is nothing more than a little hole in the dry-stone walling. It's very easy to miss – and back in 2018 I did in fact miss it, walking quarter of a mile down the adjacent track to a farmhouse, getting lost before I had even begun and reprimanded by a woman hanging out massive bras from a laundry basket. It's odd in a way that the mother of all trails is so humble and non-descript in her beginnings. There's no golden archway, no fanfare. It's pleasantly unsensational when you think about it, but the cold open meant I would need to conjure my own sense of drama. I made Jon pose for photos by the start line while I took a series of deep thespian breaths, gently stretching the hamstring which had torn only four months ago and which was now strapped in the finest lycra cladding that Millett's provided.

'You're taking a lot of deep breaths for someone about to go for a walk,' Jon said. 'Is there a scuba diving section I've not been made aware of?'

'Yes, did Maria not pack your trunks?'

'Pass me that walking pole, and when I lift it we'll go.'

I handed Jon one of the two fibreglass rods I had brought with me to aid knee support and to stab a cow if the occasion called for it. Jon held the pole in front of me like a car park barrier, then raised it into the air with a flourish and a shout of, 'And they're off!' And I began to walk very slowly towards Scotland.

I had crossed a border into the unknown, and I was refusing to go home until I'd crossed another one.

The first hour of the Pennine Way is a joy – a kind of conciliatory honeymoon period for newlytreads. You follow a little streambed out onto open pasture then undulate slowly along a flagstone path, up and down tussocky banks with Derbyshire's pastoral hills generously arrayed on all sides, the odd clump of hawthorn trees adding texture to the scene. There's a load of sheep muck, too. It's the sort of opening sally that could convince you walking the Pennine Way was a good idea. It's like mastering a new computer game, only to discover that the difficulty is set to 'Amateur' and the levels go up through 'Still a Bit Rubbish', 'Intermediate', 'Grisly Veteran' and finally, 'Get a ******* job, mate, you don't have a pension to fall back on'. That misplaced self-confidence is soon to change, though.

After an hour of walking, having descended through the straggly hamlet of Upper Booth and been told off by a dog, we reached a quaint packhorse bridge marking the start of a climb known as Jacob's Ladder, the second steepest climb of the entire 270-mile trail and an absolute swine of a thing. It's very much the door supervisor for the Pennine Way – it could do with a 'You must be this tall to ride' sign at the foot of it. Faced with this first major incline my pack suddenly felt heavy and unwieldy and I realised I would need to lighten my load. I wordlessly handed Jon a spare jumper; he wordlessly handed me a Mars bar in return.

'I wouldn't like to be a pregnant lady,' I said.

'At the foot of this slope, Andy, or just in general?'

I had confused myself with the comment and so I perched on a swell of tussocky grass and ate my chocolate in silence, studying a scanty stream as it scintillated silver-white along its guided tour of the valley. If I looked anxious to Jon (and I know I did look anxious because he actually said you look a bit anxious and that was the clue) it was because of this: I hadn't climbed any hills since I tore my hamstring. I had walked an average of 30 km per week for the past couple of months, experimenting with different loads on my back – from the contents of my sock drawer to old university textbooks to the smaller of my children – but a lot of my training had been carried out around Sherwood Forest, whose paths are flat and well-maintained and where renegade bands of archers are nowhere near as prevalent as the stories would have you believe. I had hoped that just grinding the miles out would build up the muscle's resistance levels, and that might be true, but I didn't know for sure. The hamstring had ruptured on an incline less pronounced than this, and my worry was that I'd get halfway up the ladder and my right thigh would just disintegrate like a homemade biscuit.

I started to climb: one foot at a time, my legs moving at the speed of a sundial, as though ascending through a minefield, constantly monitoring the inner weights and balances of my body, expecting at any moment to malfunction and leave Jon no choice but to carry out a mercy killing. The ascent was long and arduous, my calves shivering seismically with each step. Flagstones gave way to a winding uneven path that angled demonically upwards, and the wind circling predatorially as we left the valley's protective shield.

'Even angels would need a breather up and down this ladder,' Jon said, though where he found the spare breath I have no idea, because I was steadily deflating. Both pack and ribcage felt heavier than they should have done and my breathing was the sound of a surgeon's saw mid-amputation. If walking was soup, I concluded, then I was a fork.

But this was only thumbnail pain, a small picture of what was really to come. What made it worse was the sight down in the valley of a blurred figure moving towards us at great haste, translucent and unfathomable like the nameless terror in an M.R. James story. Up the terraced hillside it skipped, defying physical laws, lithe and sprightly and Legolas. My ability to take in oxygen was currently set to 'Still a Bit Rubbish' and every expansion of my diaphragm was like trying to work an old water pump in the middle of a village green, which bore a small plaque that read: "This pump is purely decorative. It no longer pumps water. All the best."

The blur flew up the steep path like a plastic bag caught on the wind. In no time at all it reached us, stopped, and said: 'How you doing, Andy?'

It was Phil, my ultra-running, fat-shaming friend.

'Stop it,' I replied, raking out the words as though it was my first time using this mouth.

'Stop what?'

'It doesn't play well, you know, this… (I flapped a hand at his nauseatingly lithe frame) this superhero card you keep using.'

'Oh… sorry,' said Phil, looking a bit downcast that he'd come all the way from Leeds to offer moral support and was instantly being abused.

'Apology rejected,' I replied, and to this day I stand by it. It was his own fault for turning up with about 3% body fat. Not for the first time in adulthood I had massively overestimated my required winter fat reserves, and even after months of training I was still more voluptuous than anyone who isn't a swimsuit model or a bottle of perfume would want to be. Phil on the other hand looked like he'd been punished with an angle grinder. 'There are no straight lines in nature,' my old art teacher Mr. Baker loved to say and I now understand that he was either lying or senile, because Phil was a human diamond. If his body was a temple, mine was a soft play where a toddler had just been sick in the ball pool.

We all stopped for a rest at the top of Jacob's Ladder, knowing that the hardest climb in the first week of the walk was over and done with. Knowing, too, that the ascent had been much harder than I expected and that I still had about 14 miles to go on Day 1, when really I was ready for a nap and a bath and maybe a sequel nap. I lay down to die on a gale-smoothed slab and let the mothering wind flannel me with its chill.

'Just remember,' said Phil, 'that it doesn't always get worse.'

I was still annoyed with Phil for being incredibly fit, so I just said, 'Yes, it does,' and stared off towards Chesterfield.

There is at least an aesthetic reward for completing Jacob's Ladder, for we were now up onto the shoulders of Kinder Scout, the highest point in the Peak District and the world's largest peat bog showroom. More on that shortly but, Oh!, how very English England seemed from up here; how very splendid! Gazing over the dales and peaks, how stirred one might be, high above the waterline of tribal politics and sniping social media, to see a Union flag furling and unfurling in the heaving British air, the breeze suffused with scents of Elgar, the hillsides brailled with rumours of Austen. Drive west for an hour and you'll be in Wedgewood country; swing east and you'll find the resting place of George Stephenson, the father of railways. Down amongst the cobbles of northern England the bones of empire and poverty crunch unavoidably beneath one's feet, but here, atop hills where deceit and despair carry no coin, the spring of purity continues to quench the thirsty drinker. Whatever others encrypt into the phrase 'Proud to be British' – and it galls me that many modern advocates have about six neck tattoos – up here, wind-thrashed and exhausted albeit, I was contentedly an Englishman.

Having refilled our air supplies – during the process of which I, very unlike a proper Englishman, retched three times and sicked up some Mars bar – we wended our way along Kinder Low through a mouth of gritstone teeth towards Kinder Downfall, a modest but impressive waterfall, the number of whose kind is higher than you might expect along the length of the trail. Moss and bilberry skirted the path and off to the left the view stretched out in lush greens towards Manchester, with Kinder reservoir winking chummily in the late-morning sunshine. Oh yes, that reminds me. One thing I do want to say before we go any further is this: I shan't be using the word 'dappled' at any point in this narrative. While it's a lovely word – up there with 'lagoon' and 'salubrious' in my book – it has been hijacked in recent times by peat-bog-standard writers who use it in the first paragraph of their novels to add a sense of atmosphere, and quite frankly I've had enough of it.

Nobody really knows why Kinder Scout is called Kinder Scout. I don't wish to go full Ron Burgundy here but scholars maintain that the translation was lost hundreds of years ago. Specifically, the place is mentioned in the 1086 Domesday Survey as "Chendre", whilst Phil was able to tell me (although I was deliberately unlistening) that 'Scout' is from the Norse word 'skute' and means a high overhanging rock. I spent a few minutes rolling Chendre Skute around in my mouth, and a few minutes more thinking about changing my name to smouldering mystery man, Andy Chend. My knees were aching and felt like they might have been mentioned in the Domesday Book too, so it seemed apt.

One thing I do know is that this area is hallowed ground for any lovers of outdoor rambling. Around these craggy clefts, one Sunday morning in 1932, the famous 'Mass Trespass' took place in which 400 walkers marched up onto the grouse moors of Kinder Scout to protest the appalling lack of public access. This was the era of smog and grime and mass unemployment, and escape to the hills from the smoke-saturated city was one of the small comforts for the proletariat – or would have been, had the whole area not been designated out of bounds save for grouse shooting and menacingly guarded by gamekeepers. It all kicked off on that sabbath day, the wave of stoical ramblers overwhelming the fierce-but-thin defensive line of gamekeepers and joining with hundreds of others who had made their way up from the industrialised zones – a sort of *Peaky Blinders* touring production. People were hurt and arrests were made that led to imprisonment, but a beacon of activism was lit that day which couldn't be extinguished. Gradually over time public access increased, and then in 1951 the Peak District National Park was opened. Now you can wander wherever you like on this moor – although you shouldn't because it's like an undercooked souffle and you genuinely might perish. Furthermore (and here I'm very grateful for Mark Wallington's lovely book, *Pennine Walkies*), it was as a direct result of the 1932 protest that a journalist named Tom Stephenson mooted the idea of a long-distance footpath following the Pennine chain. It took many years before rights of way were negotiated, but eventually, in April 1965, the Pennine Way was opened as a complete entity and has been popular with people (mainly but not exclusively people who look like retired geography teachers and Channel Island football managers) ever since.

Through and around rocky outcrops we wove, the trail becoming a sandy path scattered with puddles as we headed toward Snake Pass, that ominous sounding A-road through the Peaks which closes at the first sign of weather. Phil explained to Jon and I, his words occasionally pinched and pilfered by the wind, that his current (unappreciated) fitness levels were due to him taking part in the Summer Spine Race, an Ultra-Running challenge in which competitors run the first 100 miles of the Pennine Way from Edale to Hawes, without sleep and carrying nothing more than a little head torch for the long night shift.

'With any luck I might make the Top 10 this year.'

'Excellent!' Jon said. 'What made you want to do it?'

'I just like getting to the top of hills. It's about showing the world who's boss, even if we do it on our hands and knees.'

'Rather you than me.'

'Do neither of you fancy it then?' Phil asked with a smirk, stroking his handsomely shaven head.

'Oh, I don't think so,' Jon replied earnestly. 'I don't think Maria would be happy with me going all that way without a permission slip.'

I refused to dignify Phil even with a response and then started calling him Paul for a while to chip away at his self-esteem. A steep-stepped descent towards boggy moorland signalled the end of our traverse along Kinder Plateau's western rim, and also marked the turnaround points for my caretaker companions.

'Do you want your waterproof trousers back?' Jon asked.

'No, thanks, they're too bulky. I'd rather have wet legs than flayed lungs. Give them to a museum if I don't make it back.'

'Right you are. If you finish the walk, I'll make you something nice in my woodshed.' He smiled his guileless smile and held out a hand. 'Good luck.'

'Thanks, Jon.'

'Just remember,' said Phil, 'that it doesn't always get worse, OK? You can do it. Trust the process.'

Phil finally got a smile from me, then an awkward hug. 'Thanks. I really appreciate your support. Just promise me, when all this is over, that you'll start eating loads more cake.'

'When this is over,' he replied, 'I will never stop eating cake.'

Off they went: Phil skipping and skating his way back along the sandy track; Jon taking his time, eating a banana, probably thinking about how many dowel joints in a litre or something. I had been glad of their company, and I'm delighted to say that they are both still alive. Phil would go on to finish in an incredible 3rd place at the Summer Spine Race, while Jon would also go on to do things – I was quite sure of that. Within minutes of their departure, however, the sun clocked off for the day. It started to cloud over, the sky turning the colour of a day-old bruise, then the rain began to fall.

'Well, Phil's obviously a massive liar,' I said to Alan. 'Stupid Paul.'

I stood with my back to Chesterfield, staring bitterly into my immediate future, and a feeling of isolation and dread seeped over me. The honeymoon period was already over.

CHAPTER 4
POINTLESS

I don't know whether you've had a short break between chapters or whether you're cracking straight on, but either way I'm exactly where you left me.

Looking back at Kinder Edge from its northern side it appears as a huge sweeping tidal wave of granite, tantalisingly held back from overwhelming you. For North-to-Southers (people who start the Pennine Way at Kirk Yetholm) it might well appear as the ominous final enemy. To me, it felt good to have such a powerful landmass at my back, washing me ashore out of the turbulent Derbyshire seas.

The sodden moorlands loomed ahead of me and coal-dark clouds were descending like a baler. Feeling suddenly lonely and looking for a spot to sit and devour my lunch, I crossed William Clough (a stream that sounds like a naughty Victorian schoolboy) and sought comfort on a large cairn – a game I would play and constantly lose over the next week. I don't know when the last time you tried to sit down outside was, but it's harder than it looks because there are *no* cosy seats in nature – the Great Outdoors isn't there to accommodate your coddled, self-entitled bottom, and for the 21st century LazyBoy-ensconced binge-napper this can come as quite a shock. Nature rightly garners a lot of negative feedback for being 'red in tooth and claw', but where its detractors could really turn the screw is by pointing out that, far worse than blood-soaked antipathy towards sentient life, it just isn't very comfy.

An Irish couple in their early twenties were seated across the path from me, their attempt at a romantic picnic thwarted by the constant need to rein in their Hungarian Vizsla, who was belting around with the zestiness of a dog who'd put 'A day out grousing' at the top of his Christmas list and now believed in Santa after so many years of agnosticism.

'How are ya?' the man said.

'Top… Greetings!' I replied.

You'll no doubt be aware that 'Top Greetings' isn't a common rejoinder. What had happened was this: I had started to say 'Top o' the mornin' to ya', inclusive of accent, but at the last moment had managed to swerve that head-on collision with cancel culture. I had still mounted the curb with 'Top Greetings' however. The two Irish picnickers glanced at each other sceptically, perhaps searching the other's face for recognition of the phrase 'Top Greetings', finding none.

'Are you quite well?' the woman asked, noting the misery of my situation. 'You look like you've come out for a morning's suicide.'

'Thank you,' I said. The top greetings I'd offered them now seemed premature and overly charitable.

I was very hungry. I took Alan out of his pack to sit next to me, then loosened the duffle on my pack and drew out a reassuringly large brick of tin foil with the glee of a prospector who struck silver on his first day at the job. The couple were still looking at me curiously, and I chose not to colour their scepticism further by confessing that my mother had made me a packed lunch for Day 1.

'I made these myself,' I told them, playing it real cool.

I unwrapped the hefty foil package with the taut anticipation of Charlie Bucket, then whooped with glee at the sight of my golden ticket – Coronation Chicken.

The Irish lass gave me a look that might have voiced itself as, 'That was a surprising reaction from someone who not only made but insisted on telling us that he made his own sandwiches.'

'I just love opening presents,' I said, smoothing things over with debonair charm. The couple packed up their own picnic and moved on within 60 seconds. Their Vizsla stalked back on the pretence of giving Alan a suspicious sniff, then raced off into the heather in search of something less stuffed.

'There's a storm coming,' the Irish gent said over a cold shoulder, pointing a digit at the darkening sky.

'I know.'

I sat with my back to Edale, the flagstoned moors stretching out before me, wondering how long I had before my sandwiches became waterlogged. Wondering, too, whether there's anything more comforting than eating a packed lunch made by your Mum. (NB. There is an acceptable reason for my Mum making me a packed lunch. My parents live in Newcastle-under-Lyme, just under an hour's drive from Edale. I had stayed with them the previous night and was awoken to the most insistent lunch I've ever been given. 'It could be days before you have a proper meal,' Mum had said, mistaking the Pennine Way for the Russian Steppe or a desert.) Chewing into my sandwich, I dived headlong into memories of all those school trips where my *Count Duckula* lunchbox had tethered me to maternal reassurance. Whatever the backdrop – the turrets of Warwick Castle, the lion enclosure at Chester Zoo, the boarding gate for a flight to Hamburg – the sight of a Wagon Wheel or a Capri-Sun was always that symbol of, that signpost to, home. Mums: they wrap up their hearts for us in clingfilm.

When I was 10 or 11, I got selected to represent Newcastle-under-Lyme at a football tournament in Montreal-la-Cluse under the shade of the French Alps, against a misfitted selection of teams ranging from the local village school to Inter Milan (who by sheer miracle somehow won the tournament). It was only a two-day trip, but it was the first time I'd ever been away from home on my own. We were housed with families for the weekend and the abrupt exposure to a strange language and culture completely unseated me – I basically blubbed my way through the whole excursion, pausing momentarily to help the team cruise to a four-goal defeat against Inter, after which at least I was able to claim my tears were down to some criminal defending.

The thing that had made me cry the most that weekend was unvelcroing my shin pads to find three packets of Fruit Pastilles, tightly wrapped like contraband, landing at my feet.

'Do you not like Fruit Pastilles then?' Marky Denson had asked, singularly missing any sense of emotional nuance. He has since been in prison, which I offer without comment.

At the time I remember thinking that I was just a bit of a cry-baby (NB. This was in the days before 'triggering', when you couldn't just have someone arrested for challenging your most transient feelings). I reflect now though and think that, actually, I just had a very well-defined idea of *home:* what it was, where it was…who it was. A few years later I signed up to the French Exchange scheme, spending a fortnight with a French lad named Fabien and his family over Easter before returning the favour in the Summer. I cried a lot then, too. Half a decade later I studied Modern Languages at Warwick University and spent a whole year living in Chartres, an hour's train ride from Paris, teaching English in a lycée. It was unequivocally terrible, but I never cried once – I had finally crashed through the fear barrier, victorious if not unscathed – and maybe there was a lesson in that for me now. But during each one of those trips, regardless of length or the state of my well-being, she always sent Fruit Pastilles. Sometimes, I think, knowing you can go home keeps you going while you can't.

'Sorry, Alan,' I said, snapping back to the present, 'all this talk of mothers must be hard given that you were mass-produced in a factory.'

Alan remained stoically tight-lipped and stared at the ground. Fair enough. It was time to move on.

Metal-grey clouds were covering the sky like a winter duvet slipping off a bed. There were plenty of miles left to cover before a hot bath and a cold pint, and it didn't look like the afternoon session was going to be fun. Nor was it.

Having walked the first day of the Pennine Way (16.5 miles) twice before I had a sense of where I was and what it would involve. On both prior occasions I had really enjoyed that opening spree, but this time, whether through over-familiarity or a sense of foreboding, I found myself adopting an unsentimental workmanlike approach: head down, shoulders hunched, one Meindl boot in front of the other. There would be plenty of time to absorb the scenery, but today had become about the result, not the aesthetic. It had rained for the whole of the previous week and, after the brief sunny morning respite, the rain clouds seemed to have abruptly nipped back like someone forgetting their wallet and keys then deciding to work from home anyway. Any desire I might have had to enjoy walking in the company of sphagnum moss and deep heather was then nipped in the bud by the onset of an unwelcome hailstorm. Frozen pellets exploded against the slabs and agitated the marshy pools tight up against the path, while the rain streamed down my face like someone else's tears. Still, these sodden paths were far preferable to the desert roads of the pandemic. My body was aching but not idle; not languishing on a settee with a flag of victimhood fluttering at half-mast. Walking stops us from drifting.

Reflecting from a comfy chair some time later, I'm struck by just how arduous Day 1 is. In the second half of the day you cross Snake Pass, then have to climb Devil's Dyke up towards Bleaklow Hill. There's a reason why these places aren't called Gushingjoy Lane and SuperHappyFuntime rise. These are Ronseal places. Devil's Dyke is a sunken trench with high-sided grassy parapets on either side; a former riverbed which, with the newly arrived downpour, seemed to be regretting that hasty decision and was now considering coming out of retirement to be a riverbed again – nature's version of getting the band back together. The terrain in these parts feels mildly apocalyptic like the set of a 1960s BBC sci-fi series, bleak but eerily so, as though the air is somehow squatting, refusing to circulate according to the natural order. You cross and recross Hern Clough (William's brother) with the groughs and peat hags observing you eyelessly from either side. The path is unclear here and the gloopy terrain refuses to negotiate with signposts, so at unsatisfactory intervals the letters PW had been painted onto stones like modern-day runes.

You reach Bleaklow point, a terrible rockery on an ocean of peat bog (the sort of structure I would make if all the *Garden Rescue* team rioted and quit and I was brought in to finish the job at short notice) and it's downhill all the way to Crowden from there. But I would quickly learn and come to recite *ad nauseum* the phrase 'The Last Three Miles Are The Worst.' By this point the rain and cold were tyrannical, a swaying lashing turmoil, my fingers drained white from osmosis, my whole being leprous with damp. I felt as though I'd been left too long with the teabag in. I tripped and slipped and aquaplaned down to Crowden, trying not to swear, saying things like 'flipping pig' and 'blimmin' bloody baskets', while nameless birds shrieked angrily from their makeshift hideouts. Streams with names like Wildboar Grain tumbled down in the direction of Torside reservoir, just up the road from which, I knew from last time, was my accommodation for the evening. It would be a welcome sight.

Finally, after a lot of squelching and far too many blimmin' baskets, and resembling a leftover scarecrow from last year's Halloween, I reached the Torside Reservoir, took a hard left and schlepped up the hill to The Old House, ecstatic torrents of water fluming down against my march. The bunkhouse shelter was already unlocked and I appeared to be the only guest staying on that Monday evening, so I didn't have to put up a pretence of being happy or in any way enjoying myself, waving cheerily at other guests with calls of 'Not too bad, was it?' and 'I could do that one again'. My room was clean and anonymously comfortable, penitential more than palatial, as though it wanted to be your ally but didn't want you getting to know anything about it – like Ben Affleck in *Argo.* I removed my boots with the sound of a man falling down a huge well and felt better for it. I peeled off my soaking gear, draping it over radiators and bed struts and open cupboard doors. Whatever I had meant by it earlier in the day, I was glad not to be a pregnant woman.

Once showered, changed and filled with several cups of tea, I towelled off my phone and Facetimed the family.

'Day 1 is done, guys!'

'Well done, Daddy! Do you feel old?'

'Yes, very old, darling. I've just been taken over by the National Trust. Only 15 days to go though!'

'You can do it, Daddddoooоiiuuuuuyyyyyy…' the signal glitched, dropped and then cut out. I was left with a blank screen. Still, they knew I was safe and to a lesser extent well. I downed several more cups of tea and switched on the TV to watch *Pointless,* the soothing sight and tones of Alexander Armstrong restoring me to partial normality as the rain continued to smash unrelentingly against the outside world.

'I might struggle to finish this thing if the weather doesn't change,' I told Alan.

'Let's see if you're right, let's see how many people said it,' came the reply from the TV.

Later in the evening, the landlady of The Old House offered to get Bertrand to give me a lift to the Peel's Arms, the nearest pub just a couple of miles down the road in Padfield. I thought it only right that I treat myself after my gruelling foray across the antagonistic morass, so I accepted the offer. Betrand shuttled me along the intervening country roads, handling the car like a man who was a huge fan of The Stig but hadn't actually learned to drive himself.

This belief was given extra credence when, every time he rounded a sharp bend, he made the sound of a racing car rounding a sharp bend.

'Let me know when you're done and I'll come pick you up,' he said as I poured nauseously onto the pavement outside the pub.

'Is it always you who does the ferrying?' I asked.

'Used to be mi dad, but he's dead at the moment.'

'At the moment?'

'Yeah, he died last year. Let me know when you want picking up. Have a lickle drink for me.'

I was too tired to ask any of the 30 questions that had sprung to mind during the death-defying short drive to the pub. I found a table, ordered a hanging kebab with a side of chips, then ordered more chips for dessert.

'You want chips for pudding, too?' The serving boy looked at me as though I'd hidden his X-Box in a geocache and refused to divulge the coordinates.

'I've lived through a pandemic, young man,' I replied. 'The old ways are dead.'

I had budgeted to allow myself one beer per night so I ordered a Guinness, and then had another two after that because being in debt is the one game in which my generation has reached 100% completion. The pub was fairly empty, a brace of local workmen peering warily from well-worn barstools, but a posh-sounding bickering couple seated across from me had the aura of people also walking the Pennine Way – not least because they were ordering a glarss of wine and saying how much they enjoyed their barth. Maybe I would meet them on the road tomorrow, but for now I kept myself to myself, resting in the throaty warmth of the tavern, letting the beer do its job of glueing my emotions back together.

Bertrand picked me up about 10pm and catapulted me back to The Old House.

'I'm in the university now,' he told me proudly, taking a corner like a coked-up Chris Hoy.

'Oh, are you? What are you studying?'

'Yeah, I'm in the university. It's dead good. Did you have a drink for me then?'

'Yes,' I said, 'I had a Guinness. Are you paying for it, then?'

'Can't, I got to pay for mi books.'

'OK.'

In the morning, I would repent of the suspicion that Bertrand had been recruited directly from The Island of Dr. Moreau, but for now I just sat white-knuckling my way back to the B&B, glimpsing the panicked hedgerows as they thrashed wildly by. I got back to my room and found my clothes still dripping wet but unsure what to do about it. I rummaged in my rucksack for a phone charger and pulled it out along with a knotted wrap of clingfilm. I chuckled, already knowing what was secreted within.

I sat on my creaking bed, looking out onto the coal-black night, chewing pensively on Fruit Pastilles… thinking of *home.*

Day 2
Crowden to Diggle
15 miles

"A Dungeon horrible, on all sides round
As one great Furnace flam'd, yet from those flames No light, but rather darkness visible
Serv'd only to discover sights of woe,
Regions of sorrow, doleful shades, where peace And rest can never dwell, hope never comes."
John Milton, Paradise Lost

'Your pain has just begun.'
Darth Vader, Obi Wan Kenobi

CHAPTER 5

GAWAIN AND THE GREEN EYES

'How do you like your coffee?'

'With lots more coffee.'

I was sitting at a small breakfast table with a view down into the Longdendale valley. Outside, the Trans-Pennine trunk road was already groaning and Torside reservoir lay topaz beneath me, its surface fretted by the early morning rain. This was the third time I had stayed in Crowden, and the weather never seemed to change its socks.

'Is it ever sunny here?' I asked the landlady.

'There were rumours of something like that happening years ago, between the two wars like, but I don't believe it.' She slipped a silver cafetiere onto my table and pulled out a notepad.

'Raight, I can do you a continental breakfast if you like, but in my vast experience you'll just be wanting a full English – am I raight?'

She was raight.

'Raight then. Pork sausages or veggie?'

'Pork.'

'Hash browns?'

'Yes, please!'

'Fried tomatoes?'

'No, I hate hot fruit.'

'Me too. And your eggs – with a kiss?'

'No, with more coffee – and scrambled.'

'White or black coffee?'

'Black.'

'…as black as the mood of a Pennine Way walker. White or brown toast?'

'White.'

'…As white as the sheets that soften your passing into sleep.'

I wasn't comprehensively sure what was happening – whether she always brought out the freestyle poetry with the breakfast menu – but this whip-sharp repartee was a sunny contrast to the scene looming outside.

'OK, it won't be a minute – I'll get Bertrand on that now.'

I could already hear Bertrand through the swing door to the kitchen, laying down his own lyrics over Classic FM. If he cooked like he drove (or like he sang) then breakfast would arrive in 20 seconds and look like it had suffered a nervous breakdown. On the subject of which my attention was now drawn to the dining room doorway, in whose gloomy light was silhouetted the form of what at some point in the past must have been a man, but was now a Lowryan mockery of one – pallid and matchstick thin and unfeasible. He wandered into the dining room, lowered himself into a chair at the adjacent table and just sat, as if the act of sitting down had inadvertently flicked his off switch. He was wracked with something; seemed to be full of some long word that I haven't yet learned. Only his eyes moved, flickering under their lids as though trying to process intense trauma. Had he just received tragic news? Should I ask? Probably not. I decided I would.

'Excuse me… is everything alright?'

His head flicked in an almost imperceptible jolt to stare at me – the signature move of creepy dolls in haunted houses and no less disconcerting in live humans.

'Yes. Yes, fine, thank you.'

He wasn't fine. He was just being British.

'Are you working nearby?' I asked, keeping my tone light.

'No. I mean, I do work not too far from here, but no – I'm on my final day of the Pennine Way.'

The washed-out trauma victim sitting in front of me had come from Kirk Yetholm. The Pennine Way had done this to him. This was not the news I wanted to open my day with. Why couldn't he have lost his job or something?

You're about to observe me ask the stupidest question of the last decade:

'And have you enjoyed it?'

The man showed no sign of emotion. 'It's not been too bad.'

I wasn't wishing to break this guy under questioning, but I needed to know just how terrible things might get. Anticipation of death is worse than death itself, so they say (although I'm not sure who *they* are) and my thinking was that if I could manipulate this guy into vomiting out all his woe, I may be able to pick through it for some helpful tips and march victoriously to Scotland over the bones of his martyrdom.

He could see that I was still staring, my attention encircling him like press-ganged sailors around a craggy old sea Captain.

'I got a blister crossing Hadrian's Wall. It got infected at Alston. I don't know how.'

Before he could say 'Would you like to see?' and I could say 'Absolutely not, sir', he stripped off his cotton sock and showed me something that might have just won 'Wound of the Year' at the annual WTF? awards. His right foot looked like it had been hunted for sport. And this had happened at Hadrian's Wall – this poor bloke had walked for over 10 days with a foot that belonged in a medical textbook if not an abattoir. I could tell you a lot more, but what have you ever done to me that I should persecute you so?

'Why didn't you just stop?' I asked, several octaves higher than normal.

'I couldn't,' he replied, turning in his seat to look over the fir-covered valley. 'I needed to finish. I… I just needed to.'

I stared avidly and silently at him for a few moments more until…

'Bloody 'ell, put that away, will ya?!' the landlady barked as she carried my plate of now-less-appetising breakfast into the dining room. I poured myself another coffee and considered asking for a partition.

'What's your reason for doing the Pennine Way?' the man asked as he gingerly replaced his sock.

'I don't know yet,' I shrugged.

'Well, it's good to have a reason. Work it out as you go along, maybe.'

I finished my breakfast (except for the bacon because it reminded me of the man's foot), bade the chap farewell and went to kit up, leaving him to stare a thousand yards down into his coffee. I have no idea what that man's name was, nor how he got on during that final gruelling leg of the journey. But I hope he finished it. I could see in his eyes that he needed to.

* * *

I started Day 2 as I would start all my days, by reading a verse from *Hebrews 12*: "Let us run with perseverance the race marked out for us." My dad had mentioned it to me the day before I set off and it would become a great epigraph for each phase of walking. Running might be a bit of a stretch, but then the writer of *Hebrews* didn't know I would be carrying a DLX Twin Peak 45 litre rucksack so you have to take context into account, and a little bit of hermeneutics goes a long way. I slotted Alan (my mascot/novelty Christmas fox/doorstop) into his pouch and off we went.

Today would see me leave Chesire (whose border I had silently infiltrated at dusk the previous day) and enter West Yorkshire, the third of nine British counties in whose company I would take a stroll over the next two weeks – unless I developed a wound like the one I'd just seen back in The Old House, the memory of which was even now trying to coax my breakfast back into the open. If I picked up that sort of injury then Northumberland and

Roxburghshire would need to find alternative travelling companions.

My fear was not an irrational one. In 2018, when I walked from Edale to Malham, I died of blisters early on Day 2 and had to endure rather than enjoy the remainder of the walk. It seemed inevitable that I would get blisters at some point this time around, even with my top-of-the-range, military grade, *they cost ******* how much?* Meindl boots, but the longer I averted that scenario the better. After that it would just be a battle of wills. Walking is a competitive sport – your adversary is you.

What's more, and you probably don't need me to tell you this but good boots are the second most vital thing to take on a long trek (the most important being the weathered feet that slot into them). "When you see someone putting on Big Boots," wrote A.A. Milne, "you can be pretty sure an adventure is going to happen." However, if you want that adventure to finish with a smile then those boots need to be made for walking – and lots of it. No matter how fit you are, without proper footwear you might as well strap into the nearest Nissan Qashqai and set a course for the moon. You can live without most things over long distances – screens, hot meals, Alan etc. – but the power of life and death is in your boots.

Today's opening half mile was a term my guidebook described as "bonus walking", which translates quite accurately into English as 'extra walking' – a less psychopathic way of saying that when the guidebook tells you there's only 11 miles of hiking today, it is lying. I took to the road and trudged noisily down it to where a dam wall offers safe passage across the reservoir, early morning commuters on the B6105 apparating out of the morning mist then swerving to avoid manslaughter on their way to work. Almost immediately there's a short stretch of track through a copse of firs, bouncy under foot and pleasantly sappy, which could easily mislead you into thinking today might be spent under canopy. Interestingly, only about 10% of the Pennine Way passes through woodland and most of that is found in Kielder Forest over 200 miles north of here. You quickly leave the motherly embrace of the firs and cross the A628, then climb to reach a small hillside plantation of spruces. The ascent to Laddow Rocks rises ahead and the smell of bracken wafts down the pass to meet you. After yesterday's baptismal exertions, a mere 18 km of trail looked to be a relatively palatable tonic – a first timer might well imagine themselves lightfooting and quickstepping their merry way over the hills to Standedge in time for afternoon tea and crumpets.

But I had been here before, and I knew different. Under my boots I was wearing £40 worth of waterproof sock, bought specifically with today in mind. Nothing baits a blister's hook better than a wet foot and so the exorbitant price seemed reasonable under the circumstances. I would simply adjust my life budget by cancelling Netflix for a few months or just not taxing my car.

Day 2 is technically the shortest day of the Pennine Way, but it might also be the worst. It has 'small man syndrome' or, to put it in canine terms, is an absolute Shih Tzu. You climb to the gritstone outcrops of Laddow Rocks, the rich coppery hues of soggy bracken skirting your path, and all seems well: the trail is clear and obvious and the first couple of miles can be chalked off in well under an hour. The march along the top of Laddow, as it contours the hillside precariously, is exposed and blustery but the views are staggering, having that immemorial feel that all unpopulated countryside possesses. Mauve and primrose colours skip amid the greens, and that singular scent of wet earth sieved through bracken snuggles up in the nostrils. That's about as good as it gets, though. Once you hump and lump your way down the hill the bogs along the route become as ubiquitous as they are treacherous – I passed one woman who had fallen pride-first into one and looked as though she'd just completed some sort of horrendous spa day. Then you have to cross a couple of 'streams' which look fairly innocuous on the map, but on this day Lady Arwen had hexed them in elvish to prevent Black Riders getting at the Hobbits. My

£40 waterproof socks were performing admirably by all accounts, until I had to literally wade through three feet of torrenting water and treat them to a white-water rapid ride they never signed up for.

'I should have spent another £60 and gone for the "biblical-deluge-proof" pair,' I told Alan, who seemed to agree. I did manage to laugh at this point however, although it wasn't mirth-oriented. The guidebook, which a mere hour previous had told me to enjoy some "bonus walking" (I shan't name the book because I'm planning to track down and assassinate its author and I don't want to leave an obvious trail – much like the author himself, it seems) was now reassuring me in plain and published text that Crowden Brook would almost certainly seem little more than a trickle, rather than the enraged Brahmaputra sweeping over me that probably had crocodiles in it. I gave serious thought to heaving the book into this so-called 'trickle' and watching it cascade away downstream like a Viking funeral, but I had only borrowed the book from the library and would need to return it. I would therefore treat it henceforth like an unruly prisoner that I was escorting through Injin country, keeping it safe while fully distrusting anything it had to say, and ready to drown it in a creak if it made another wrong move.

'What happened to our precious book?' the librarian would say.

'I'm so terribly sorry, there was nothing I could do. He's with the angels now,' I would reply.

In case you're in any doubt, my feet were soaking, and it was only going to get wetter. The aesthetic pleasantries of the preceding valley had tapered into mired wastelands polka-dotted with bog cotton, while the fossil grey clouds dominating the skyline didn't prophecy a bright afternoon. Stupid Phil had told me yesterday to 'trust the process', but it seemed as though the process hadn't been informed of my fealty and had quickly moved on to other projects. Needing to recalibrate therefore, and having not attended a school that offered a GCSE in raft-building, I decided to halt and have brunch before making the grim ascent to Black Hill. In the Bible, Elijah had a snack and a nap and didn't want to die any more, thus a flapjack and a Capri-Sun would stabilise my energy levels and perhaps transmogrify me into Elijah reborn. Scrambling down to the shelter of an overhanging rock, I spied an incongruous pair of peat-painted boots dangling out from the shadow.

'I lost my mother, I don't suppose you've seen her?' a voice said. Whether this was a genuine question or in fact the opening line to an upsetting folk ballad, I wasn't sure and would need more information before committing either way.

'Erm…'

The voice belonged, I now saw as I skirted the rock whence it came, to a cross-legged woman in her early twenties, with green eyes and cropped hair and a face that looked like it might be permanently amused by something just off-screen. She was chomping her way through a bag of mixed nuts as she sat on the only dry spot for miles around.

'Have you passed anyone in the last hour?' she asked, at which point the penny dropped.

'Oh, right, your mother. Small woman? Rucksack? Massively covered in mud and on the verge of tears.'

The green eyes glinted. 'Sure, that'll be her. I told her to wait for me but she was keen to crack on, so she was.'

'You're Irish?'

'Gillian of Belfast.'

Don't say Top Greetings, Alan whispered from his pouch. I was determined not to, but while my mind was engaged in cordoning off that phrase with painstaking imprecations, my mouth was left open for the phrase 'Aloha' to just wander brazenly out.

'Aloha?!' Gillian asked with alacrity. 'Where are you from now – Hawaii?'

'No, I am not,' I replied, and refused to discuss the matter any further.

You know, you could just say 'Hi,' Alan pointed out.

A curlew screamed overhead in low-level flying manoeuvres. Droplets of rain started coming to find their friends already having fun at ground level.

'Is it OK if I sit here for a while?' I asked, unsure what the safeguarding regulations were in these parts. Gillian's look of amusement widened, absorbing as it did so a hint of slight scorn.

'Sure, work away…' She rummaged in her bag of nuts and brought out an almond which she tossed into the brook, 'just bring a DBS certificate next time.'

'Ah, I knew there was something I'd forgotten to pack.'

And thus, having established consent, I sat down on a big stone, took a bite of flapjack, and set about removing my river-soused boots.

'Aren't you worried you might lose your mum permanently, Gillian of Belfast?' I enquired, trying but failing to inject the paper straw into my Capri Sun.

'Not at all,' she said composedly. 'She can't go very fast and she won't go very far. And if I'm Gillian of Belfast, who might you be?'

'Ser Endrew Kynde,' I replied.

NB. That is not my real name, but there was a point somewhere before the pandemic when life's most pressing task was figuring out what your name would be if you were a noble on *Game of Thrones*, and it was nice to finally feel vindicated in having taken the time to do that.

'Ser Endrew Kynde? Cool name.'

'Indeed, 'tis I, Ser Endrew Kynde of…'

'of the South Pennines?' Gillian suggested.

'Ah, forsooth, my reputation precedes me then, good… damsel? I'll stop speaking like this now (Gillian nodded appreciatively). Are you doing the Pennine Way?'

'We are, but not all in one go. This is our fourth outing – we started in Malham a few days ago. We did Kirk Yetholm to Dufton years ago now, but Mum's not very well at the moment so she's keen to finish it in case her health gets worse.'

'Got to have a reason for doing it, hey?'

'Aye, so you have.' She pointed a pistachio at me. 'What's yours?'

I shrugged. 'I don't know yet. Work it out as I go along maybe.'

Gillian shuffled around for a comfortable new sitting position and I saw that her pack looked even heftier than mine. Tent pegs jutted from a side pocket and a Calor gas stove was wrapped efficiently in a foam lilo.

'How is it that you're nearly at Crowden and it's not even midday yet?' I asked. I knew categorically that there were zero places to overnight between The Old House and Standedge.

'We're wild camping.'

'Seriously?! Where did you camp last night?'

'Well… outside. I didn't take the grid reference.' She seemed completely unfazed.

'Isn't it illegal to camp out on the moors?' (It is. It's also very dangerous – which is partly why it's illegal. The weather in these parts operates on a kind of spin-the-wheel axis, clacking between arctic and sunny and back again, sometimes within the hour.)

'So it is, but look at the state of that sky – there's no policemen coming onto the moors in this weather.'

I laughed incredulously. I had thought I was being stoical attempting to walk the whole of the Pennine Way on my own, but this woman was sleeping in swamps and had even brought her mum along.

'You're braver than I am,' I confessed.

'Is that terribly hard, Ser Endrew?'

I didn't answer that. She wasn't trying to shame me – wasn't making a genuine inquiry, even – but that question would be squelching about in my brain for the next few days.

We sat together under the overhang for 10 minutes, her munching mixed nuts, discarding into watery oblivion the ones she had no time for; me, rounding up stray oats that had fallen onto my trousers, changing into dry socks, slurping noisily from my Capri Sun. (Update: The biodegradable paper straw had failed catastrophically in its attempt to infiltrate the pouch, so I had used the miniature scissors from my Swiss Army knife to decapitate it. On a side note, it's a jolly good job the straw was 'recyclable' because it wasn't at all suited to being a straw, and it was reassuring to think it might still find redemption as a toilet roll or something.)

'I've got one nut left,' said Gillian. 'A walnut. Do you want it?'

'No, thanks, I don't like them.'

Then suddenly a memory, spiking my conscience like a tent peg driven into pitch. *A 5-minute walnut…* where was that from? Oh yes, that's right, that was it – one of the first messages she ever sent me, telling me how she was just a short walk from her friend's house, but she hadn't checked autocorrect so instead she outed herself as a '5-minute walnut'. I smiled into the beaded curtain of rain. The memory faded like highland sheep into the misty uplands.

'I'll take it – I'll take the walnut!'

'Thought you said you didn't like them?'

'Let's say it's a symbolic reason, shall we?'

Gillian smiled, tossed me the cellophane bag with the solitary walnut and jumped down from her perch with nothing more than a cushioned, peaty thud.

'Well, I should go and make sure my mother hasn't been eaten by the creature from the Black Lagoon. All the best, Ser Endrew. Fare thee well, brave knight, and all that jazz.'

'You too, Lady Gillian of Belfast.'

I bowed, clipped up my bag, tightened cords and zippered pouches. The plasticated walnut I stored in the inside pocket of my raincoat. I made the short climb back to the path expecting to say a final farewell to Gillian, but she was already 50 metres hence, jumping puddles and glistening over rocks. Already a memory. At least it prevented me from ending our short time together with something like 'B-aloha', I suppose. And that is a very reassuring thought.

I turned both body and attention once more towards the North and its great grey coat. In reality, British Summer Time was already two months in. But over the summit of Black Hill ahead of me, it looked very much like winter was coming.

CHAPTER 6
THE GOOD LIFE

In public speaking they talk about the power of the pause – those instances as an orator where you pitch your tent for a moment, let stillness in, and allow the impact of your previous words to settle in the hearer. And it's all about timing, of course: a pause that lasts too long becomes an awkward silence, but pound your tongue relentlessly and you drown your audience in a river of sound – an overwhelming Crowden Brook when they expected a trickle.

What you need to do is 'empower the pause'.

It's a rule that's applicable holistically, I think. Human beings weren't made for incessant action, any more than we were wired for indolence. And yet most of us struggle to find that narrow path between industry and apathy, between busyness and burnout, and some don't look for it at all. I've heard three people in my life tell me that 'I'll rest when I'm dead', and tragically two of them now are – and neither had reached retirement age. Because resting *isn't* retirement. It isn't a retreat. Certainly, rest too long and you'll end up loafing; but fail to rest at all and you'll end up losing – your peace, your mind, your relationships… your life perhaps.

Resting is what steak needs to do to taste delicious. It's what the fields need if the farmer wants to reap what she sows. It's the human translation of the I.T. guy's advice to 'turn it off and on again'. I only mention this now because my little traveller's tryst with Gillian had made me feel a lot better about things. My rest had been restorative. The day wasn't going to get any easier, and my hopes for an untroublesome Stage 2 had already been brutally shattered, but isn't life just made up of broken expectations and their subsequent decisions? Tennis supremo Roger Federer won close to 80% of the matches in which he played over a 24 year career, claiming over 100 titles and a record eight Wimbledon triumphs. But how about this: he only won 54% of the points he ever competed for. The greatest tennis player of all time won just over half the skirmishes he fought in – and he just tried to win the next one. There's something in that, probably. Life is a walk through a hall of cracked mirrors. All we can do is decide how to face the reflections.

* * *

At 1900 feet (one thousand feet shorter than Cross Fell, the Pennine Way's highest point), Black Hill is no great physical challenge. You're aided by the hallelujah-inducing appearance of flagstone slabs, repurposed legacies of the Industrial Revolution and a good example of a redemption story. I followed this narrow patio up and over, safe from sinking, crossed a rusty red stream and then climbed to the Manchester-Huddersfield road at Wessenden Head. A certain guidebook, now figuratively handcuffed within my pack, had told me to expect the tantalising aroma of frying bacon from the food van parked in the layby. Nope – more nonsense on stilts. The layby was home to a couple of discarded tyres and a spoiled mattress, but I didn't need a nap or scabies, so I just carried on.

What makes the area around Black Hill so bleak is simply the inherent unearthliness of the place. The terrain is uniformly bland, implacably inhospitable. As Guy de Maupassant wrote in his short story, *Love:* "There is at times nothing more disquieting than bogland." The sky hangs in 50 shades of grey, draining – suctioning – all colour, all joy from the place. The supporting slabs notwithstanding, with each step across the morass you can feel the whole earth sigh beneath your feet, an interconnected hive-mind of malignant gloop – *Stranger Things* set amid the dark satanic mills of Northern England. To make matters worse, you're now crossing the epically tragic Saddleworth Moor, where I imagine even on a sunny day it's impossible to feel too carefree.

It used to be even worse before the slabs. In the early days of the trail, it's said that the bogs of the South Pennines were so treacherous, about half of all prospective Edale – Kirk Yetholm wayfarers gave up before they reached Yorkshire; before local dialect changed 'ayall raight' to 'ow do'. While the surrounding land may no longer be mortiferous, it was still unnerving, discomfitingly silent like a sleeping bear. As Mark Wallington remarks in *Pennine Walkies*, "there's a sense of being in the presence of something very powerful, something temperamental which is being lenient with you for no reason."

The successive afternoon hours string together a necklace of reservoirs, completed in the year 1800 to serve the construction of the Huddersfield Narrow Canal and, today, maintaining a Victorian formality which I much appreciated – a reassuring rationality and order amid the otherwise eldritch chaos of the landscape. I plodded on. Another curlew made its tweeting reconnaissance mission over Wessenden Reservoir while, several thousand feet above it, one of its evolutionary progenitors carried her retweeting cargo to a place where summer had already arrived and poles were for rude dancing, not just checking for potholes. Down at marsh-level I was wet without and miserable within, but just up ahead a real bright spot was awaiting me – and, by association, you. I found them near Wessenden Lodge, picnicking by a welcoming waterfall, hailing and hallooing me with plastic champagne flutes and trumpeting prose.

'Greetings, come and have a tipple!'

'Yes, you look tired – have a drink, damn you.'

Nestled under the protective ledge of an overhanging cragg a tartan rug had been stretched out, upon which was laid a banquet of parma ham, sun-blushed tomatoes, exotic-sounding-and-erotic-looking cheeses, pork pies, tins of olives and a bottle of cider. It wasn't hot enough for this to be a mirage, and while this could have been a trap set by bounty hunters, I wasn't currently wanted as an outlaw by any of the major police forces. Assuming then that a Shirley Hughes drawing had somehow sprung to life and made its way to a narrow valley in West Yorkshire, I unslung my pack and joined the picnic. And with that tiny perturbation of chaos theory, I met Geoffrey and Margot.

'Who are you, and why?' Geoffrey demanded to know, foisting a flute of cider upon my person while I was still halfway through my groan of unburdening relief. I told them my name (it's the same as the one on the cover of the book) and explained the reason for my presence. Geoffrey wanted to see my driving licence as validation, but Margot batted his hand away and apologised, explaining that they'd been walking all day, hadn't had much in the way of lunch and that this was Geoffrey's second bottle of cider.

'Cheers to that!' Geoffrey declared, chinking his plastic glass against the pork pie I was holding.

They were a pair of retired doctors from London who, from what I could tell, seemed to own about seven houses and were treating life like one big game of *Monopoly*. (NB. The most expensive thing I own is my waterproof socks, and they are huge failures.) I learned in addition that Margot and Geoffrey were walking the first 10 days of the Pennine Way, and so I might well have the pleasure of their company for the next week or so. This sounded like good news to me, particularly with the promise of more bounteous feasting, and it became my sole intention to ingratiate myself with my new companions so that they might, you know, let me have one of their spare houses. We chatted and feasted for a while, empowering the pause, and there was something so charmingly incongruous about these two – so uncannily out of place – that I couldn't help but chuckle to myself as we finished our picnic by the rapturous waterfall. Geoffrey in particular was such an anatopism, so wonderfully archaic in his use of language, it was unclear whether they had started the walk in Edale or at some point during the late 1800's. As we packed up and tracked together over the next few miles of sodden heather, Margot narrated the tale of how they had both caught Covid the previous year.

'I was pretty ill, dear, I don't mind telling you, and Geoffrey actually died from it.'

I had just been talking to Geoffrey and was now incredibly frightened. Reassuringly, Geoffrey looked almost as perplexed as me.

'I think you mean I nearly died, darling,' he cut in, just as I was Googling a number for the Ghostbusters.

'What did I say?' Margot asked.

'You said I actually died of Coronavirus.'

'Oh, don't be silly, of course you didn't. You wouldn't be here now, would you?'

'You're hysterical, dear. Let's take another breather.'

I picked up speed and put some grateful distance between us. I knew they were staying at the Diggle Hotel in Diggle, just up the road from where I was staying in Diggle, and so I would almost certainly see them later.

'Thank goodness I wasn't talking to someone who wasn't really there,' I confided to Alan.

The last three miles were the worst. The final stretch of the day drags you across tawny grasslands past Swellands Reservoir (whose dam broke in 1810, sending a deluge of peaty water down into the village of Marsden in what became known as "The Night of the Black Flood".) I took the ground one boot at a time, pondering the path of my feet, whittling down the steps in tiny splinters, the marshes an immovable object against my easily resistible force.

The day's official walk ends at Standedge Cutting on the A62, at which point the Peak District National Park ends and you can officially say, whether you feel like saying it or not, that you are now in Yorkshire. But don't worry, because there's some 'bonus walking' for all those hardcore hiking masochists, an extra mile or so trudging downhill to reach your accommodation. Worse, it had started to hail again – and badly. It seemed that the Atlantic Ocean was staging an airborne invasion of northern England; I could see cars dissolving on the A-road below. The writer John Ruskin once said that 'There is really no such thing as bad weather, only different kinds of good weather.' John Ruskin died a long time ago, and I'm happy about that.

'It's bloody May!' I screamed at the landscape. 'Pick up your end of the settee, nature.'

Had I not walked this section of the Pennine Way before, I think the last two days would have been enough to send me back to hearth and house. *It had rained all day.* By 4pm, I wasn't sure whether I'd actually seen blue sky in my life, or whether it was just something Aesop had slotted into one of his fables to teach children about the value of low expectations. As I galumphed down a twisting farm track towards Diggle I was soaking, frustrated, cold and aesthetically thwarted. I shambled into my accommodation and buried myself up to the neck in towels and self-pity.

Sunfield Bed and Breakfast was charming and sprawling, with room decor based – I can only assume – on my Great-Great-Grandmother's Pinterest account. It wasn't the whitewashed cottages of Madeira or the terracotta glamour of Venice, but it would do very nicely. I upended my saturated boots onto a radiator, showered myself and my mud-obsessed clothes, had three cups of tea, as many biscuits, and a short but welcome nap. Maybe it's just me, but there's something about the sound of a boiling kettle which hints that life might turn out OK after all.

After that I decided to call the girls. There was no wifi in the guest house and although there was 4G in the village of Diggle, the 'G' stood for goats. Unwilling to have a Facetime with my daughters that resembled found footage from the *Blair Witch Project,* I did what people used to do in the olden days when everyone spoke like Geoffrey – and made an honest phone call.

'Day 2 is done, my darlings!'

'Wow, Daddy, have you finished now?' Heidi asked.

'Well, no – I've still got quite a lot of walking to do, love.'

'Are you feeling old, Daddy? asked Alice, repeating yesterday's question.

'Yes, very old, my love – I'm expecting a letter from the Queen any day now.'

'I don't know what that means, Daddy.'

Without the focal point of my face both my daughters were easily distracted, and before too long they bade me farewell and good luck. Still, it was nice to hear their voices. I fell back onto the bed with a pathetic groan, and stayed there until my need for food finally overtook my desire to never move again. Around 8pm, with the gloaming smudging away the lines of cottage roofs through the window, I reluctantly redonned my soaking boots, not bothering to tie the laces, and lolloped down the drizzly road towards the Diggle Hotel. Geoffrey and Margot were already in there, strikingly obvious the moment I ducked under the door beam. Margot fluttered a hand at me, ordered Geoffrey to open his eyes, and insisted I join them for dinner and give my gossip some ale.

'Are you married, Andy?' Margot asked during the meal, pointing a morsel of battered fish at me.

'…I am, yes.'

'You mean she didn't fancy doing the whole walk with you?' Geoffrey put his hands on his hips in mock disbelief, then laughed at the fact that he'd made such a good joke.

'I think she would have done a few years ago,' I said. 'We've got two daughters now though, so….'

'Oh, wonderful!' said Margot. 'How lovely.'

'We've got two wonderful children as well,' Geoffrey said. '…Three children in total.' At this he punched the air and roared with delight at having made another good joke.

'Geoffrey!' exclaimed Margot, forcing his fist back to its normal height. 'That's a horrendous thing to say.'

'I was joking.'

'Which one of our children don't you like?'

'I like them all!'

'Well, you should love them all, not just like them.'

'I do love them all.'

Margot shook her mass of hair. 'I hope you and your wife don't bicker like this, Andy.'

'I can honestly say that we don't.'

'Good for you. You don't want to end up like us.'

Around 10pm, after a couple of hours of spirit-raising chatter and a couple of pints of pain-numbing amber, I took my leave of the Diggle Hotel and wandered back through drizzle and mizzle to bed. I used three of the four goats to ring my parents and assure them I was still alive.

'That's good, then,' Mum said. 'Although the prospect of being away from your two girls for two weeks must be hard.'

'Three.'

'I'm sure you only have two children, Andrew – I think you must be delirious.'

'Three weeks, Mum – I'll be away for three weeks.'

'Oh, well that's not good – but better than having a surprise child we didn't know about.'

I thanked her for the Fruit Pastilles and passed on a message to Dad that I was finding comfort in *Hebrews,* then rang off and collapsed once more. It had been a hard day – really hard – but I was 15% of the way to the finish line and I didn't have any blisters or injuries. Oh, and for the first time in nearly two years I had made some new friends, and with that pleasant thought I sank low into slumber's marshy depths.

I could give it one more day.

Day 3
Standedge to Calder Valley
15 miles

"The sour spring wind is blurting boisterous-wise,
And bears on it dirty clouds across the skies…
'Nature, you're not commendable to-day!'
I think. 'Better tomorrow!' she seems to say."
Thomas Hardy, An Unkindly May

"From this moment I began to conclude in my mind that it was possible for me to be more happy in this forsaken, solitary condition than it was possible I should ever have been in any other particular state in the world; and with this thought I was going to give thanks to God for bringing me to this place."
Daniel Defoe, Robinson Crusoe

CHAPTER 7
AN UNKINDY MAY

I woke to the sight of a dragon staring at me through the window. It was actually a pea-hen, but it was still mildly terrifying. It made some kind of pea-hen sound (I can't do the accent) and strutted off to do whatever pea-hens do all day. I'm sure there must be books on ornithology where you can discover precisely what that is, but this isn't that – sorry not to be more helpful.

Alan, still alert after his all-night vigil on the windowsill, kept an eye on its departure.

'Thanks for taking the graveyard shift, Alan. Goodness knows what that pea-hen might have done to me if you hadn't been on guard.'

It's what I'm here for, sire.

'No, it's not. I have something else I need you for later on.'

Now look here, I'm fully aware that Alan isn't sentient and the conversation I was having was with myself, but anything I could do to conjure up the perception of companionship seemed like a worthy endeavour. I wouldn't be the first man to try it, either. Nietzsche once wrote, "I am walking a lot, through the forest, and having tremendous conversations with myself." So there. For balance, the great German thinker also wrote, "When you go to a woman, take the whip along." So perhaps he's not the best role model for an impressionable young 40-year-old.

The morning had tiptoed in, not wanting to rouse or disturb. It was raining outside – still or again, the distinction didn't seem important – and sullen clouds stretched tight over the valley like the dust cover on a snooker table. I exhumed myself from the bed, unsure whether the creaking sound was the weary wooden frame or just me. Either way, something needed replacing.

To claim my boots had dried on the radiator overnight would be villainously dishonest: the radiator was presumably just for show, and so my boots looked, felt and smelled like they had been excavated from the Mariana Trench along with a handful of pirate doubloons. Maybe I could walk to Hebden Bridge in bare feet like a hobbit? Nevertheless, the smell of cooked meat hung in the air. I followed it nose-first like an episode of *Looney Tunes* and found my way into the spacious dining room, where a wall of muskets, antique pistols and the odd blunderbuss provided an oddly menacing decor, a lost-property box for highwaymen.

The breakfast was hearty and heart-attacky, just as I liked it, with a sausage so long it looked like a corner flag, two hash browns and an extra one wrapped in a napkin for me to eat later. (I did eat it later – on the way back to the room after breakfast.)

There were no other guests staying that morning – or else they had hoplophobia and were confining themselves to quarters – so the proprietor very generously ferried me the short distance back to the Standedge Cutting (and with Diggle situated in a valley and the near-constant rain, it very nearly *was* a ferry ride). The man drove slowly, cautiously, my safety his priority, like an anti-Bertrand.

'Is that pea-hen yours?' I asked him as we trundled down the cobbled street.

'Yeah, that's Gladys. She's a pervert.'

'In what way?' (I thought this a pertinent question.)

'Constantly looking into people's rooms and that.'

'Oh… well, yes, she did that to me this morning.'

'She does it to everyone. I'd like to bayonet her, but mi wife says I can't.'

'Oh, that's a shame,' I said noncommittally.

'Aye,' he said. 'Aye.'

My driver, whose name I once knew and have since forgotten, dropped me back at Standedge. I said 'b-aloha', he looked confused and drove off, then I paused to make my routine checks in the gravel car park.

Rucksack: snug

Water bottle: full

Boots: laced up tight and soaking

Poles: clutched

Alan: secured

Guidebook: a d***head

The wind was awake and finding its morning voice, soughing like a toddler demanding to be seen to, while the sky was blubbering but not yet sobbing. I crossed the road, a slick, oily snakeskin in the cutting's shallow grave, resolving once more to spend an entire working day putting one wet foot in front of another. There's a neat simplicity about that, really – even in barbarous weather. I had a day's walk ahead of me and a whole day to walk it in. I would hear no gossip, watch no news, neither start nor finish an argument. My body might ache and my knees might buckle, but pre-arranged pain – the sort you're expecting, braced for, that meets you head-on along the agreed route – carries far less potency than that grotesque surprise pain which stalks you in the shadows, feared but never seen, felt but never comprehended, pleaded with but never bartering.

The pain of walking is a good pain – a reasonable pain. You chose it, first of all. But after that it charts your progress, and it pushes to the periphery for the time being those other, non-physical, non-voluntary pains. As Bill Bryson says in *A Walk in the Woods,* his famous book about hiking the Appalachian Trail, "All that is required of you is a willingness to trudge." Cheers to that, Bill.

In screenwriting terms, these West Yorkshire legs of the pilgrimage mark the start of Act II. We've had the inciting incident (man starts walking the Pennine Way), we've got a basic grasp on the lead character's major desire (he wants to finish walking the

Pennine Way) but also his major flaw (not very good at walking, easily distracted/upset). It's a strong set-up and we're now into the Second Act: the stage of *confrontation,* where the journey really gets going and the forces of antagonism mass as we head inexorably towards the crisis point.

Generally speaking, there are three things I don't like to be in. Those three things are debt, a helicopter and West Yorkshire, and you need to hear me out on this lest the entire city of Leeds flocks to my door with pitchforks. I used to live quite close to Diggle, you see: just down the road towards Slaithwaite, up above the mists on Bolster Moor, out of sight… going out of my mind.

My family had settled on that high hill with such high hopes. Running a retreat centre, we thought, would be an exciting new challenge – *The Warden of the North* I had taken to calling myself. But… well, let's just say I should have set better lookouts for what was coming towards me down that dark Colne valley…

No, no. I couldn't allow my feet to follow in the direction my mind had started to wander. I punched myself in the face and turned around.

What I can tell you, having learnt it in that former life, is that Standedge is fairly well-known in Yorkshire for its canal tunnels. There's a little museum you can visit and a short tour they can take you on, during which you'll be told that Standedge tunnel was once 'the highest canal in all Britain', a boast with the same level of kudos as having 'Europe's Dampest Lawn' or 'World's Hairiest Bottom'. They do make nice hot chocolates though.

The poor weather wouldn't ever really lift for this third day, and although the rain would only make irregular forays to ground level the shekinah of grey cloud would hang ominously above me for the next eight hours.

I was heading for the Calder Valley. By all accounts, Day 3 of the Pennine Way is one of the least interesting for South-to-Northers, but that's fine though isn't it because I'm not writing a travel guide – please, I beg you, do *not* use this book as a travel guide – and so I'm happy to montage a good portion of the 15-

mile walk to Hebden Bridge for us. The beauty and the awe were to come; for now it was enough just to make progress and be happy about it. "How few sufferings are felt by man living in a state of primitive simplicity," as Jean-Jacques Rousseau said. Cheers to that, Jean-Jacques, and I agree: to get everything you want, sometimes you just need to desire less.

An enthusiastic traverse through the mists along Millstone Edge opened the day's proceedings. Any highwaymen loitering in the vaporous shadows would have plenty of time to prepare an ambush, the squelch-squit-squirch of my boots announcing my arrival to anyone within half a hectare, my only hope being that they'd left their pistols on a dining room wall back in Diggle.

Geoffrey and Margot's current whereabouts were uncertain, and possibly a matter of national security. I didn't know whether they had left the royal suite of the Diggle Hotel and I'd find them fine-dining alfresco along Blackstone Edge, or whether they would eventually find me, sitting dank and miserable and dead somewhere near Rochdale. I had been assured by a couple of local Digglites (Digglians?) that a food van awaited me just shy of the M62 motorway, roughly an hour's walk away, and that I'd be able to purchase lunch from there. That needed to be true, because my only remaining provisions were a banana from the guest house and a small walnut inside my jacket pocket, but I was saving that for something or other. P.S. I hate bananas.

As it turned out, the food van was indeed squatting there in a layby, cooking up bacon and coughing out fumes. I stocked up on pop and chocolate bars and sausage rolls, the sort of diet only feasible for long-distance walkers and fictional pupils at Grange Hill. Then I crossed the M62, which was opened six years after the Pennine Way was settled and is technically 'on our patch'. The resultant expanse of conciliatory bridge crossing the motorway may as well be strung together with rope and mantras for how dipping and vertiginous it is. I hesitated before crossing, staring down at the flying ranks of traffic below, aware of how curiously alien they looked after just two solitary days in the wild, a Union Pacific railroad to my Cherokee chief.

'Don't be a coward, people have been crossing this bridge since 1971,' I rebuked myself, shouting so I could hear me above the roar of traffic.

I found Margot and Geoffrey over the next ridge, brewing up next to a semi-circular cairn shelter. Margot started waving manically whilst I was still 100 yards away.

'Ah, Andy, there you are! Good morning, dear. Geoffrey, give Andy something.'

'What do you want me to give him, £20? I'm not made of money, you know.'

'You are made of money, dear, but I just meant give him a sandwich. I hope you didn't buy anything from that ghastly food van, Andy, did you?'

'What food van?' I said, playing it real cool.

'I don't know what they put in their bacon sandwiches, but I could tell by the smell it wasn't bacon.'

'Probably cat,' Geoffrey said. He appeared to be erecting some sort of miniature Bedouin tent.

'Yes, it's probably cat!' Margot said, shaking her tousled head with incredulity, as though her own wild speculation was all the proof she needed.

I sat with my new friends, surveying the ancient moorland – common ling and bell heather laying a cordial carpet beneath the sky's splenetic ceiling – and listening to the hum and whir of anachronistic traffic somewhere back there.

'Do you know why it's all so boggy?' Geoffrey asked me, turning big owl eyes in my direction.

'Actually, I don't.'

'Excellent. I'll tell you then.'

He cracked his heavy knuckles, took a copious swig of tea, and began the history lesson.

The British Isles were once covered almost completely in trees – everywhere except the sandy beaches and highest mountain peaks were wooded. From Guildford to Edinburgh, lions and tigers and (oh, my!) bears prowled the forests along with rhinos and elephants, having a fantastic time by all accounts. Then along came early man. The primitive Britons, those axe-wielding forebears of ours, felled the trees for building and farming and weapons, which prevented the latent groundwater from being evaporated by the trees. Add into the mix the impermeability of the underlying gritstone and the saturated vegetation rotted in its boots, forming what we have today: an all-you-can-eat buffet for people who only eat peat.

Geoffrey sat back on a travel cushion and looked pleased with himself.

'That's fascinating,' I said truthfully.

'Yes, I'm very knowledgeable, aren't I?'

'Incredibly.'

'Oh, Geoffrey, give Andy a packet of peanuts – he's only got one left.'

I had been rearranging the contents of my pockets during the seminar and Margot had seen the solitary walnut.

'Don't worry, Margot,' I said, 'this is more of a macguffin than a snack.'

'A what?'

'You know, a macguffin – that object in a film that's integral to the characters but doesn't have any importance to the audience. The mysterious briefcase that is never opened, for instance.'

'Oh goodness, well, I never knew that. Seems you *can* teach an old dog new tricks. A macguffin – Geoffrey, did you hear that? Andy taught me a new word: macguffin.'

'How wonderful.' Geoffrey was resting his eyes now.

'Have you heard from your wife and girls this morning, Andy?' Margot asked.

'Yes, they sent a little picture of themselves on the way to swimming.'

'Oh, how lovely.'

'I went swimming once,' Geoffrey said, eyes still closed but with his lips twitching. I could see what was coming.

'What on earth are you talking about, "once"?' Margot chided him.

'…It was yesterday, walking the Pennine Way! Ha!'

There it was. Margot actually afforded him a small chuckle at that. 'Silly man.'

Leaving Geoffrey then to bask in the glory of yet another good joke, I took my leave and trudged on, north by north-west under the light rain, gnawing at the miles in small bites, finding my own pace and maintaining it. Walking with other people is ideal for banter and downright chats, but it's not great for rhythm. When you hike in a group you're forced to jostle and hamper and march to someone else's drumbeat, taking point and covering the rear as required. You don't so much walk as swarm – you become *legion*, something other than yourself.

Walking alone is 'setting oneself apart'. It allows you to find that golden mean between haste and speed, to breathe and roll and tick, tick along. You're not just walking in time but walking *alongside* it, accompanying it – matching Chronos step for step. More than that, walking with a set destination in mind guarantees two things: purpose and progress. You know where you're going, and why, and how far you are from finishing – and how often can any of us say that? Sometimes too, you're leaving the remains of the old life and journeying to what remains eternally new: the present.

* * *

Time passed. Horizons shifted. I flirted teasingly with the Lancashire border without ever fully committing to it long-term. I was sure it would find someone else though, a good-looking county like that.

Heading for the old boundary marker of Aiggin Stone I crossed the once-dreaded Redmires (now a paved paradise) then wound my way through boulders along Blackstone Edge, a remarkably rugged kink in the fitted sheet of land stretched out to the West. Daniel Defoe, who wrote *Robinson Crusoe* and other things which it's possible to find out that he wrote, crossed Blackstone Edge in 1724 in a blizzard… in August (knowledge bestowed upon me by Cicerone's *Pennine Way* guide by Paddy Dillon). He said this: "The narrowness of the way, look'd horrible to us. We knew nothing where we were, or whether we were right or wrong." Obviously, there's a strong chance he'd simply been reading the guidebook I'd used for the first two stages of the walk, but it was humbling to reflect on what hill-walking would have entailed 300 years ago. Your boots would have been hobnailed; Gortex was still over 200 years in the future; no NHS, so even a mild blister required immediate amputation; and worst of all, with mortality rates being what they were, there was the likelihood of returning home to find at least three of your 12 children dead from any number of poxes.

At the far end of Blackstone Edge I reached the 600-year old standing stone of Aiggin – a bit like Stonehenge, but where the other stones pranked him by not turning up. This took me left down an old supposed Roman road, where the view seemed to take a deep breath and hold it. The wind farm across the valley was laundering away, layering modern grace onto a base of ancient nous, and I lubricated myself on clean air.

There's some debate about what influence the Romans actually had on the area. They definitely carved out paths, but whether they had any lasting influence beyond that is up for grabs. I had read that back towards Crowden there have been curious sightings over the years of a Roman Centurion out on the moors at night, looking for his lost legion. I like stories like that – I think it adds mythos to a place – but it also sounds very much like what happened on a friend's stag do, only the Centurion got lost in the centre of Nottingham and had to get a taxi back to Crewe.

Much farther north than here the Pennine Way crosses Hadrian's Wall, so I could think more about the Romans another time, and how pretty much the whole of England between Edale and The Wall used to be home to the Brigantes tribe under their fierce female leader, Cartimandua. If you observed the landscape from certain angles, shielding your view from the industrialised valley floors and leviathan windmills, it wasn't a huge challenge to imagine yourself there, out on the hills in primitive dress, chopping down trees willy-nilly, subjugating the terrain, occasionally getting run over by a chariot. Happy times, I'm sure.

CHAPTER 8

THE FOLLOWING CONTAINS SCENES THAT SOME VIEWERS MIGHT FIND OFFENSIVE

This whole area of Yorkshire is one big reservoir junkie. The afternoon session started with a long flat bout of walking past man-made lakes with names like Warland and Light Hazzles, during which time the environment began to feel lived-in again, somehow tamer. The rain had been fitful and petulant but it hadn't properly lashed out, the blue-jacketed sky seeking to unify the heavens while the grey cloud waged defiant civil war against it.

Piercing the new horizon the monolith of Stoodley Pike stood sentinel, a staunch monument of northern England and the walker's next waypoint – a waypoint, I might add, which never, ever, ever seems to be getting any closer (NB. There's an outside chance that I still haven't reached it and my mind has simply shattered into a very lucid fever dream). During the long stalking drag towards Stoodley you regard its implacability, a single blackened finger raised questioningly: 'Do you really want to do another fortnight of this? You must be so tired, and I can hear the squelch of your boots from here. Don't you want to be back with your family?'

'Yes, that is what I want.'

Don't listen to him, sire, Alan came to the rescue.

When I finally reached Stoodley Pike in the winter of 2045, I stopped under its eerie sundial shadow to down a can of pop and munch a cat-meat sausage roll. A man from one of the underlying villages was thrashing his dogs across the hillside, while somewhere up on the monolith a pair of pigeons were having an animated conversation in pigeon (I can't do the accent).

The monument actually has a quirky backstory, if that's of interest to you? Apparently the site of an ancient chieftain's burial cairn, it was built in 1815 to celebrate Wellington's victory at Waterloo and the end of the Napoleonic Wars. Rather ominously, the 37-metre needle collapsed in 1854 just as Britain was entering the Crimean War. Two years later, at the end of that conquest and having given Tennyson a chance to pen *Charge of the Light Brigade,* the memorial was rebuilt and has stood resolute ever since, branding the hillside with its searing mark of ownership. There's a lookout floor accessible from inside the tower which you can reach by climbing 39 steps, but I've read a book where that didn't end well so I decided against it, and besides, I'd done enough climbing for the day. Which was auspicious, because the remainder of the afternoon's walking was a staggered descent into the bustling, beckoning promise of Hebden Bridge: a charmingly Lovecraftian reimagining of an industrial town, where you're as likely to drink a vial of potion as a pint of Theakstons.

Into the valley of life walked the one.

I was blister – and injury – free and my walking poles had been quite good entertainment as twirling batons, but the drawn-out tedium of walking all day in isolation had left me feeling bored as I made my steady descent into the Calder Valley. The valley acts as a natural escalator, conveying you through various department store-style floors of habitat, from windswept moorland past cattle-studded farm pastures, down through sweet-smelling groves of oak and birch, and finally to the cafe-strewn waterway at ground level. I landed alongside the Rochdale Canal, opened up Google Maps (shielding my phone from a fresh influx of raindrops) and triangulated my position in relation to my accommodation. The route took me strolling back along the canal and through the gentrified streets.

A former textile town (previously a jungle of chimneys held together by its own grime) Hebden Bridge has more recently been upcycled and re-upholstered into a hive of hippyfied fashion and liberal values, with a hint of the dark arts lurking somewhere beyond the wall of sleep. Some guerilla graffiti on a road sign said "Freedom for all", whilst under an archway down a sidestreet another Turner Prize contender had spray-painted "MASSIVE TITS". The whole place felt otherworldly, but maybe I just hadn't seen civilization for three days.

"Expect nothing and you'll always be surprised," Daniel Defoe wrote. Today was to be the only time on the walk when I would stay at a private residence – a back-to-back terrace newly listed on AirBnB – rather than a bespoke walker's inn. My hosts were an Austrian couple in early retirement named Werner and Ingrid, and Werner had come across as very enthusiastic in his correspondence. I arrived at 4:30pm, the hour when the soul sinks lowest, and after ringing, hammering and wailing 'Pleeeeaaaasssseee', I waited outside in the now pouring rain for an hour because they must both be out. As it transpired, only Werner had been out. Ingrid was in the whole time but suffers from depression so doesn't answer the door unless she feels like it. On this occasion, she didn't.

Werner finally arrived, opened up and welcomed me in, leading me through into what can best (perhaps only) be described as an Aladdin's cave of psychedelic erotica. Ingrid was apparently a very talented but quite rude artist, and had adorned practically every surface and wall with quasi-spiritual and fully-pornographic paintings and sculptures, including one just above the Aga of my two hosts wearing coy smiles when underwear would have worked better to my taste. I was handed a chai tea and engaged in avid conversation by Werner, while never really being able to take my focus off the acrylic of his liberated genitals perennially in my eyeline. Seemingly an acolyte of the realist school of art, Ingrid had not *ahem* been kind to Werner in the scale of her work – a creative move I would have applauded had my hands not been otherwise engaged in forcibly detaching my retinas.

'That's certainly me!' Werner chuckled shamelessly.

No wonder she's depressed, Alan whispered. I told him not to be crass and took another long, studious sip of chai, closing my eyes to fully appreciate the delicate oriental flavours and also to block out the baying mob of willies nestled in my peripheral vision.

I should have just left at that point. "It is never too late to be wise," Daniel Defoe wrote in Robinson Crusoe. I really could have done with reading about Daniel Defoe before I started walking the Pennine Way – he seems like my sort of guy.

'Would you like to have a bath?' Werner enquired of me after a blessedly short but completely harrowing tour of the house.

'Yes please, but on my own if possible,' were my exact words. If live conversations had an edit button, I'd almost certainly look to redact the 'if possible' part on the second run.

'Ja, that's possible,' Werner replied. Not preferable, notice – but possible.

'How long will you be?' he asked with slight consternation.

'Erm, I don't know, I was hoping to have a long soak.'

'It's just that we only have one toilet in the house and it's in the bathroom. What if I need to do a wee?'

'Maybe you should go and do a wee now?' I suggested, really starting to project manage this crisis.

Werner went for a wee while I stood outside with my towel. He was out quickly enough.

'Hang on, let me just check with Ingrid – she's upstairs painting. Ingrid? Ingrid?!' Werner called up to the attic room.

'Ja, wass?'

'Andy chooses to have a bath. Do you need to do a wee first?'

There was a delay while Ingrid divided her daily fluids intake by the average length in minutes of a domestic soak, timesing that by the urgency of whatever bottom she was painting.

'Ja, Ok, I come and have a wee too.'

'Ingrid comes to have a wee too,' Werner informed me.

'Yep, I got that.'

Ingrid came down the stairs, ghosted past me into the bathroom to have a wee and, surely contravening all unwritten lore of hospitality, also a massive poo. Six minutes later and Werner and I were still standing there.

'I think she may be taking a poo as well,' Sherlock Werner confided. 'I'll just check. Ingrid? Ingrid, are you taking a poo, too?'

Less of a pause this time.

'Ja, sicher.'

'She's taking a poo, too,' Werner confirmed.

'Thank you.'

I was changing my mind about this bath. On reflection, that hour standing out in the pouring rain had got me pretty clean. More than that, it had been a magical time, a golden age of innocence.

Over a late-night potion of homemade kefir – which Werner brought into my unlockable room while I was trying to Facetime my girls, staying there until I hung up – he laid out his plans for breakfast the following morning.

'Usually, we eat around 9:30am, a breakfast of oatmeal and melon tea. How does that sound?' His ingratiating smile suggested he was expecting me to gush gratitude.

*Is he ******* joking,* Alan asked from the windowsill.

'Do you have any hash browns?' I asked.

'No.'

I had found myself in a culinary cul-de-sac, and there was no way to reverse.

'Oatmeal and melon tea sounds… just like breakfast to me.'

'Ah, wunderbar, excellent.'

It was 10pm and I was exhausted. A perfect time for Werner to dive headlong into a no-context diatribe about vaccinations, casually admonishing me as he did so for getting my Covid jab.

'Don't have your second one, whatever you do – you'll be dead in three years.'

I glanced around at the swirling pantheon of aggressive nudes, recollected the odious bath from earlier in the evening, and sloshed some of the sour yoghurt bacteria around in my mouth.

'Good,' I said. 'I want to be.'

Day 4
Hebden Bridge to Cowling
19 miles

"Be with me always – take any form – drive me mad!
Only do not leave me in this abyss, where I cannot find you!"
Emily Bronte, Wuthering Heights

"They all march in line, not swerving from their course.
They do not jostle each other."
Book of Joel, Chapter 2, NIV

CHAPTER 9
VINO VERITAS

'How's the oatmeal?' Werner asked, sipping appreciatively from his fruit tea. It was 8am and he was in loose robes – robes, I'm keen to mention, so hastily and randomly fashioned that they looked to have been woven using the 'infinite monkey' theorem, by giving a chimpanzee needles and wool and telling him to knit without a toilet break until he conjured the full range of Coco Chanel. These robes were, I suspected, an early prototype in that process.

'Mmmmmmm,' I responded to the question about the oatmeal, as though my tummy was revving its engine at how well refuelled it felt. In truth it was one of the most disgusting things I've ever tasted (and I once mistook bird droppings on my sleeve for Cornetto). Knowing I had a gargantuan 17 miles of walking ahead of me, Werner certainly hadn't stinted on the oatmeal, ladling scoop after hideous scoop into my bowl like a detestable remake of *The Magic Porridge Pot.* My secret plan was to foist handfuls of it into my North Face pockets when he wasn't looking, and then shuffle it out from the bottom of my trousers like *The Great Escape.*

The burlesque kitchen was snug and cosy at least, the Aga sending warm vibes into the retro wood-panelled walling, blending with the aromas of fresh basil, dill and parsley that hung like dress wigs next to a sculpture of a big erection.

'You know something, Andy?' Werner asked, and I quickly braced for a quick game of "Whose Penis Is It Anyway?"

'Not until you tell me, probably,' I replied.

'I've been researching you.'

This wasn't the sort of forensic background checking you expect from a B&B, and Werner's Austrian accent added a sinister note that I could have lived without.

'It's true, Werner,' I confessed. 'I *am* the tenth dentist – the one who keeps refusing to endorse all those new toothpastes.'

'AndyKind.co.uk,' Werner said slowly, enunciating every syllable with relish, as though uncovering some great conspiracy.

'That is the name of my website, yes.'

Werner seemed impressed with his own sleuthing. 'You're a preacher!'

I shrugged. 'A comedian mainly. I preach too though, sometimes, yes.'

'The Christian religion though, no?'

'I'm a Christian, that's correct.'

'OK… and why are you right? What makes you think that?'

Werner's spine had straightened and he looked mildly indignant, part way through a conversation that he and nobody else had started.

I wasn't on an itinerant preaching tour, and it was the green pastures and still waters on the other side of Calder Valley (rather than those found in *Psalm 23*) that concerned me that morning. Still, Werner looked genuinely interested if not a little antagonistic, and anything I could do to avoid another mouthful of oatmeal had inherent value. So I told him that I didn't think it was a case of me being *right* and anyone else being *wrong*. Doubtless, I am right and wrong about a good number of things, but here it's not so much a question of who is *right* as *what is true?* And, I told Werner, I believed that the story of Jesus was true, and that the central claims of Christianity made the most sense of what I already believed about myself: that I wanted to be loved unconditionally; to see justice done; to experience real joy and freedom and hope; to have a spiritual home from which I would never be turned away. As F.W. Boreham wrote, "Christianity enables man to burst the links of habit, break from straitened ways, to walk with buoyant stride a wider world. It provides him with an escape." (Maybe that's why I found myself on this here trail, at least in part.)

Werner nodded away, not receiving anything, merely counting the beats until he was able to transmit the message he had ready and prepared.

'I believe God is like an elephant,' he began when I took a vile sip of fruit tea. 'God is like an elephant and people are like blind men brought in to feel different parts of the elephant, to guess what it is like. And one blind man feels the tail and says, "Ah, the elephant is like a snake." And another man feels the leg and says, "No, no, the elephant is like a tree." Another feels the ear, another feels the tusk, Andy. And everyone goes away thinking they know what the elephant is, but...' Werner's eyes flashed from under his cotton-wool eyebrows 'it's all the same elephant, ja? And that's what I think God is like.'

It's a nice analogy, and an old one – first recorded about 500 BCE in the Buddhist Tittha Sutta. But it relies on the fact that somebody actually does see the whole elephant and understands its true nature. Consequently, it's not the all-inclusive monistic rallying cry it claims to be, because someone – or some group – actually does see the reality of the elephant for what it is. All truth claims are ultimately exclusive.

But I wasn't there to win an argument; wasn't there to save a soul. Maybe I should have been – maybe, pre-pandemic, I would have been. But I wasn't playing the role of preacher. Here, I was just a pilgrim.

'Elephants smell,' I said, stretching my facial muscles into their first smile of the day.

'Aha, yes!' Werner clenched his fist triumphantly, 'But so did you when you arrived last evening!'

He chuckled, and I chuckled with him. Then he stood up and his dressing gown slipped open and it was too late because I'd seen everything.

9am, I was at the front door, everyone was fully clothed, and there was another pleasant surprise.

'Your boots were soaking wet and filthy,' Werner confided, looking suddenly a bit sheepish. 'So I dried them in the airing cupboard and brushed them down a bit.'

He handed me my boots, which looked, felt and smelled unrecognisable. This was an incredible gesture, especially given that my footwear was the least vegan thing in all of Hebden Bridge.

'They smell like Christmas stuffing,' I said, slightly awed.

'Ja, we have sage hanging in the airing cupboard. I hope you don't mind that I took them without asking.'

'You didn't just take them, Werner. You have resurrected them!'

'Aha, yes! Resurrection – like Jesus, ja? Das ist perfekt!'

I slipped on and laced up my transmogrified boots, offered Werner my hand and gave him my own version of a pre-prepared spiel.

'Danke für ihre gastfreundlichkeit… das Frühstück war lecker.'

I was lying, of course, but to an A-level standard.

As a final parting gesture Werner handed me a snack for the day's march – two slices of pumpernickel bread and a handful of odd-looking beans. I would plant the latter in the next valley and check the BBC news every day for updates. I didn't see Ingrid, presuming that she was mid-diarrhoea somewhere, but I shook Werner's hand with gusto and crossed the morning threshold. Stepping out onto the cobblestone street, across from which pretty raised beds of dahlias and geraniums were swaying through their early matins, something caught my attention, an old friend I hadn't seen in a while but news of whose demise had been greatly exaggerated: blue sky. The sun had risen, shaking its holy joy like crumbs from a picnic blanket.

'Hey there, Mr Blue,' I nodded.

It was going to be a good day.

* * *

I had noticed over the past few nights that my sleep pattern had changed, and I was amazed at how awake I felt. And not just awake, either – alert! I had been expecting to want to sleep all the time; to reach my destination at the end of each stage and lapse into a coma from which I'd need to be roused the following morning by a kindly nun holding smelling salts, or to be doused in the contents of a bedpan by a cantankerous matron. When I'm sleeping in my own bed, anything less than eight hours leaves me feeling sluggish and mildly homicidal for the remainder of the day, but it was different on the Pennine Way. I was operating on about five and a half hours of sleep each night, waking at first light, harmonising with the songbirds' melody, feeling chipper and adrenalised. Sore and aching, yes, but bright and beautiful and raring to go. It was as though my primitive hunter-gatherer, lying dormant in my psyche so long that they'd called off the search, had suddenly stumbled out of the wilderness, roused by three days of continuous primal movements – stride, push, lunge, bend, grunt – to take my body by the reins and lead me along neural pathways long untrodden. I was still flabby around the middle, still exhausted and mewing by dusk each day, but my synapses and sinews were starting to pulsate with evolutionary energy. I was shaking off the sedative effects of a Netflix-driven life, the soporific symptoms of a locked-down existence. Each morning on the Pennine Way signalled the day of a big exam; each evening marked the night before another one. A sort of Christmas Eve for masochists.

In his ludicrously pleasant book *Walking Home: A Poet's Journey*, Poet Laureate Simon Armitage quotes Richard Holmes's book *Footsteps: Adventures of a Romantic Biographer*, in which Holmes quotes Robert Louis Stevenson:

"For my part, I travel not to go anywhere, but to go…the great affair is to move; to feel the needs and hitches more life a little more nearly; to get down off this feather bed of civilisation, and to find the globe granite under foot and strewn with cutting flints."

You'll notice that's me quoting Armitage quoting Holmes quoting Stevenson. Not a bad relay team, and you must feel free to quote me on that.

I was to be joined for Day 4 by Tony Vino, my friend of 17 years and a man of such joyful constancy, the fact that so much of our fellowship time has been red-carpeted with benign chaos no longer bothers me. We had met at the first comedy gig either of us ever did, and were both terrible; but in that fiery crucible a tungstenian bond was formed which has so far proven unbreakable. C.S. Lewis wrote in *The Four Loves*, "Friendship…is born at the moment when one person says to another 'What! You too? I thought that no one but myself…'" So it was with Tony and myself.

You tend to acquire fewer and fewer friends the older you get, I think – although I don't have a wide-enough social circle to carry out any kind of meaningful research. People dip their toe into the shallows of your life for a time, paddle about a bit, and then move off down the beach to where it might be warmer, to where the seaweed doesn't entangle so much, or where the moral sewage leaking from you won't spoil their life out at the seaside. For lots of us, the pandemic exacerbated that by taking a clean reaperish blade to so many connections we had thought of as 'friendships', scything them down to 'acquaintances', to 'somebody that I used to know'.

But whatever our souls are made of, mine and Tony's are the same. He had kept steady pace with me through the metaphorical dales of adult life, and now I would reward him by thrashing him over literal ones. What a tremendous thing it is to have a friend.

He was due to meet me at Mytholmroyd, Hebden Bridge's less gentrified outlier, which lay a mile down the road and offered some – massive cheer, please – 'bonus walking' to reach the day's official start line. I headed off from Werner's house, stump-clacking over cobbles, whistling a happy tune, greeting shopkeepers like a post-redemption Ebenezer Scrooge, grinning at the light dappling the laconic Rochdale canal. It was well with my soul.

I crossed a lovely stream, saw a sign for Midgehole, stopped, opened my pack, took out a map, checked it, realised I'd been going the wrong way, swore, replaced my map, zipped up my pack, crossed the stupid stream again. It was *not* well with my soul. I clack-stumped back down the road, remembering how much I hate the word dappled, shunning shopkeepers like a pre-redemption Ebenezer Scrooge, blowing aggressive raspberries. The day was already due to be 17 miles (the longest stage so far) and I had just added on an extra one because I was a complete and massive idiot – there simply isn't a better way to describe that situation.

Just before 10am (much, much later than you want to be starting a day like this) I reached Mytholmroyd, pouting grumpily. And there was Tony, sitting on a dry-stone wall, smiling insouciantly, not really dressed for walking so much as smuggling contraband across the straits of Gibraltar – mustard brown jumper; bizarrely billowing Kappa tracksuit bottoms; Christmas socks.

'I'm throwing all these clothes out, Kindy, so I thought I'd give them a nice day out before I take them behind a barn and execute them.'

This raised as many questions as it answered, still, he'd brought cooked meat for lunch and a flask of coffee, so Tony was basically the hero that Bonnie Tyler had so aggressively demanded back in '84. He had also memorised W.H. Davies' famous poem *Leisure,* that he wanted to recite before we started. Without permission he clambered up onto a ledge of dry stone wall.

'What is this life if, full of care,
We have no time to stand and stare?
No ti…'

I cut him off. We were behind schedule, and I didn't want experimental theatre slowing me down even further.

'You can recite the next stanza when we stop to take on water,' I said. 'This isn't a holiday, Vino.'

'But I brought you coffee and meat…'

'Oh? How's bragging camp going?'

The opening act of this stage of the Pennine Way takes no prisoners. It's a slow, trundling rollercoaster up to and over Heptonstall Moor, an inverted toboggan run that slaloms painstakingly round tapering country lanes and past unfeasibly perched allotments, with Stoodley Pike staring daggers at your back whenever you stop for a breather. There's an immediate precipitate climb up slippery cobbles towards an overgrown graveyard, brambly and nettlesome, which feels uncommonly untended for Britain's best-known National Trail. Pinkish-purple foxgloves line your way and look beautiful, but get any of their toxins in your eyes and those bell-shaped flowers will toll for thee.

I informed Tony as we walked that I wouldn't need the map today, that I had vanquished this section twice before and it was pretty straightforward all the way to Old Bess Hill.

'But Kindy, you managed to turn the wrong way out of your front door this morning.'

'That is of course true, Tony, but…' I explained that the town of Hebden Bridge isn't actually *on* the Pennine Way – it's just near it. Now that I was back on the trail proper it was simply about muscle memory.

30 minutes later we were lost.

'Kindy, I'm not sure if it's relevant but there was a sign about 20 minutes back saying Pennine Way to the right.'

'Not sure if it's relevant? How could that possibly *not* be relevant?'

'You said you knew the way.'

Tony refused to budge an inch until I let him read another stanza of his poem. I took the opportunity to down a beaker of hot caffeine solution while he stood, legs dramatically akimbo, one foot perched on the step of an old barn, and his stentorian voice swept clear along the valley.

'What is this life if, full of care,
We have no time to stand and stare?
No time to stand beneath the boughs

And stare as long as sheep or cows…'

'Quite finished?' I asked.

'For now, Kindy. For now.'

'Wonderful.'

'Pass me that coffee. And tell me more about that Austrian guy – did you really see his entire willy when the dressing gown fell open?'

'The whole lot, Vino. I was just glad there weren't a load of blind men groping around the kitchen for spiritual enlightenment.'

'Oh, of course. Imagine the heresies.'

* * *

Chaos – in this case, being lost – like boredom is a great motivator. It's a literal ground zero from which you can only build and seek, and stimulates maybe the most important desire for any human: the desire to be found. These sodden lumps of truth did nothing to cheer me as we cut off the track and walked steeply uphill for a mile to regain the path. Navigation would be 'muscle memory' I had said, but after three kilometres of sheer incline my muscles were going to need CBT to cope with some of these flashbacks. By my reckoning I had now managed to extend the day's projected footfall by more than two additional miles – and it wasn't even lunchtime. Fieldfuls of sheep and cows raised ruminating jaws to stare at us ambivalently (having, according to legend, loads of time to spare) while Tony spent much of the corrective diversion remixing the Proclaimers:

'Oh, Kindy would walk 10,000 miles, and Kindy would walk 10,000 more, just to get from Hebden Bridge across the moooooorrs to flippin' Ickornshaw.'

Twelve times in total he sang it. I haven't forgotten. I won't forgive.

'Should have just let me recite my poem then, shouldn't you Kindy, you old miser.'

We entered the village of Colden, spying a reassuring acorn signpost which meant we were back on track, albeit late, sweaty from the detour and with irresistible Scottish folk-pop now lodged in my head. Still, we were no longer lost. A humble plywood strut, nailed onto a stretch of fencing and bearing a simple painted message, caught my eye:

MAY'S SHOP 50m
SELLS OWT THA WANTS

Even with Tony's salvific meat-and-coffee errand, the opportunity to buy extra provisions is something no walker should turn down, ever. Whether it's a farm shop or a village store, or just a creepy shack with a beckoning hag saying 'Enter, child' from the folds of an adumbral cloak, you go in. You just do.

The door looked like a tight squeeze, so I unbuckled my pack and searched for a place to hang it. Tony, carrying less of a wide load, made straight for the entrance.

'Check for hags please, Vino.'

'Always.'

Moments later he reappeared, or at least his head did, poking through the doorway like a whack-a-mole.

'Kindy… there's something you need to see.'

'What's the matter? We can't dally.'

'Just come.'

And it was incredible. Inside the small, nondescript outhouse was a bijou supermarket. No, no, better than that – more like an award-winning quartermaster's or a hobbit's pantry, shelves stocked and ripe with tantalising food, quenching drinks and delicious toiletries. There was everything a wayfarer could dream of: terraced rows of chocolate bars, foil-wrapped meat pies, the full executive range of mints and sucky sweets. I looked around in wonder.

'As God is my witness, I'll never be hungry again.'

'Aye, that's how most people react.' A lady behind the counter smiled. This must be May, the shop owner.

'How is this possible?' I asked. 'How have you done it?'

'We do our best for yer, lad,' May (presumably) said stoutly. 'People call this the Aladdin's Cave. One walker last week said this was what heaven must be like.'

'I can understand why.'

'Aye, 'appen. It's reyt nice to see people's happy faces. We do our best.'

'Do you have any Bertie Bott's Every Flavour Beans?' Tony asked from somewhere deep in the confectionary.

'What yer see is what's there,' the woman who I'm convinced was May answered.

I purchased a meat pie for now, a Danish Pastry for later, another Danish Pastry for now and a balanced diet of Tic Tacs and Trebor Extra Strong Mints. The incontrovertible May also let Tony serenade her with a few bars of his poem, which they both seemed to appreciate very much.

With our spirits dry-cleaned we pushed on, eager feet trying to make up time ('No time to see, when woods we pass, where squirrels hide their nuts in grass'). Through shady dells and dry stone-walled pastures we marched, down over the peaty wastes of Heptonstall Moor, talking at intervals, watching the slowly shifting landscape, stopping occasionally to sip from a canteen or point at a goat. There was a nice confluence of babbling brooks at Graining Water, then an amble above the stream towards the Walshaw Dean reservoir trio ('No time to see, in broad daylight, streams full of stars, like skies at night'). Cloud shaped like commas punctuated the sky, hinting that the rain might have reached the end of a clause without coming to a full stop, but the sun was out and about too, infusing the afternoon air with a gorgeous peroxide glow.

'Come on, Vino, we can get this back if we really work at it. 90 minutes is nothing.'

'You know that song?' Tony asked, as he watched me make clumsy work of a walled stile.

'Which one?'

'The one where the sun has got his hat on.'

'Oh yes – hip hip hip hooray. That one?'

'That's the one… just give me your rucksack and I'll pass it over the wall to you – this is like watching an elephant try and climb a ladder.'

'Thanks. What about it – the song?'

'Well, what exactly is the sun shielding his head from?'

I stopped and leaned back against the drain wall. We were at the bottom of Withins Height Hill, my eye tracing the sinuous line of slabs towards its peak.

'You know what, Vino, that is an excellent question, and it's never even occurred to me.'

'I know. That's the problem with the school system, Kindy – they teach kids what to think, not how to think. Here's your pack.'

Tony jumped down onto the turf and I rewarded his intrepid mind with a cascade of Tic Tacs.

'I'm waiting for an answer, Kindy. Why is the sun wearing a hat?'

'I'll be completely transparent about this, Vino – I have no idea.'

'Oh. Do you know anyone who might?'

'I don't, I'm afraid.'

'Never mind, then.'

'Let's get up this hill. 90 minutes is nothing – we can get this back.'

'Hang on…

No time to turn of Beauty's glance,
And watch her feet, how they can dance:
No time to wait till her mouth can
Enrich that smile her eyes began…

Now you may walk up that hill, Kindy.'

CHAPTER 10

A SHADOW OF THE PAST

We were now in Brontë country and approaching what is, arguably, the most touristy part of the Pennine Way – which isn't something that counts as an accolade, in the same way that you wouldn't tout the most enjoyable aspect of a factory fire.

Over the crest of Withins Height and sitting desolate amid the tawny moors is the evocative site of Top Withins, rumoured to be the muse for the house in Emily Brontë's most famous novel; but nothing more than a dilapidated ruin to the illiterate.

'Apparently, Wuthering Heights is based on this,' I told Tony as we bobbed across the wilderness towards it.

'Wow, cool. Is that the one that goes "Ayyyaaah, Babooshka Babooshka"?'

As I say, nothing more than a dilapidated ruin to the illiterate.

Thousands of literary boffins make their devout pilgrimage to this site and nearby Haworth each year, which is an odd thing because there's diddly squat to look at, the place being nothing more than a tumbledown farmhouse with a caved-in roof. It might just about provide shelter for a walker caught in a storm, but it's not even the best-maintained bothy on the Pennine Way. Compounding the anti-climax is a wall plaque from the Brontë society which reads:

"The buildings, even when complete, bore no resemblance to the house she (Emily Brontë) described but the situation may have been in her mind when she wrote of the moorland setting."

Don't pull any punches, Brontë Society. You tell all these American and Japanese tourists struggling up here in sandals exactly how pointless it is them turning up. Why not add a short postscript: "Btw, while we've got you here, Santa isn't real, and you're probably adopted. All the best."

Nevertheless, Top Withins remains unfathomably popular for those wanting to chase dreams of Heathcliff and find literary inspiration – it's essentially grave-sucking for authors of romantic fiction. A Canadian lady, sitting pensively inside the ruins, told us how she'd written her Master's thesis on landed gentry in Victorian novels. She looked a bit underwhelmed by Wuthering Heights, but she cheered up when I offered her a Trebor Extra Strong Mint, and so she should.

'I read that Charlotte Brontë died from walking over the moors in the rain,' I told Tony as our boots rehit the path.

'Oh dear. Probably should have checked the weather app before she left the house,' he replied. 'And who's Charlotte Brontë?'

'Oh, just a friend of the family.'

I was just glad I hadn't told him we'd passed near Sylvia Plath's grave back in Heptonstall. He'd memorised one poem and that was enough English lessons for this academic year.

The trail surrounds and then finally pounces on Ponden Reservoir, a really pleasant spot, spoiled slightly by the fact that a local farmstead has turned the approach into an unofficial car graveyard, the skeletal corpses of Ford Mondeos hedged up against the dry-stone walling.

'That one looks how I feel,' I quipped to a guy sanding down the paint on a cadaverous Rover Metro, assuming that, like plenty of the wayside dwellers, he'd be receptive to a bit of playful chitchat. Instead, he stared at me as though I'd written my Master's thesis on just how much of a wally he was.

'Tough crowd,' Vino whispered. 'Don't offer him a mint.'

A surprising number of writers bemoan the presence of so many reservoirs during these opening days of the Way. I have to say, I don't get what the problem is: the sight of a glass-bottomed valley, an island of satin blue in a sea of greens, browns and greys; the defiant horizontal slash cutting order across the unruly wilds; the promise of succour for the parched wanderer. What's not to appreciate? And Ponden Reservoir is a place to tarry a-while; to breathe easy, glug from a canteen, eat a slightly squashed Danish Pastry and watch the incongruous windsurfing lessons taking place on the water's surface. So tarry we did.

I was feeling heavy and jaded, a direct result of treating the whole day like one big game of catch-up. That tactic seemed oddly facile on reflection, for who was I trying to catch? What goal would be missed by turning up in Cowling 90 minutes later than planned? My accommodation was booked and I'd still have the whole evening to recover and recline, to write my notes and ring my girls and read a book. Why had I worried about being out of time?

Wait! Hang on…

With a shuddering jolt from my memory I realised that this was the exact location where my attempt to walk the Pennine Way back in 2003 had failed. This reservoir was where I'd run aground and abandoned ship.

That previous walk had stopped being fun somewhere around Black Hill (NB. We walked during a baking hot August, and I'd developed what I now understand to be plantar fasciitis). Upon reaching Ponden Guest House with its home-made scones and comfy mattress, I had decided that enough was enough, and so the fresh-faced, lithe-limbed 22-year-old had taken the easy way out and gone home along the path of least resistance. My friend Matt had soldiered bravely on, but he too gave up after a few more days owing to the oppressive heat.

Another 100 metres and the 40-year old would overtake his younger, former self. And that was something to celebrate.

'Finish your poem, Vino,' I said. 'Do it all in one go. Let me appreciate every nuance.'

I de-pouched Alan and we formed a modest but committed audience. Verge-side daisies held up small clean faces, with wall-climbing ivy creeping up to the balcony seats. The reservoir shivered pink and silver under the afternoon sky, and a party of mallards dipped in and out of earshot. Head held high, arms outstretched as though preparing for ascension, and with feet ludicrously wide apart, Tony recited his poem:

"What is this life if, full of care,
We have no time to stand and stare?–
No time to stand beneath the boughs
And stare as long as sheep or cows:
No time to see, when woods we pass,
Where squirrels hide their nuts in grass:
No time to see, in broad daylight,
Streams full of stars, like skies at night:
No time to turn at Beauty's glance,
And watch her feet, how they can dance:
No time to wait till her mouth can
Enrich that smile her eyes began?
A poor life this if, full of care,
We have no time to stand and stare."

I applauded and threw a dandelion at him. Alan was too emotional to comment.

'Bravo, sir!'

'Thanks Kindy, thanks Alan. Right, my work here is done – let's go!!' Tony hoisted his pack.

'Not yet, Vino,' I said, gazing across Ponden Reservoir back towards 2003.

'Not just yet.'

'OK, perfect,' Tony replied. 'In which case, I have also memorised the song *Jellicle Cats*. Take it away – and a one and a two and a…'

* * *

Eventually we walked on. I saluted Ponden Guest House as we overtook it, wondering whether the same scone-making lady still dwelled there; imagining her staring through her garden window with a fresh bake, winking knowingly at my oh-so-tiny victory.

The weather had devolved again, Mr. Blue Sky knocked off the top of the charts by Rain Clouds. I had drunk a lot of water and was running low, and we still had Bare Hill and Old Bess Hill to negotiate before day's end. As Providence would have it, coming to my rescue as it occasionally did, I spied an outside tap lodged conspiratorially inside a gated farmyard. A notice daubed in menacing red paint said: "Private Property – KEEP OUT."

'I'll grab us some water,' Tony said.

But then another memory straddled my path – that of Gillian of Belfast asking if it was hard for anyone to be braver than me.

'I'll do it,' I told Tony firmly.

It was silly. Staying off private land isn't cowardly, nor was syphoning tap water an act of undaunted courage. But I was Ser Endrew Kynde of the South Pennines and I was on a mission. I removed my pack, checked the angles for sheep dogs and ornery farmers, leapt the wall and scurried to the tap, refilling first Tony's and then my own bottle from the sputtering faucet, before making a glorious retreat back over the gate. This must be what being in Special Forces is like. It must be.

We struggled up among barns and lambing sheds towards Crag Nook Farm, overtured all the while by the persistent cry of a peacock reverberating off the hillsides, a shrill siren notifying the next valley that I had done it, I had beaten my past and escaped… for now. The creature sounded sad, doleful, as though calling out for someone. I thought back to the pea-hen in Diggle and joined a couple of disparate dots in my imagination.

It's me, your Cathy, I've come home...

The last three miles are always the worst. Why is this so, we may ask? Well, firstly because it feels like such a small percentage of the day's walking – 'I've trekked 15 miles already, another three is nothing' – but also because you sense that you're nearly *there* and you've let your mind's eye range to the finish line, to thoughts of beer and burgers and baths. That's when you start to notice your body, its pain and aches: that nettled calf, that stone under your heel, the tug of your pack and chapped skin of your shoulders. You stop breathing and start panting, become petulant and entitled. The stoicism which has carried you so well so far gets usurped by an epicurean obsession with rest and reward. The only cure is to reel your thoughts back to where two tired feet are walking slowly but surely, one step at the time. When walking long haul, the mind needs to stay just above shoulder height.

And while the climbs on the Pennine Way may sap you of your energy, it's the interminable descents that surgically remove your inner joy and suture in a Sartrian angst. After 17 miles of hard graft, we tumbled discordantly down Old Bess Hill to Cowling, by which time the rain had abruptly returned for an encore none of the crowd had demanded, like a meteorological Joe Pasquale. Tony's wife Claire and his two children, Jojo and Myla, were parked up on the road waiting for him. We waved and blew kisses and bowed to them, and Claire wound down the window and told Tony to hurry up and get in the car. In her defence, we were 90 minutes late and also morons, and I noted with some interest that Tony didn't even attempt to placate her with recited verse – the blunt prose of his wife's expression putting a big fat full stop to his career as a performance poet.

'Good luck, Kindy Kindy. I might be able to walk another day with you next week, but I'll see how I get on. You're going to smash this walk, though.'

'Cheers, Vino. Thanks for being my friend.'

'Always. If you don't make it out alive, do you want me to avenge your death?'

'Erm… yes. Yes, I think that would be a nice gesture.'

'I'm on it.'

The Vino family headed back along the Pennine Way towards Manchester, taking the rain with them. Like a mysterious wizard or malaria, Tony would return to me further down the line.

My muscles were tight and my limbs were loose, and I shambled into base like a backpacking Boogeyman. Reprieve was at hand, though. Winterhouse Barn B&B sits on the main road through the village and was set up specifically for Pennine Wayfarers, and I had booked the Summerhouse for the evening. That sounds fairly grand, but it was essentially just a shed with a fake ID. Still, it was only £10 including breakfast, and on arrival I was asked by my host Trevor whether I would like some wine. This, I decided, was how I wanted all future conversations to start.

'I have been known to go back for seconds at communion,' I replied.

Trevor looked delighted and shuffled off past his flower beds and his "Trespassers will be composted" sign. I heard clinking and uncorking, and he returned moments later holding a carafe brimming with crimson wonder. The carafe itself looked as though it had been exchanged for Esso tokens back in the late 80s – Trevor probably had a commemorative coin of Gary Linekar stashed somewhere in one of the outhouses, too. I wasn't complaining.

'It's mi own brew and it may be reyt strong – see what yer think.'

It was 5:30pm. I'd walked 19 miles and not yet eaten dinner.

By the time Trevor's wife Olwen turned up 15 minutes later to hand me a fresh towel, I had drunk a single glass of homemade wine and was absolutely obliterated, smashing out *Babooshka* like it was a football chant.

I wasn't fully aware of the effect the wine was having on me until Olwen gently highlighted, 'I think you've caught the sun,' in response to which I pointed directly at her and said, 'I think YOU have!!'

Olwen spied the jug of homebrew on the table and sighed, then engaged me in conversation to stop me from blacking out. I somehow managed to maintain cogency, although at points my mind fuzzed over and I mistook her for my grandmother. She and Trevor had been housing weary pilgrims for years, and even though the B&B wasn't technically open because of Covid she had refused to close her doors completely – hence the use of the 'Summerhouse' exclusively for walkers. She asked if I was married and I said yes; asked if I had kids and I said 3, then 2. She discovered I was a preacher and tried to find common ground by remembering the name of a local vicar she used to know.

'Kevin Ass….'

'Kevin Ass?'

'Ass ass ass…'

'Why do you keep saying ass?' I may have been tipsy, but this woman was in her late seventies and no amount of subliminal messages would convince me to take a chance.

'Kevin Aspall, that's him. Do you know him?'

'No.' Although after two glasses of Winterhouse Shiraz, I was struggling to remember who *I* was.

A homemade beehive shaped like a chest of drawers was vibrant with activity on the other side of the garden. Tiny black shapes were circling and landing, storing away pollen for the honey judging contest at the Skipton Summer Fayre.

'Those bees aren't going to swarm, are they?' I asked Olwen, concerned.

'Only if the Queen dies.'

'How would they know, though?'

'The Queen Bee, love, not the one in Buckingham Palace.'

'With you now, makes sense,' I nodded.

'Try and drink some water,' she said, and bustled off back to the house.'

'How old are you today, Daddy?' Alice asked me over a brief Facetime.

'I once had tea with Mr William Shakespeare, my darling,' I slurred down the phone. 'And a fine chap he was, too.'

'Oh, yes, you are quite old then.'

'Your face is very red, Daddy,' Heidi said, peering into her side of the screen.

'Oh, well, as your great-grandmother told me earlier, I've just caught the sun.'

In the distance I could see a couple of Trevors, both quite blurry, bringing me another sloshing jug of joy.

'We miss you Daddy! Byeeeeeee!!'

'I miss you so much! Speak to you tomorrow!'

The call ended.

I miss you.

It had been a gruelling day, albeit waymarked with points of interest and various genres of Vino. Nevertheless, I still had no injuries and no blisters and I could sense the landscape brightening as I headed for the limestone of the Yorkshire Dales. And by the end of tomorrow I would have trudged as far as I'd ever managed to trudge before. I lay back and elongated myself on the Summerhouse's camp bed as the moon clocked on for its nightshift.

Unlike the 2003 edition of Andy Kind, I could do one more day. In an accidental move he would have very much approved of, I was ******* hammered.

Day 5
Cowling to Malham
17 miles

"Here today, up and off to somewhere else tomorrow! Travel, change, interest, excitement! The whole world before you, and a horizon that's always changing!"
Kenneth Grahame, The Wind in the Willows

"Sole lord am I of all this realm of sight,
These swinging meadow sweeps, this delight
Of ranking hills, these clouds just out of fold.
Stoutly the sturdy road beneath my feet
Rings me a morning welcome. Rise, my soul..."
A Morning Walk by Amos Russell Williams

CHAPTER 11
BEASTS OF BURDEN

Today the sun came *out,* out. Today the rainclouds fled like no-good hoodlums at the first wail of sirens. In short, today was amazing, a rare and disingenuous act of benevolence from Britain's most gruelling footpath.

It didn't start particularly well. I bolted awake at 5am, confused and a little frightened to find myself locked in a shed. Why was this? Had I been taken hostage in a bloody allotment turf war? No, no, that couldn't be it.

My immediate surroundings adjusted into focus. A pair of tumbledown boots lay on the floor, while on the small bedside table a jug of ruby liquid stood resplendent and half-full. Oh yes, I remembered now – I was walking the Pennine Way and I had been spiked by an old man.

With the flood of panic at having been kidnapped now receding apace, I was still left with the not-insignificant problem that my brain was on fire. The second carafe with which Trevor had furnished me last evening had been of a different vintage to the first, tasting of blackberries soaked in raw diesel. I had still partaken in a glass, not wishing to appear rude, but the grape had been so strongly fermented that I could now smell colours and potentially see through time. I downed a handful of Tic Tacs from May's Pantry in the hope that they were also secretly paracetamol. At least they would prevent Charon the Boatman from mistaking my mouth for the gateway to Hades and trying to sail into it.

I opened up the summer house and welcomed in the wave of pastille light lapping across from the east. Dug in between the agrarian bulwarks of the valley, Olwen's garden was almost arcadian, with rows of fuchsia and marigold technicolouring the soil and tomato plants potted here and there like candy trees. With brain throbbing and mouth dry, I padded down the patio in bare feet and drank all the water from the garden tap like The Tiger Who Came to Tea. Next, I filled my canteen for the day's endeavours, re-rolled the two pairs of walking socks I'd left draped on a bench overnight to dry, then stood long under a portacabin shower, abusing the hot water supply and slapping myself round the face.

At 7:10am a back door opened, and Olwen came cheerfully along the patio carrying a plate of bacon baps and a full cafetière. She had been looking after Pennine Way walkers for years and she knew precisely what was needed of a morning: cooked meat, strong coffee, minimal chat.

'It means you can get an early start, young man. You'll be heading across to Malham today, I assume?'

'That's the plan, yes.'

'Well, it's a beautiful day of walking. Me and Trevor used to walk it a few times a year, but we're too old for that now. Just leave the plate and cup on the table and I'll clear it up later.'

'Thank you, that's very kind.'

Olwen started to tootle back inside, then asked in an almost prescient over-the-shoulder way, 'Would you like a couple of paracetamol as well?'

'I would kill for them.'

She gave a rueful chuckle. 'Ah, yes. Trevor loves having tasters for his casks, but it *can* have the occasional downside. We once had a pair of chaps have to stay an extra night because they were so hungover.'

'Ridiculous,' I said, opening a new tab in my mind entitled 'Plan B'.

'Pick yourself some tormentil – little yellow flower that looks reyt like a buttercup. Good for headaches, they say. And don't forget to sign the guest book. Tek care, love.'

Packed, strapped, laced and liberally dosed up, I made the short walk up the road to where the emblazoned acorn of a Pennine Way signpost pointed me off and down to the right. Clouds skudded above me, heading my way towards warmer climes, so I would trust their nose and follow. Blue sky and sunlight are the best disinfectants for a polluted brain.

Day 5 of the Way is a saunter. It's easy on the eye and the feet – although not so much on the ear, as we'll find out. First there's the quaint village of Lothersdale, easy Loversdale, the last of the South Pennine mill towns. From here the country starts to transfigure as you prepare to enter the riverlands of the Aire Gap, a broad tract of land separating those ancient adversaries, the Peaks and the Dales – similar to the Jets and the Sharks but with absolutely no dancing. Lothersdale is the sort of village where you might expect to find a vicar's daughter reading Jane Austen under a tree, or a couple of flat-capped scamps catching sticklebacks in an old tin can, both of whom go on to get wounded during the Battle of the Somme.

And why shouldn't walking be a saunter, after all? It's the best method yet discovered by humans to move at a pace which balances speed and energy. (If you want to go faster, hire a bike or a donkey.) Hiking may be a sport, but it's not a performance. As Frederic Gros says in *A Philosophy of Walking*, "When you are walking, there is only one sort of performance that counts: the brilliance of the sky, the splendour of the landscape."

Walking then, across a constantly self-painting canvas, is more like art appreciation: it invites you to be an active spectator, interacting with the tableaus as you find them. By doing that it reaches down into your soul and retrieves, from where it had been stuffed beneath waterproofed pragmatism, the simple serenity of just *being alive.* Aesthetically, it's as though you're moving rhythmically down the wide corridors of a Constable exhibition, only without needing to have your bag inspected on arrival.

There's no entrance fee, no need to show off your own talents, and the only tools you need are charmingly rustic: two willing legs and two big eyes to drink in the scene. The industrious walker is also – as far as time and schedule allow – an unashamed bystander.

At the top of Pinhaw Beacon I found one such bystander, a man in a bright blue top staring through a pair of binoculars – though thankfully not at me.

'What's the view like from up there?' I asked.

'Here, take a look.'

The chap handed me his binoculars, and after a couple of gentle clicks of the dial I was afforded a staggering northward view of distant peaks, majestic and mercurial, the most impressive vista since Kinder Scout. "Because without a view," Simon Armitage writes in *Walking Home,* "the whole enterprise is pointless, a futile schlep, hours of visual confinement with nothing to see apart from your own feet."

Malevolent skies turn even edenic places into dystopias, but the newly-clement weather was like a swooshing off of a blackout blind.

'Wow, amazing,' I said dreamily.

'F****** beautiful, isn't it. See that prominent shelf on the horizon? That's Pen-y-Ghent, where we'll be tomorrow.'

'How did you know I was walking the Pennine Way?' I asked. *And also,* I didn't ask, *where did that F-Bomb come from?*

'I guessed that you were,' he answered. 'Lone walker, out on the hills before nine o'clock, big f****** pack.'

And so I met Rob, an endearingly foul-mouthed 28-year old from Nottingham with a pleasant boyish face and a shock of brown hair. He was walking every one of the 270 miles to Kirk Yetholm and had apparently started only a couple of hours after me from Edale. He was camping, roughing it for the most part, which was why his path hadn't subsumed mine until now. He had set off from Derbyshire with a work colleague, but that poor bloke had been 'Pennine Wayed' early on Day 2. I smiled at the use of adjective. I'd been there.

'You must be Herman,' Rob quipped, pointing at my chest.

Let me explain. My primary hiking t-shirts, breathable and climate-defying and extortionate, had both been worn twice so far and needed some time on the subs bench. Squad rotation and limited budget meant that I was now wearing a Ben Sherman t-shirt from the early 2000s, suitable at this point only for decorating or turning into a duster. The stitched lettering across the chest had already started to perish – the opening 'S' had gone off to work on solo projects – and so my t-shirt read 'Herman'.

'My name is Andy.'

Rob smiled. 'Nice to meet you, Herman.'

I didn't at all want to be called Herman, but I felt excited to have a new travelling companion, particularly one with his own binoculars and – I would later find out – coffee stove. "The fastest way to make a friend for life," A.A. Milne wrote, "is to travel with a stranger." Journeys are made alone, but adventures must be shared. Which reminded me – where on earth were Geoffrey and Margot? I hadn't seen them since Lancashire.

'You haven't seen a posh couple, have you?' I asked Rob.

'What do you mean by *posh?*'

'You haven't, then. Trust me, you'd know. Do you want to be friends?'

'OK,' Rob replied, probably rationing his emotion for when we were farther north and better acquainted. Not how I would have played it, but that was *his* choice. We descended Pinhaw Beacon together and walked on.

Another pretty village in the shape and name of Thornton-in-Craven was next, charming and blooming and bunting. I nearly got stung by a bee here, in what the British Film Institute would call "a scene of mild peril", stooping to inspect the flower in which it was doing its chores. Vexed at the interruption to its working day it definitely went for me, in response to which I ran 30 yards then gave it a bit of a telling off from a safe distance, trying to point out in a very reasonable way that he wasn't going to get very far in life if he couldn't handle social situations. It's possible that I misgendered him too, but I already have a lot to remember. Eventually I calmed down and acknowledged that I don't like to be distracted when I'm busy either, and besides it was too nice a day to hold a grudge. I thought I handled the whole thing with a lot of dignity.

There's a lovely stretch along the Leeds-Liverpool canal which brings the Pennine walker up to lunchtime, with riverside cafes and whimsical barges and erratic geese. Late Spring was moving in the air above and in the earth below, and that long courting passage gave me a chance to question my new friend on both his origins and future intentions. I learned as we stepped out together that Rob was an engineer, getting married next summer and so trying to burn a hole in his waistline whilst enjoying an manhood-initiating journey into the wild. He was told I was married and asked me, as we crossed the wildflower-speckled meadows between East Marton and Gargrave, whether I would still recommend it a decade after making my vows.

'They're not decade-long vows,' I said, wondering whether those flowers were buttercups or tormentil. 'It's not a contract, but it *is* a covenant – which is better.'

'Hard though, would you say?'

'*I would say.* You have your dales and you have your peaks. But Rob, that's why covenant is so special, because you know you're on the path together. And (I raised my arms to incorporate the surroundings in my description) you know yourself from the last four days, what do you do when you find yourself in the bottom of a valley with steep hills all around?'

Rob smiled wryly. 'F****** start climbing.'

'Absolutely. You flipping start climbing. But you don't run.'

There was no climbing for us though, not really. If crossing the South Pennines is like scurrying through an orc-less Mordor, the

Aire Gap is a live-action roleplay of *Wind in the Willows*. It's as though the Pennine Way hastily stuffed and pummelled all its philanthropy into a single day like a sleeping bag into its carrier. Route-finding wasn't always a cinch, but by shambling in roughly the right direction, usually following the babbling procession of a stream or rivulet, it was never long before the sturdy oaken signposts beckoned us onwards, invisible little hands pulling and tugging us into splendid spaces. We'd be at Toad Hall in time for tea and crumpets.

Leaving behind the millstone grit of the previous days we crossed about 300,000 stiles, which unearthed an almost maternal longing for household doors that I never realised I had. Then there were handmade farmer's signs with imprecatory messages such as: "Don't Feed the Horses". Believe me, I wasn't going to try and feed a horse – I act like I'm in the evacuation scene of *Titanic* whenever I'm walking through the park and a goose looks at me. I understand it's an irrational fear and smudges my otherwise impeccably-burnished masculinity, but unless an animal – and I mean pretty much *any* animal – is on a leash or behind six feet of electric fencing then I'll keep my distance, thanks everso. I mean it. I once stayed with some friends in Surrey who had a pair of incredibly cute (to everyone else) lop-eared house rabbits. These beasts would hop around without consultation, blithely sit next to you at dinner, eat of your treats, and I refused to even get out of my car until they were securely back behind glass. I just couldn't rid my mind of the idea that at some point, with my defences lowered after a glass of wine and some light singing, one or both of them would leap for my jugular. I shared none of this with Rob, of course.

Later on, just shy of pretty Airton (a watercolour challenge of a village) another sign declared: 'Warning – Otters'. Whether it was breeding season or just that Airedale otters were known on the circuit as being particularly badass, I didn't stick around long enough to find out. 'God has not given me a spirit of fear!' I prophesied, as I edged past a cow which refused to move from the path.

CHAPTER 12

STYLING IT OUT

'Why are you wincing?' I asked Rob after lunch. We had feasted, like a couple of feudal lords, on egg mayonnaise baguettes from Gargrave's Grade II-listed Dalesman Cafe. Since then I had purchased, penned and sent a couple of postcards, crossed and recrossed the dainty stepping stones over the river Aire, and we were now banking up from the Pennine Way's lowest point over the springy turf of Eshton Moor, lubricated on fresh coffee and azure skies.

'My thighs are chafing a bit,' Rob replied. 'I've got some moisturiser but it's my girlfriend's and I'm trying to ration it.'

'Let me show you my pants!' I declared, and before Rob could shout 'Stranger danger' or claw at me with his nails I had excitedly opened the top of my bergen, whipping out a handful of shimmering polyester which I now presented to him.

'Have a feel of those!'

They say that the best way to get a great idea is to have a lot of ideas (Nietzsche said in *Ecce Homo*, "Do not believe any idea that was not born in the open air and of free movement.") And I'd had this great idea to avoid inner thigh chafing, the most nefarious of all hiking wounds, by wearing cycling shorts under my cargo trousers. The plan had initially been thwarted – the majority of cycling shorts are too restrictive for the task and contain a sewn-in seat which makes you look foolish and incontinent. However, having spoken to a teenage boy in Decathlon about polyester crotches for far longer than I ever wanted to again, I discovered that you can purchase online a thinner undergarment – a cross between a leotard and a pair of long johns – which is flexible, comfortable and keeps thigh-rub resolutely at bay. And here you find me.

'These look brilliant,' Rob said.

'A finer pant I have never experienced,' I confessed. 'It's the same material they use for elven cloaks.'

'Really?'

'I hope so. Please, keep those – they're so light, I've got six pairs. Go and try them on, I'm pretty sure they're uni-fit.'

'Try them on? We're in the middle of a f****** field. There's a road over there.'

'Hide behind a cow.'

'No.'

'OK, well you can just slowly bleed to death then, can't you.'

I'm not usually this passive-aggressive, but I was just incredibly keen for the man I'd only met that morning to take off his pants and try on mine. Where I come from, a man who doesn't upgrade his underwear when he has the chance is no man at all.

Rob eventually found a clump of mature trees to act as a changing room and wandered back out a few minutes later, now smiling winsomely rather than wincingly, but refusing to sashay or catwalk in any way whatsoever despite lecherous wolf-whistles.

With both of us now wearing delicious pants, the day's final section towards Malham Cove along the chattering Aire was an absolute delight – a soft gliding into unfathomable lushness. Clouds like snags of wispy sheep's wool breezed overhead, while outposts of alder and willow hung maternal branches over the playful waters. I skirted the bank, scanning the shallows for signs of tiny fish – without success – but the river was weaving itself into my heartstrings, changing my tune, and carrying negativity away over tiny rapids. After the *sturm und drang* of the opening stages, I wondered whether the Pennine Way and I had finally reached a state of cordial détente and may soon become friends. I was dismally wrong, of course, but let's just enjoy the river for now. Rivers know there is no hurry.

Searching for areas of common interest and tracking down a few, Rob and I passed a good riverside hour listing our top computer games of all time, Rob treating me like a nerdy Elrond as I recalled the original version of games he had only played on emulators.

'For me, Herman, you can't beat a bit of *Goldeneye* on the N64. Do you remember it?'

'I was there, Rob. I was there 3000 years ago when it first came out.'

'What about the one with all those little football men?'

'*Sensible Soccer?* Awesome. Even better was *Sensible World of Soccer* – what a game.'

It's surely true that too many people waste too many hours of empty pleasure on gaming – it had been true for me in my teens and early twenties. But looking back from the distant peak of early middle-age, I find that erstwhile pleasure wandering back towards me as something else – as *joy* – less intense perhaps, but more rounded and fulfilling. Pleasure is a matter of visceral encountering. When you're no longer chasing the pleasure in something, no longer under the law of diminishing returns, the pleasure seems to return to you recloaked in nostalgia. I look back at my younger self and see him locked not just in a room but in a memory, safe and secure in his world. Which is all he ever wanted anyway.

The same is true for walking. There may be pleasure to be found in the repetitive rise and fall of a boot, the kinaesthesia of your body in its most primitive natural activity, but the joy of a good walk grows in the retreading through one's memory. If pleasure and happiness occur when the senses are intoxicated, joy, it strikes me, is what happens when the soul and mind are watered with something profound and unquenchable.

We entered the treasure trove of Malham itself at 4pm on Bank Holiday Friday and I raised a single hand in modest triumph. On both previous attempts to walk the Pennine Way I had failed to progress beyond this point, and that was simply not going to happen now. My first step tomorrow would take me farther than I'd ever walked before, and after that I'd be smashing PBs all over the place. And I still had no blisters and no injuries. Everything was beautiful and nothing hurt.

Rob hadn't pre-booked a campsite and so, looking a bit perplexed but very comfortable still in his new pants, he stomped off to try and secure a pied-à-terre between all the tents and caravans and motorhomes currently converging on the place. I took off my big flipping pack and raised my face heavenwards, letting the sun colour my skin, letting the shadow of the past fall behind me.

But then, unbidden, I started to experience a bizarre enochlophobia about so many other human beings wandering around. The Buck Inn, where I had planned to devour meat as a way of reasserting my authority over the animal kingdom, was buckling with day-trippers, part-time walkers and – worst of all – happy families. After four days detached from communal existence this sudden reattachment of the umbilical cord felt mildly suffocating, and I stood in the middle of the road looking vexed.

'Hey… hey, mate… mate,' a still small voice behind me said. I turned around, to see that a group of blokes had annexed the local bus-stop and upcycled it into an outdoor tavern, all bubbling pots and sloshing ale. They beckoned me over conspiratorially.

'You have the look and rucksack of a man who is walking the Way,' one of them said.

'Most assuredly,' I replied, in a needlessly Elizabethan fashion.

'We're doing it North-South as a group. Can we tempt you to some bread and ale?'

'That would be incredible.'

I ensconced myself in their midst, gratefully resting my bottom on something that wasn't a root, and we started sharing stories from our respective journeys. They told me how Tan Hill was incredibly boggy but Scotland was beautiful. I told them how I'd fed all the horses I could find because that sort of thing just doesn't faze me at all.

'And is that a toy fox hanging from your pack?' a privately-schooled voice asked me.

'He's more of a novelty doorstep,' I replied, tearing off a hunk of bread and dipping it into a tankard of IPA, 'but yes, he's called Alan.'

'Alan the toy fox?'

'Most assuredly,' I said, and I literally had no idea why I kept speaking like that.

All that was left was to check into the Youth Hostel and get an early night before an early start. Back in the olden days the Pennine Way was awash with hostels, but now all-but-one were temporarily barred or permanently boarded up. The YHA at Malham was absolutely rammed but I had managed to pay over the odds for an outdoor camping pod in the grounds – something that looked half-Scandinavian, half-Martian.

'Do you have any photo ID?' the lady behind the counter asked. She had a smile which ran dry before it could trickle into her eyes. She also looked like a cat, and I intend that neither as a compliment nor a criticism.

'I don't have photo ID, no,' I replied, 'but I have my booking reference on this email and I have my bank card, and also I'm not trying to cross the Mexican border – I'm walking the Pennine Way.'

'Sorry, we need to see some photo ID.'

'Why do you NEED to see it??'

'You could be anybody, sir.'

'Do you get a lot of problems with imposters?' I asked, my large internal grace tank springing a leak.

'With…?'

'With imposters. I can see that gangs of louts or underage sex might be something to guard against here, but I can't fathom why confidence tricksters would specifically target the Youth Hostel Association. What am I going to do, steal a table-tennis bat?'

This drew a laugh from a Duke of Edinburgh Bronze Award group waiting behind me.

'The table tennis is out of use because of Covid, sir,' the counter woman countered. I was sure this was actually adding weight to my argument, but she didn't see it that way.

'Er, miss,' one of the teens piped up, 'please can you just let this man in – he smells really bad.'

'Thank you very much,' I said.

'That's fine,' the teen shrugged, in an act of classic Gen Z virtue signalling.

The counter woman rolled her eyes and handed me my key. They didn't serve breakfast, so I purchased a Muller Fruit Corner for the morning and went to locate my pod. I could finally bathe in the success of a day well-trod, but before that I must literally bathe.

My self-imposed mandate of an early night was torn up the moment Rob suggested a man date at the Buck Inn. I padded down there in my socks, the sweetness of the evening advancing on tiptoe, and we chewed on meat and supped on ale, heroes fitly feasting after a fifth consecutive day's victory. Whatever traits of pilgrimage my journey bore, the vow to asceticism was not one of them. It was not the sort of night for bed, anyhow.

'I haven't asked you why you're walking the Pennine Way, Herman,' Rob said. The 'n' on my t-shirt was on its last legs and by tomorrow I'd be known as Herma.

'You didn't,' I replied. 'Although I don't think I've worked it out yet anyway.'

'Oh, OK. Tell me more about the olden days of gaming, then. What about that one with the little shooty men?'

'*Cannon Fodder*.'

'How did you get that from little shooty men?'

'Looked like the lads from *Sensible Soccer* had been called up to fight in Vietnam?'

'Yeah.'

'Sure, *Cannon Fodder*. What a game, Rob! What a time to be alive.'

Rob chuckled at my earnestness and I smiled back, for we had just become friends, and we both knew it.

When I finally buried myself in my camping pod at 11:30pm, the sky was still clinging nostalgically to some of its residual light. And who could blame it, when yesterday wasn't ever coming back. Tomorrow, on Day 6, I would need to climb Pen-y-Ghent, the mountain seen from Pinshaw Beacon that morning. But I was a real walker now and real walkers don't worry about pathetic little hills like Pen-y-Ghent, do they?

I drifted off to sleep whilst scrolling through pictures of our most recent family holiday to Alnwick. Why did I smile in photos like a hostage trying to send a message with his eyes? Why did they stop making *Sensible Soccer* when it remained so superlative? And why, when Rob had asked my reason for walking the Pennine Way… why didn't I tell him the truth?

Day 6
Malham to Horton-in-Ribblesdale
15 miles

Sam: This is it.
Frodo: What?
Sam: If I take one more step, I'll be the farthest from home I've ever been.
J.R.R. Tolkein, The Fellowship of the Ring

"The last word always belongs to the mountain."
Anatoli Boukreev

CHAPTER 13
WALKER WITH THE DAWN

'Why would you put your faith in an old book?'

The challenge had been posed over a flat white in Coffee St. under the shadow of Chesterfield's famous crooked spire. A friend had recently taken an interest in Christianity and wanted to interrogate me about the Bible over cake and caffeine – which is hardly the fiercest persecution a Christian has ever had to face.

The question winged its way back to me now across Kinder Scout and Stoodley Pike and the peak of a pandemic because I had once again got lost. It was 5:55am. I was standing at the apex of Malham Cove, a huge curving limestone amphitheatre where nature continues to stage one of her longest-running and most virtuosic shows. The previous day's trodden ground lay emerald in shadow, and for company I was content with the swallows and jackdaws swooping in and around the cove like circus performers.

Having woken up feeling exultant, clear-headed and cocksure, I had decided to go old-school and use for today's navigation a copy of the *Pennine Way Companion (A Pictorial Guide)*, originally published in 1968 and written by Alfred Wainwright, the godfather of modern wayfarers. An insanely meticulous parade of hand-written notes and sketches in which Wainwright's passion, fierce intelligence and contemporaneous chauvinism ooze from every nook and crevice, I had brought the book along on the journey more as a talisman than an instructive manual – a sort of King's seal, to be presented on capture and thus ensuring my safe passage through the wildes. Given that the book was written seven years before the opening of the M25, walking between the terminal points of Edale and Kirk Yetholm required something a bit more en vogue; however, this morning's assignment – climbing up out of Malham Cove and circumnavigating Malham Tarn – seemed innocuous enough to let Alfred take the lead. And yet, here I was, lost and confused while everyone else was still in bed.

The misplacement didn't last long. An early-morning farmer walking his border collie, both of whom looked like extras from an episode of *All Creatures Great and Small,* took me by the arm and used the crook of his walking stick to point me back in the right direction. I thanked him and he made some kind of guttural Yorkshire grunt which I shall refrain from trying to recreate here. His appearance provided a decent response to the question, though: Why would you put your faith in an old book like the Bible? Answer: You wouldn't.

For someone easily outable as a preacher (as Werner had proven) that answer might seem coquettish if not downright capitulating, but I believe it's true. Books can offer us lots of things – insight, knowledge, guidance – and that's helpful, because plenty of us are looking for a code, a moral guidebook to help straighten out our crooked spines. And obviously, the fact that a book is old has no bearing on its truth content; indeed, in this case the reverse is possibly true: if we're searching for truths about eternality and spiritual roots, one might expect those signposts to have been dug in from the start. It's simply chronological snobbery to believe that fact and fashion are symbiotic, that truth is the same as trend. Progress along a national trail isn't an infinitely upwards curve, and so it is with wisdom and morality – the historical map of human ethics has as many valley floors as liberating peaks.

But concepts only take you so far. Words on a page only get you so far, particularly if the author isn't there to explain what they meant by those words. As Wainwright says in his *Pennine Way Companion,* "A guide is supposed to help, not confuse. This one will help if it is used as it is intended to be used." Books, both old and new, can operate as spiritual or ethical satnavs, and all guidebooks can help to a degree if used as intended. But what we really need is someone to find us when we're lost and shepherd us towards home (guttural Yorkshire grunting optional). Where the Bible is at its most successful is in those places where it tells us about the one who offers to do that.

The worst guidebook of all time was a guide to the English language written by a man named Pedro Carolino. In 1883, his pioneering phrase book *English As She Is Spoke* was published to help Portuguese speakers fit in with the natives of Victorian England. A noble aim, but one perhaps not best suited to Pedro given that he spoke very little English and didn't even possess a Portuguese-English dictionary, having to dredge all his attempts at everyday idioms through a Portuguese-French and then French-English index. Having studied French at university myself, I know first-hand that idioms are weird and taxing enough without the unnecessary middleman. For instance, if a Frenchman said to you (and I'm not saying they are definitely going to) 'Je suis comme une poule qui a trouvé un couteau', you might initially be taken aback by the revelation that he's like a hen who has found a knife. Idiomatically though, it just means to be at a complete loss.

But Pedro Carolino was a flagship for 19th century swagger. His death-defying leaps of mistranslation exhibit a felicity of language that might otherwise be achieved by putting the works of Mark Twain into a tumble drier. The book kicks off with some 'Familiar Phrases' which the Portuguese holiday maker might find helpful, including 'This hat go well', 'Dress your hairs' and that well-known phrase, 'Exculpate me by your brothers'. General proverbs such as 'The walls have hearsay' will keep you out of the hands of the secret police, while in the section economically entitled 'Eatings' you'll learn how to order food such as:

Some boiled meat
Some fritters
A stewed fruit

Some jelly broth
Some wigs
A chitterling sausages
Some dainty dishes and, of course,
Hog fat.

I slid old Alfred back into a side pocket and retrieved my guidebook of choice: *Trailblazer's Pennine Way* by Edward de la Billiere (the son of Peter de la Billiere, former head of the Special Air Service).

I stepped nimbly over the chequered limestone pavement at the top of Malham Cove – very dental-looking, an exposed jaw of giant's molars – with my dew-freshened boots leaving time-sensitive clues as to my passing. I had messaged Rob about my dawn departure, inviting him to join me on the early shift. He had demurred in lavish Anglo-Saxon but hoped to catch up to me before Horton-in-Ribblesdale. At my current rate I wouldn't take much catching.

The air felt coy and economical up here. I wasn't that high up, but it was as though the austere nature of the landscape had encouraged the air to be prudent in who it gave itself to. It's here that a section of *Harry Potter and the Deathly Hallows: Part I* was filmed, but it's arguably the most boring scene of the worst of the Potter films, which is probably why Wainwright neglected to mention it in his book.

Regardless, I had never stepped foot here before. Everything from this point on was nascent and uncharted, and I had learned the lessons handed down from the past.

In 2003 (my first attempt at reaching Scotland on foot) the plan had been to walk the Pennine Way until it stopped being fun, which was a moronic thing to think or say. The Pennine Way isn't fun. It might be majestic and live-giving and imperious, sovereign as it is over other long-distance footpaths, but it is not *fun.* Playing Hungry Hippos is fun.

More recently, in 2018, I attempted to walk half the Way before moving my life over to Chesterfield. I chose to wear Karrimoor walking shoes, which offered as much protection and comfort to my feet as would a Muller Fruit Corner, and by Day 5 my heels looked as though they'd been flayed for refusing to deny Christ in front of a North Korean court.

No such problems this time around. My top-of-the-range Meindl boots were like personal butlers, allowing me to eat my breakfast Fruit Corner in peace. Gone are the days when you had to break in a new pair of boots like a skittish horse, wearing them to bed and at dinner parties and in the bath. Still, I'd already done plenty of miles in Jeeves and Carson (the titles I had given mi boots, sir) and history wasn't going to repeat itself for a third time. I may be 40, but I couldn't remember feeling this spritely. As I marched on into the untrodden future I felt like John Colter, mountain man and pioneer, hacking through the weeds that had stunted my personal growth.

Watlowes, a dramatic dry valley of enclosed cliffs, was boundaried by a Natural England gate and accompanying stile. I grabbed a crumbling wooden post, heaved myself up, lost my footing and, without an elderly Headmaster to shout 'Arresto Momentum', came crashing back down onto limestone, back- and pack-first. For a good minute I just lay there, elbows bleeding, the clangour of water bottle and mess tin galloping down the valley like Minutemen crying, 'The red cuts are coming!'

Nothing was broken, but nor did anything feel healthy. My body was like an Ikea wardrobe put together by a group of the king's horses.

Eventually I rolled over, graduating from supine to prostrate to hominid to homosapien. I checked my rucksack for signs of damage and tearing, but aside from a couple of dents in my water bottle all seemed well.

'Are you OK, Ala…'

I turned back towards Malham Cove and started walking.

I had left Alan at the Youth Hostel.

CHAPTER 14
BADGE OF DISHONOUR

By the time I successfully crossed the gated stile an hour later, the rescued fox now tucked back in his pouch but refusing to talk to me, I had been given quite the rollicking. Alan had told me in no uncertain terms, borrowing from Rob's lexicon of lavish Anglo-Saxon as he did so, that I really couldn't carry on like this, starting days with flights of frivolity and then having to turn back shamefaced. It was down to a negligence of mental sobriety, he informed me; a deficit in my moral fibre. If I wanted to dance the hokey cokey then I could catch a locomotive back to civilization and leave the rest of us to it. As an Englishman, I really must do better.

Suitably chastened, I trudged on.

I stepped nimbly over the chequered limestone pavement (reprise), then meandered round to the glassy tanzanite lustre of Malham Tarn, indisputably the most impressive view of the walk so far, gorgeousness and gorgeosity made flesh. The whole of Malham Dale is absolutely hench, rippling and flexing with primal authority, geological drama leaping out at you round every corner. You get the impression that you're welcome here, just remember who's in charge. As Mark Wallington says in *Pennine Walkies,* "it had the feel of a theme village, as if all things geologically impressive had been bought, uprooted and re-erected on this site."

It wasn't yet 7:30am, the sun was up and about but the heat of the day was still waiting for breakfast in bed. Speaking of which, I also hadn't eaten any breakfast beyond my yoghurt. I had two dehydrated Beef Stroganoffs in my pack in case an astronaut turned up wanting a romantic dinner, plus I knew I'd be arriving in Horton for lunchtime, but I'd failed to recognise just how vital a good breakfast is for a walker's chemical and psychological well-being. Big mistake – huge.

The path curved pliantly round Malham Tarn and its reconstituted manor house, then bended a knee away towards Fountain's Fell, the first of the two mountains to be scaled today. By now the small community of Malham would be a nest of activity: family tents would be unzipping, gas stoves would be sizzling and day walkers would be booting up for a jaunt towards Gordale Scar. A small gang of ultra runners jogged past me during their warm up.

'Where you 'eaded, mate?'

'Scotland.'

'Nice. Can we come?'

'If you agree to slow down a bit, sure.'

'Maybe not then. 'Ave a good' un.'

The sun's heat finished its brekkie, downed a couple of Pro Plus and came out to play, and by 9am it was absolutely sweltering. The sky was fairytale blue, cloudless and regal, but as I plodded on a growing sense of dread started to overhang me. I was drinking plenty of water and making striding progress, but the minimal sleep (four hours), meagre breakfast and intense early-morning exercise was sending my body into the early stages of survival mode. Already, necessary nutrients were falling back from my extremities to reinforce the inner keep.

At the peak of Fountains Fell (668 metres), having skirted deserted mineshafts and leapt over sinkholes, I saw the valley suck the high ground away in an almost tidal ebb. And there in front of me, cresting its own monstrous wave, was the peak of Pen-y-Ghent.

As a one-off climb it looked doable, but I'd already walked 10 miles, was feeling isolated and paranoid, and my mood had passed my body on the stairs, dropping as far as my legs had climbed. I couldn't remember feeling this tired this early.

I stood at the foot of Pen-y-Ghent with the same sort of vertigo you get on the clacking ascent of a rollercoaster or the obtuse climb of an aircraft. Despite the increasing heat I had started to shiver, and I sat down at the side of the path feeling completely discombobulated. I frantically messaged Phil, my Spine-racing friend from Day 1, to ask what was happening to me.

'Sounds like you need fuel pronto. Get yourself some nuts or an energy bar asap. And keep drinking water.'

Then, for the first time in my life, I started to hallucinate. Not one of those cool hallucinations where an ancestor you never met appears to you and offers benevolent guidance. Not a prophetic vision to be interpreted using Scripture and brought before the King. First, a tree uprooted itself and started walking along the valley floor swinging its branches. Then a sheep grew to the size of a horse and started galloping towards me. I don't know what happened subsequently because at that point I simply blacked out and collapsed. I can't have been out for very long, but the whole experience was terrifying. Today was supposed to be about setting new personal bests – but 'first hallucination' and 'most dramatic swoon' weren't on the bucket list.

What saved me was the swell of bank-holiday picnics peppering the Yorkshire Dales. Having spent 10 minutes desperately trying to compose and re-orient myself and taking on as much water as I could, I staggered over to a motorhome parked under the shadow of the mountain and sought succour. The hallucinations had ceased by this point, but my dignity was a beach at low tide, an ebb without a flow. A Spanish mother, a Scottish dad and a brace of Spottish children gawped at me like the post-apocalyptic vagrant that I had obviously become.

'We don't have any energy bars,' the mum said, 'but we got lots of nuts – ooh, and a couple bananas.'

'That would be phenomenal, gracias,' I said, using literally the full extent of my Spanish. Shame she wasn't Portuguese – I would have been able to ask her for some jelly broth and other dainty dishes, but not every story has a happy ending.

'Sorry we cannae drive ya back tee Scotland, but yall be OK in a wee while,' the dad said.

'Thanks, mi hearty,' I replied, not really knowing any Scottish lingo and so hoping pirate talk would get me close enough.

My energy levels gradually stabilised and my metabolism came out of its coma. Nevertheless, the ensuing 15 minutes climbing to the 2280-foot pinnacle of Pen-y-Ghent were the longest and hardest of any walk I've ever done, as I panted and creaked and blimming-bloody-basketed my way to the summit. To make matters worse, fresh-as-a-fruit-corner fell runners were out for their weekend sortie. Halfway to the top, an unfeasibly nimble satyr of a man leapt past me, all glistening triceps and heroic nipples. He was followed shortly after by a lady who can't have been far off 'oldest woman in the world' territory, but she made me look stupid as she triple-jumped her way heavenwards.

'Morning!' she called.

*P*** off,* Alan said under his breath. I told him not to be crass and sat down on England's most uncomfortable rock for a rest.

My pack was hefty rather than heavy, but you feel every single ounce of that when climbing – and you really are climbing. My front satchel was helping to distribute the weight around my body, but it was destabilising up this cliff and I was teetering like a Weeble. I needed to lose weight from somewhere, and three lockdowns had ensured it wasn't going to be from my waistline. These fell runners, aerodynamic loons that they are, probably tanked up on kiwi smoothies before a day's exercise, but kiwi tastes like it's trying to murder you and it's in a hurry. My heart was set on a mid-afternoon kebab as a joint lunch and dinner present.

Phil pinged me another text: 'Remember what I said the other day, mate – it's about showing nature who's boss, even if we're crawling on our hands and knees.'

I strung a list of post-watershed expressions together and Alan told me not to be crass.

Finally, finally, I reached the top of Pen-y-Ghent. The most arduous of the Yorkshire 3-Peak Challenge (which also includes Ingleborough and Whernside) it lords it over the surrounding hills like the first boy at school to get pubes. The views from the top were expansive and high definition, but I was really too overwhelmed to appreciate them. Rambling clubs and ultra runners and abusive parents who want their child to be the next Bear Grylls, all of them were milling around, snapping selfies and opening hot flasks. I found a spot away from the mad in-crowd, unstrapped my rucksack and front satchel (I would empty the latter and hurl it into a gulley before the descent) and lowered myself to the ground with the care of a pallbearer. I stayed there for half an hour, hardly moving, regretting everything I'd ever done. My face felt like one of Dali's melting clocks – my eyes seemed to want to relocate into my nostrils, while my tongue appeared not to be there at all. A concerned man in a running vest wandered over to see if I was OK, but I just didn't answer him – I couldn't remember how to.

In that moment, if someone had offered me an easy way out or a ticket home, I would have taken it without guilt. My sense of resilience was a late-stage Jenga tower.

All that was left of the day's walking was the long slide down into Horton-in-Ribblesdale, but that wasn't nearly as fortuitous as it looks on the map. Alfred Wainwright said that the 3-mile descent from Pen-y-Ghent to Horton was 'very, very good', but I'm sorry Alfred – I've never heard such errant dross in my life. That hill is an absolute monster, a vaudevillian childcatcher, the Cruella Devil of walkways which, were it human, would surely list its hobbies as 'setting fire to kittens' and 'ordering soup as a main course.' A limestone honeycomb of passages and potholes opens onto the hillside like bloodless wounds, a knuckle-cracking threat for people ascending Pen-y-Ghent from the Ribble valley and a final mocking

'You shouldn't have messed with me' for those of us descending like a coffin, borne to rest by the solemn procession of a walled lane.

The ancient lady fell runner, who had taken a long break at the apex to eat seeds and hemp and possibly to fashion something using a loom, skitted past me on the slope with a completely inappropriate mega-watt grin.

'Two more miles and then stop for a tiny bit of cake as a treat,' she called over her shoulder.

'Consuming a tiny bit of something isn't how treats work, Madame – you're thinking of inoculations,' I lacked the energy to say. But I planned to consume so much sugar, all that would remain was for some Oompas-Loompas to turn up and sing a creepy song about me.

I crash-landed into Horton in the baking heat with a snarling lip and a locked jaw, haemorrhaging hope. My body was on the brink of Civil War, my knees and hips looking to secede with immediate effect, and my feet were in agony, hot and pounding. I found a wall and removed my impeccably mannered Meindl boots.

I had three blisters, and they did not look at all happy.

I unzipped a trouser pocket and took out my phone, and stared at it dumbfounded. *That can't be right, surely?*

It had just turned midday.

And I wanted to go home.

* * *

At 3pm, I was sitting at a Parisian bistro table outside the Old Post Office cafe in Horton-in-Ribblesdale. I had been there for three hours, like a chicken who has found a knife, and with all the agility of rotting driftwood on a stony beach. My legs were two flat tyres, and my tortured feet would have ratted out their own mother for a commuted sentence.

Three cans of Coke, a pot of coffee and an Oreo milkshake crowded on the table in front of me like liquid courtesans. My backpack was lying in state next to me, while Alan was face down on the adjacent chair.

'Does he need help?' a man lining up for ice-cream with a toddler on his shoulders asked.

'He's just climbed Pen-y-Ghent. Please respect his privacy at this difficult time.'

The man bowed his head respectfully and I nearly smiled back at him, but not quite.

I couldn't get comfy. The wrought-iron chair wasn't designed for long stretches of indolence, plus my bottom wasn't really in a 'baroque' mood, but it was the only seat available and I was staying put. I would continue to play Supermarket Sweep with the food and drink menu for as long as my bank manager would allow it.

One thing that I was refusing to buy, however, was an embroidered cloth badge displayed in the cafe window, sporting the moniker: I Climbed Pen-y-Ghent. It was a tempting purchase, no doubt, the embroidery being of superior quality, an exhilarating flame-red stitching around its circumference – and also because there aren't really any commercial mementos you can pick up along the Pennine Way. There are no open-fronted vendors selling "I Love Ickornshaw Moor" t-shirts, or keyrings hanging on counters with the cutesy message, "I lived through a night in Hebden Bridge". However, the price of the badge was the only thing steeper than Pen-y-Ghent itself, and I decided that I'd defer the sale and put the saved money towards something of equal value, like a small vineyard in western Andorra or a space rocket.

I was cut off mid-musing by the sound of a familiar voice, shouting:

'What the ******* **** was that ****?!'

'Here he is.'

The dulcet verse of the Pennine Way's Poet Laureate infused the air as Rob lumbered into view and dropped his pack beside me like a sedated animal. He turned back towards Pen-y-Ghent and gave it both Vs, before scraping back a chair and appearing to die in it.

'How was it for you?' I asked, as non-flirtatiously as I could.

He looked up as though surprised to see me.

'It was an absolute ****show from start to finish. 10 ******* miles before you even cross that w*****.' He pointed an accusing finger back up the mountain. I thought he was making some very salient points.

'Do you want this coke?' I asked him. 'It doesn't really go with coffee and milkshake.'

'Yeah. Is Alan dead, too?'

'Just depressed. He's got some good people around him, though.'

Rob nearly smiled, but not quite.

'How come it took you so long?' I asked.

Rob sat staring into the middle distance for a good minute before he responded. Then he commenced to recount his day for me, in Spenserian stanzas, his lyricism described by one critic as "a diamond necklace of swear words snatched apart by an opportunistic jewellery thief". He explained how, first of all, he'd got locked in the campsite shower cubicle (he still wasn't sure how) and that had put him behind schedule early doors. He'd left a full pack of sausages out of his cool-sack overnight, and so had to cook all 12 of them on his stove which delayed him even further. I didn't ask if they were chitterling sausages.

'Also, my guidebook seems to have been written from memory by someone who walked the Pennine Way once, as a baby, and has since gone blind and mad.' At this he brought out the culprit and it was zero surprise to find him holding aloft the same tome that had told me the biblical flood at Crowden Great Brook on Day 2 was "nothing more than a trickle."

'Preach it, brother,' I applauded.

'Why would you let **** like this get published though?!' he demanded. 'I could write a better book using Google Streetview –

and Google Streetview doesn't even cover the ******* Pennine Way. What are these idiots playing at?!'

He continued like this for some time, using more rhetoric than you could shake a 1933 Nuremberg rally at, occasionally stopping for a glug of pop before reprising the invective.

'Then the sausages started to repeat and I got the squirts on Fountains Fell.'

I put down my Oreo milkshake.

'Are my pants OK?' I asked, like a fretting mother.

'Yeah, yeah. I'm wearing different ones today. Let me put it this way though, I hope nobody was standing at the bottom of that mine shaft.'

'I'll certainly be petitioning the Lord in prayer to that end,' I said.

'What does Pen-y-Ghent even mean anyway?'

'Hill of the winds in Welsh, I think. Or maybe hill on the border.'

'Well, I can think of other names for it…'

But I shall spare you that, friend.

We sat outside the cafe for a couple more hours, occasionally looking at each other with sympathy, yesterday's romantic view of ourselves as conquering heroes mercilessly skewered by the enforced rationality of multiple blisters. Other walkers came down the path from Pen-y-Ghent like survivors of a battle, some elated, others surrendering, but all of them safe in the knowledge that their fight was over. I tried not to think about the fact that I had 10 days left to walk, and certainly not to talk about it. As the afternoon cooled and the shadows started to lengthen, and with a Tithonian inability to move our limbs now creeping over us, Rob and I limped down the road to his campsite, communicating in little more than neanderthal grunts, our heroism cut down to sighs. It appeared that my claims to have learned valuable lessons from previous attempts to walk to Scotland had been premature, if not downright childish. At one point in Defoe's *Robinson Crusoe* the hero says, "And now I saw, though too late, the folly of beginning a work before we count the cost, and before we judge rightly of our own strength to go through with it."

That summed it up quite nicely. The mountain always gets his man.

'I might go home tomorrow,' Rob said ruefully over a plate of cheesy chips that evening. We were reclining outside his tent, heads rested on a pillow of latticed fingers, staring up into the black and gold of the earth's canopy. A symphony of irascible parents trying to lull and threaten their camping children to sleep played on repeat in the background. Rob had been shuttling to and from the campsite toilet all afternoon and was in real danger of diarrheaing himself into oblivion.

'Do you actually think you will?' I asked. 'Go home, I mean.'

'Maybe, yeah. I've been away from home a week and I'm wrecked. My girlfriend thinks I should carry on, but I'm using up annual leave to cause myself a load of pain. And I miss her. I think when you're out on the moors and there's nobody around, just you and a ****load of weather, you notice what's missing.'

It would have been a good time for a shooting star to etch a path across the sky, but none did.

'I hear you,' I said.

'You must miss your wife and daughters. Facetime can't be that much of a consolation.'

'I do, and it's not.'

'Would you think about going home, then?'

I nodded. 'I want to go home, yes. I am ready to give up. But…' I leaned over and stole a couple of cheddary chips from Rob's tray. He was peering at me through the darkness. 'I can't go home yet. I need to finish it.'

I wonder if Rob had been hoping to alleviate his own guilt at giving up by recruiting me into a small team of drop-outs. Maybe he had an expletive-laden rant about why it was better to be with the people you love, not wandering painfully and haltingly over the moors and hills with strangers. But he didn't say anything else. He didn't try to stop me from carrying on. I think he could see in my eyes that I needed to.

'Most of those stars are dead,' he said instead.

'Are they?'

'They are. The light takes years to get to us, but most of those lights have already gone out. You're actually seeing a snapshot of the past.'

'That's not true!'

'I'm not ******* lying, mate. Even the North Star might just be a memory for all we know. Trust me, I'm an engineer.'

'I'm going to finish these chips,' I said. 'Do they still exist at least?'

'For about another five seconds, yep.'

'That's something, then.'

I finished the chips, and we returned to our vigil, staring up into the blackened heavens… looking curiously towards a light that had already gone out.

Day 7
Horton-in-Ribblesdale to Hawes
14 miles

"Look for me by moonlight;
Watch for me by moonlight;
I'll come to thee by moonlight,
though hell should bar the way!"
The Highwayman by Alfred Noyes

"Two roads diverged in a wood, and I —
I took the one less travelled by,
And that has made all the difference."
The Road Not Taken by Robert Frost

CHAPTER 15
BETTER A POSTPONEMENT THAN A POST-MORTEM

'How's it going, Andy?'

Jon, my inaugural travelling buddy from Edale, was checking in via Whatsapp.

'I was human once, Jon.'

'That well, eh? Keep going! I've got some nice wood in my shed to make you a prize with. What do you fancy?'

'Can you stretch to a palanquin and a team of Sherpas?'

'Could probably do a Flintstones car – I'll ask Maria if she's got enough fabric. She wants to know if you're keeping out of trouble.'

'Tell her I'm not. Maybe she'll insist on coming to pick me up.'

I had been forced to take a rest day. It was primarily down to Bank Holiday overcrowding rather than the uprising of aggressive wounds acquired on the descent from Pen-y-Ghent, which were looking to annex my right foot and turn it into a blistered caliphate. Still, I'd been glad of 24 hours without boots, convalescing by the riverbank, messing about with notes, totally at one with creation until a family of chickens wandered towards me looking threatening and I had to go inside for a while.

I had spent the morning sitting under the eaves of a willow, reading and scribbling, catching snippets of conversation from the many hikers, campers and barbecuers within earshot. Elodie and Sophia didn't want to climb a stupid hill because they were happy on their tablets. Paul was sure he'd packed veggie burgers as well as meat but his partner didn't believe him because, come on Paul, this wasn't the first time this had happened, Paul.

Margaret hadn't been back here since Clive had passed away. He used to love it here.

My blemished foot, currently languishing beneath the Ribble's ticklish waterline, was causing me some genuine anxiety. I couldn't help thinking about the shell of a man I'd met back in Crowden, and how his humanity seemed to have been surgically removed by what started out as a simple blister. I still had 10 days of walking to do – 400,000 steps – and I hadn't yet crossed the watershed of the halfway crest, after which I could maybe have trickled downhill into Scotland like rainwater.

You know you're going to get blisters. Everyone gets blisters eventually and pain can be endured and blocked out *to a degree.* But a blistered foot that keeps on hitting the ground will eventually become torture, and as the character El Mirador says about torture in Bernard Cornwell's *Sharpe's Sword,* "Everyone breaks by the third day."

I had until the morning to find a solution.

I was stabling for two nights at the Crown Hotel in Horton, a charming abode, although its description as a 'hotel' was somewhat misleading. It's not the sort of boutique establishment where power-suits phone Singapore and a jaded lothario sits by the tinted glass, twirling his wedding ring over an 'Old-Fashioned.' It's more the sort of place where you'd expect a one-eyed ostler to drag a screaming mule through the bar, a detachment of King George's redcoats marching up under a ribbon of moonlight. But that's exactly the sort of country inn where a weary traveller bent on good stories wants to lay his head: a place where you can order a 'flagon' of something and get it; where the only women's names you need to remember are Bess and Sally; where the number one cause of death is 'falling rafters'. This is England, 1786.

The place was cosy, the ale was local, and the landlord was perfectly amenable in a slightly gruff and guarded way. He carried himself like a man who had bravely broken with family tradition, entering the world of hospitality after generations of barn building and dying down mines.

I still might abandon the walk. The thought of packing up and catching a train home had its face pressed against the window, and the inveigling voice of shame was whispering sweet nothings about how I was a sweet nothing. I had heard that voice before, and I was not unaware of its schemes.

Shame is that beast in your gut, scraping away at your fragile sense of self. And the two modern responses to such feelings seem to be either to submit to it in wormlike vassalage or to rip it up as fake news in light of your main-character energy. But shame only becomes toxic when either enthroned or ignored. Enthrone it and you'll become a pulpy mess under its cruel iron fist (something less than human); ignore it and you'll veer towards grandiose self-enlargement (something more than).

It strikes me though that shame is just a messenger, reminding you of your perfectly imperfect mortality, not a spy to be off-with-his-headed or a prophesied king to swear allegiance to.

Shame is a signpost with three struts. One directs you to crazy self-loathing, another to narcissistic grandstanding. The third strut points you vaguely onwards in undespairing trudge. To take that route though – a route that may be long overgrown by now, of course – you need to believe something important. You need to believe that you are *flawed but adored.*

Flawed, yes – you *have* made mistakes and you're going to make a lot more, and it's good to regret those things and fix what can be mended. But *adored* – by the one being in the universe who loves you unconditionally, and who will never, in any weather, downgrade, discredit or disqualify you.

Shame is neither a false charge nor a life sentence. When properly understood, shame is a rutted track to freedom.

Nevertheless, I still might leave. And I found myself badly missing Rob. You don't need to spend very long with somebody out of doors, away from the feather bed of civilisation, to form a firm ionic bond with them. Shared purpose and hardship are perhaps the quickest routes to camaraderie.

I sent him a message, wishing him all the best after our brief but comradely time together:

'Great to meet you, mate! Safe journey back to Nottingham, and good luck with the wedding.'

My phone pinged almost instantly:

'B******s to that, I'm carrying on. Probably gonna have a rest day in the second week. See you down the road.'

'Top greetings to that!' I said out loud, frightening a man on a bicycle. If my friend was persisting, then I could too, and we would reunite like odd socks after a house hinching. Mark Twain once wrote, "I have found out there is no surer way to find out whether you like people or hate them than to travel with them." I liked Rob very much and was delighted that he was carrying on. I imagined him now on the descent into Wensleydale... swearing at a tree, giving an implacable hillock the finger, being generally annoyed with life. It made me very happy.

Speaking of comrades, my fallow day had allowed Geoffrey and Margot (the retired doctors who owned all the houses and weren't sure whether or not they had died from Covid) to finally catch up with me. I was reclining at the outdoor dining area of the Crown Hotel, watching a tabby cat inspect a storm drain, when they trudged up there early in the afternoon, perfectly happy, perfectly sanguine, Pen-y-Ghent having taken seemingly no toll from them. Margot stopped the moment she saw me and held out an arm to halt Geoffrey. Geoffrey wasn't paying attention and almost dislocated Margot's shoulder, then blamed her for it.

'But Geoffrey, look! Look over there, look who it is!'

'Who is it?' Geoffrey asked, looking directly at me as I waved at him.

'It's Andy, of course! Hello dear!'

Margot waded over to me, her massive bergen swelling behind her on all sides like a gaping portal. I got up from the table and she swamped me in a hug.

'We didn't know if we'd meet you again,' she said. 'We visited some old friends from medical school in Haworth, and they insisted we stay a couple of days and drink wine with them. We weren't going to refuse that, now, were we?'

'Friends with benefits, hey?' Geoffrey added.

'That's not what that phrase mea…' I began, but was drowned in another of Margot's hugs.

'It's wonderful to see you, dear! Are you staying here, too? It doesn't look very much like a hotel, does it? Geoffrey, isn't it wonderful to see Andy again – why are you dallying?'

Geoffrey forewent a hug, instead holding out his walking pole like an emaciated arm.

'Give him a shake then, you scoundrel. His name's *Rod.* Ha! You like that one, don't you?'

I invited the pair to join me for a late lunch and Margot said 'Oh yes, wonderful' and Geoffrey went to shout Bess for some flagons.

'Are you ready for more?' Geoffrey asked me an hour later over the stickiest of toffee puddings. I had just devoured an entire community of scampi like an underwater Godzilla.

'Yes, I suppose so,' I said.

'I'm spelling it m-o-o-r, because of the terrain,' he smirked. 'So, Andy… are you ready for moor?'

'Erm… still yes.'

Geoffrey laughed uproariously at his own wit, knocking over the gravy boat of custard that had just been placed on the table, then apologising profusely for his clumsiness. (Geoffrey, the cardiothoracic surgeon, apologised for his clumsiness.)

'You really are a complete oaf, Geoffrey,' Margot chided him with a look that harboured regret at the success of the Covid vaccine. She turned her back to her husband, who was now helping a barman to mop up custard and retelling his incredible more/moor zinger. The barman, for his part, looked perplexed and mildly suicidal.

'How are you shaping up, Andy?' Margot asked. 'How was Pen-y-Ghent?'

'I should like to have it burned for witchcraft and heresy,' I replied.

'Oh dear. Any injuries? Come on, dear, you can tell me – I'm a GP.'

'No muscle injuries, no – just some bad blisters on my foot. I've got some plasters though, so hopefully…'

'Hold that thought, please! I'm going to the bathroom.'

Margot left her white wine spritzer sloshing in its glass and strode off with purpose towards the bedrooms, returning in moments holding what looked like a couple of jelly moulds, which she dropped onto the table in front of me.

'What are these?'

'Silicone heels, dear, from a plantar fasciitis kit. You'll never need blister plasters or socks again.'

'Oh really?'

'I assure you, put those on under your normal socks tomorrow and you won't even notice the blisters. Trust me, I'm a doctor.'

There was of course another doctor in the vicinity, and he was brushing Devonshire custard ever deeper into a regency carpet, but Margot's silicone heels were the best shot I had at staying the course.

'Thank you, Margot, these could literally save my skin.'

'Oh, don't mention it, please. It pays to have friends with benefits.'

'You really must stop saying that.'

She gave a big, self-satisfied smile and drew a healthy draught from her spritzer, then changed the subject.

'The bathrooms here are splendidly rustic, don't you think?'

'I haven't inspected them yet,' I replied.

'Oh yes, delightfully rustic and very quaint. Very quaint.'

It should be said that I'm always wary of words like 'rustic', employed as they sometimes are to varnish criminally archaic facilities with a coat of romanticism. I resolved to wash in my bedroom sink, in case the 'rustic shower' at the end of the rickety corridor was just a smiling stableboy with a bucket of suds.

'Morning, squire, shall I wash your bottom?'

'No thank you, Edwin, I'm just here to brush my teeth.'

Geoffrey finished his cleaning chore and retook his seat. Between bustling trips to and from the bar the landlord stood congenially at our table and furnished us with tidbits of local history. He told us that in the 13th century Horton-in-Ribblesdale had been ruled over by monks from nearby Fountains Abbey. In 1597 it had been struck by deadly plague, killing an eighth of the population. And a local farmer named Malcolm owned the ugliest sow he'd ever seen.

'Pigs aren't pretty at the best o'times, but this one is an absolute monster. Honestly, I can give Mal a call now if you want t'go up and see it.'

We all thanked him, but declined the offer on the basis that we just didn't want to do that. My daughters criticised that decision over the day's phone call later on.

'You should have gone, Daddy!'

'I want to go and see a really ugly pig – that's not fair!'

'Well, put it on your birthday list, girls, and Mummy and Daddy will discuss it.'

'How old are you today, Daddy?' Alice asked.

'Still very old, I'm afraid. The Coronavirus is actually my third pandemic.'

She laughed. At this stage it wasn't about understanding the joke – just about testing Daddy's reflexes.

'Will your blisters be OK, Daddy?' Heidi asked.

'I don't know yet, love.'

'You should have rided that pig.'

It wasn't the worst logic in the world.

* * *

It was that hour of the day when every colour, every shade comes out to play. Pen-y-Ghent was still out there, standing erect and taut like someone had just played the hill national anthem, and I was unable to sidestep the dread that shouted from its eternal, ambivalent minerality. However, after a day of loafing and recuperation I treated myself to a stroll in the warm evening, mentally drafting a folk poem entitled *Margot and the Stableboy* which I quickly realised had got out of hand.

Holme Farm campsite sits on the road through the village of Horton and was frothing with campers both die-hard and amateur, showing off their fire-retardant cotton to the world after 18 months in the loft. The sounds of families together and friends reunited carried clear over the bleached grass like fireworks as I walked by.

Sitting dunce-like among the Kiowa Tipis and Klondike Grandes was a family tent which looked as though it had been straitjacketed for going insane. I felt sorry for the obviously inept city-dweller who was now voiding himself from the impossible doorway and, oh no, waving excitedly at me.

'Kiiiiiiinnnnnnnddddd yyyyyyyy!!!!!'

I was seconds too late to step in front of the Number 11 bus trundling along the main road, and instead had to enter the campsite, outing myself to the other campers as the best friend of local tent abuser, Tony Vino.

'Surprise!'

'What the flip are you doing here, Vino?' I asked.

'Surprise!' he said for a second time, perhaps unaware how surprises work. 'I've come to join you for tomorrow. You sounded really low about Pen-y-Ghent so I thought you'd be glad of company.

'You're a wonderful man,' I told him through a bear hug. 'I've seen hell, Tony – and it's green.'

'I'm sure. What do you think of my tent?'

‘It looks like it’s gone mad.’

‘I thought you’d say that.’

It turns out it’s not only dogs who end up looking like their owners.

‘Come with me if you want to live,’ I said, putting a sympathetic arm around him.

My room at the Crown Inn had twin beds, and so we left Vino’s tent to seek out rehab and start to rebuild its life somehow, and sheepishly left the campsite to cries of ‘Shame… shame’ from a man in a Game of Thrones t-shirt. The good news was that at least Tony looked like a walker this time, and not the entry-level drugs trafficker who had met me at Hebden Bridge.

Having been studying for a PHD in Victimhood only hours beforehand, Rob’s message, Margot and Geoffrey’s reappearance and now Vino’s unbidden arrival jump-started my stuttering resolve – and put me in the mood for another of Bess’s finest ale flagons. My oldest friend and I sat outside the Crown Hotel under what Robert Browning called “the quiet-coloured end of evening”, kindling merriment from our cohabited memories and laughing like simpletons, while the tabby cat continued her search for a late dinner.

I could give it one more day.

CHAPTER 16

SILICONE VALLEYS

The following day's walk to Hawes was the perfect Pennine rehabilitation. Most guidebooks gloss over the stretch between Horton and Hawes as being free from highlights and that suited me just fine, because if Pen-y-Ghent was vaunted as a highlight then I'd be happy with some gentle passing it back to the keeper and playing for a 0-0, thank you very much.

Tony and I were first on the road, "up with the ground-mists and the pheasants" (Seamus Heaney). Breakfast had been the standard fare – sausage, bacon and eggs – and many trumps were issued forth like bugle calls as we set off from the Crown. I was hardly *excited* about the day's walk, and had woken up determined to carry out from the will alone duties which had lost all relish. But revival ran along the hedge that morning and the track of Hope quickly wove back towards Expectancy. Tony would need to turn round and head back after the first few miles, but he spent most of the first hour belting out sea shanties and so I wasn't overly upset. Sea shanties, like various other fatal diseases, are catching, don't you know?

Small grey birds called wheatears tacked across our path as we followed a well-marked packhorse trail over Jackdaw Hill, which afforded splendid views of Ribblehead Viaduct on the famous Settle-Carlisle railway line. Designed by John Sydney Crossley and finished in 1874 after five years of construction, the span of limestone arches stands as another legacy of Victorian derring-do, although Crossley's feat of engineering, while admirable, paled in comparison to my silicone heels, which were acting like pull-on morphine patches, shielding my feet not just from injury but from even the sensation of pain. With each early step I expected the spell to break and to feel rapiers of violence shooting up to my brain. But they didn't. The wayfarer came walking–walking–walking, and nothing barred the way.

'Do you think I should take the tent home with me,' Tony asked while peering down into a gulley, 'or just set fire to it?'

'There might be a third strut to that signpost,' I suggested. 'But it didn't look like it wanted to be alive.'

'I just can't be bothered to load it in the car. I bought it off a man under a bridge and it was only a fiver. Claire won't want it in the house. Remember when I memorised that poem, Kindy?'

'Yes, it was less than a week ago, and I preferred it to the sea shanties if you don't mind me saying.'

'Not at all. I'm just trying to give you a varied playlist.'

The easy conversation on the easy trail took us along wall-bound stony tracks towards Ling Gill Ravine, where the beck has carved a deep gash beyond the reach of natural predators and created a unique nature reserve, a tranquil haven for trees and wildflowers and tents with PTSD. It felt timeless, and that's the joy of walking through the hills of course – the imagining yourself wrapped in a land where things are as they always were. There's an immutable in-placeness to the British countryside which is strangely comforting, as is the knowledge that, although you might be in the middle of nowhere, you are definitely headed *somewhere,* with each new footfall clothing you in a view you've never seen before. Evelyn Waugh said that "Change is the only evidence of life." Perhaps that's why walking kick-starts such primal feelings of viscerality? Out here you truly are a human being, and for once you believe it.

We ate a light snack at Ling Gill, and then Vino parted ways with me to turn back to Horton.

‘I’m just going to abandon the tent, Kindy, I’ve decided. I’ve got to get the hire car back to Manchester before 5pm anyway.’

‘What happened to your actual car?’

‘It was in for repair, but the garage got burned down as part of an insurance scam. It’s the second time I’ve given that garage a car and never had it back.’

Oscar Wilde would have had a field day with Tony, but I was tired and in a field already and I expect this sort of thing to happen to him, so I just said, ‘OK.’

‘Keep going, Kindy. The most dangerous thing you can possibly be is enduring. And if you need me to pick you up from Scotland, I’ll do it! I’ll need to buy a car first, obviously.’

‘Obviously.’

Once Tony disappeared from view and the *Some Mothers Do ‘Ave ‘Em* theme music had faded, I clambered up onto the shoulder of Dodd Fell like a cumbersome parrot, feeling content. The countryside had made no other plans for the day and neither had I; it was just the landscape and the sky and my boots and my breathing – an orchestra tuning up to play in concerted sympathy. The poundage on my back felt familiar, the wind was little more than a series of uncertain puffs, and the air temperature was what Goldilocks might call ‘just right’. The road lay bare in the daylight, and I walked with a jewelled twinkle under the yellow gold of the sun for a good couple of hours.

Dodd Fell carried me along the West Cam Road past the mysterious valley of Snaizeholme, which looks like the sort of shady dell that curious children are told never to venture in fairy tales. Maybe I would retire here if I ever came to the conclusion that human beings were no longer my cup of tea.

Speaking of which, towards day’s end a rag-tag gaggle of six teenagers staggered out of the hillside cranny in which they’d been cowering, to seek my help. Dishevelled, distraught and disorientated, they had been walking these moors for literally two hours, but without being able to press the START button and bring up an open-world map or return to their last save point, they looked – and apparently were – completely displaced.

'We're trying to get to Aysgill Force but we're lost. Can you help us, please?' a plaintive girl said.

'Tim said he knew how to use a map, but he doesn't,' a second voice piped up.

'I do!' snapped the lad who I guarantee was Tim, his hair like mouldy hay, 'just not this sort of map.'

'Should have said that then, shouldn't you, instead of lying to try and impress Olivia!'

'I wasn't trying to impress anyone.'

'Tim loves Olivia! Tim loves Olivia!' They sang with tremendous gusto.

'Calm down!' I said sternly. 'I need everyone to just calm down. Right, is everyone calm?'

Several of them nodded.

'OK, right. First thing's first, who's Olivia?'

It wasn't any of my business, but if I could help the chap out then I was more than happy to do so. If there's one thing you learn in 40 years of life, it's how to get relationships gruesomely wrong. Olivia, it transpired, was part of their rival orienteering group and she was either 'fire' or 'on fire' (I couldn't decipher all the lingo) but apparently that meant 'pretty'. The problem was that Olivia was dating Harrison, who by all accounts wasn't half the man Tim was but those were the facts. Another girl in the year, Tasha, *was* interested in Tim, but apparently she was something known as a 'slay queen' and Tim was being encouraged to steer well clear.

Compared to navigating Gen Z dialect, geography maps were a piece of cake. I hadn't been using OS maps – I find them cumbersome and too prone to slapstick comedy the moment a slight breeze picks up – but I did at least know where we were and so, using Tim's unfolded map, I was able to show them their location and how to cut across the pass to Aysgill. They were staring at me as though I was the Mentor of Homer's *Odyssey;* the Sacagawea to their Lewis and Clark; the Brain to their Pinky.

'Your pack is even bigger than ours!' A tall girl said, almost accusingly. 'Where are you walking to?'

'Scotland, with any luck.'

'Oh my days,' said a small urchin boy, placing his head in his hands like he'd just seen a zeppelin crash into a stadium.

'How do you get all the way to Scotland from here?'

'You just follow the route.'

'Yeah, but like, *how* though? How do you manage something like that?'

'Well, I don't know yet – I'm still under halfway.'

I wasn't the person to be setting up a wayside lyceum. I had no gnostic wisdom, no elixirs of knowledge to help this clan level up. But they were waiting for *something*, some inkling of guidance.

'You just have to choose it,' I said tentatively. 'You have to decide – not work out how you feel but *decide* – that you want this more than you want the alternative.'

'So what, like, pretend you're enjoying it even if you're not?'

'It's not about pretending. It's about not letting your feelings make every decision for you.'

'Oh. OK, sweet.'

I don't know whether they actually understood, or even cared, but I realised as they walked off down the yellow road that my external processing had touched on something important for me.

Feelings are authentic, but they are not authoritative. They're great servants but terrible masters. If every path you take is feelings-led then the final destination can only be victimhood, because if life is simply a story about you and your feelings are sovereign, anything which causes you emotional pain is treason – attempted regicide even. But that does seem to be our cultural trajectory. Minor discomforts waylay and paralyse us. We protect our feelings at all costs, building barricades and calling them boundaries. It's how the zeitgeist operates – it's how I had been operating. And I wanted now to take the road less travelled.

Comfort is such a natural thing to desire but such a bizarre thing to demand, as though it were itself a human right. And you can't allow the search for happiness to exercise punitive veto powers over every other human experience. Nobody likes pain, but it's not always your enemy – often, it's a sheep in wolf's clothing. And for each emotion that turns up at the prom there's an act of the will (a choice) to dance with it. The question is always: who gets to lead? As John Milton wrote in *Paradise Lost:*

> "Thae mind is its own place, and in itself
> Can make a Heav'n of Hell, a Hell of Heav'n."

Sometimes we just need to turn our prison into our playground and put on steel-toed boots in a ballet-slipper world.

The young rabble wandered off like confused cattle, one of them asking the others in a stage whisper why there was a badger hanging from my rucksack. I've edited out the part where Tim asked me if I remembered black and white television, and it's a good job there wasn't a sea in the vicinity because onlookers would have spotted me walking silently into it.

The last three miles are always the worst, even with silicone heels. Rottenstone Hill is not your friend and felt like taking the stairs down from a penthouse after the lift had broken. A quick straw poll of my body found that 80% of my joints were 'not at all satisfied' with the current working conditions. Hawes beckons you seductively from the valley floor a long time before you reach it, by which point it's got bored waiting and started flirting with someone else. Nevertheless, after the absolute pasting I'd taken over Pen-y-Ghent today had been a suitable recovery hike, the quality of its mercy largely unstrained. My blisters were sore but not excruciating and, even better, my guidebook told me that I'd now walked 100 miles since the start of the walk! This was something that seemed unlikely even 36 hours ago and was surely worthy of a mini celebration at the Wensleydale Creamery in Hawes. I treated both myself and Alan to an ice-cream and we sat down in the sunshine waiting for the Board Inn (my accommodation for the night) to open its brawny doors.

'Easy,' I said. 'Easy.' And somehow it had been.

I don't like Mint Choc Chip, sire.

'Oh, let me help you out with that then, Alan.'

In his book *A Philosophy of Walking,* Frederic Gros says, "Discipline is the impossible conquered by the obstinate repetition of the possible."

There were still nine days left to trudge, several things had already gone wrong and anything still might. But someone once said that tomorrow will worry about itself.

I didn't have it in me to walk another 170 miles. But I did have it in me to walk the next few steps; to end today's troubles by clattering over the cobbles, tramping through the now-open tavern doors, having a long shower and a light supper and a deep sleep. And that's precisely what I would do.

It's hard for an egg to turn into a bird. Harder still for that bird to start flying while it is still an egg. And there will always be old lessons to relearn and painful new ways in which to learn them. All you need to do, though, is take it one stage, one step, one view at a time.

The wayfarer came walking–walking–walking, up to the old inn-door.

Day 8
Hawes to Tan Hill
17 miles

"Up, lad, up, 'tis later or lying:
Hear the drums of morning play;
Hark, the empty highways crying
'Who'll beyond the hills away?"
Reveille by A.E. Houseman

"Come forth into the light of things,
Let Nature be your teacher."
William Wordsworth

CHAPTER 17
JUST YOU THWAITE

The opening section of Day 8, as you follow the Ure River out of Hawes and tread the soft buttercupped meadows towards the village of Hardraw, is the sort of photogenic terrain which gives people ideas of walking the Pennine Way in the first place – the landscape is rigged with love and that heavy greenness fostered by water. The day's closing section up to the old miner's drinking hole at Tan Hill, by contrast, is the sort of terrain that makes people wish their parents hadn't opened that second bottle of wine in Kidderminster, March 1980.

Reveille was at 7:30am in the Board Inn. After a hearty breakfast of meat and eggs the thud-creak of boots and the lighter tap-clack of walking poles on the exposed dining room floorboards drummed us out onto parade. Geoffrey and Margot were once more present and correct, but they wanted to potter around the small town of Hawes and its fashionable emporiums for an hour before tacking north. I was pretty well-stocked for Grandfather clocks and brass coal scuttles, so we would rendezvous that evening at the Tan Hill Inn. I did however buy myself a garish red baseball cap from a newsagents, to cordon off my bare scalp from the unexpected sunfall.

'See you later, dear! Have a marvellous walk, won't you?'

'You too! Don't burn too much daylight on retail therapy.'

'We'll be there in time for tea, Andy, never fear.'

I never quite solved the mystery of how Margot and Geoffrey reached their destinations in such good time. They never appeared hurried, never seemed to move that rapidly, took more picnics than Ratty and Moley. But they did always arrive, as Margot said, in time for tea.

Rob had taken his pit-stop yesterday and was waiting for me in Hardraw by the Green Dragon Inn, on the wall of which a sign reads:

Hippies Use Back Door
No Exceptions

When it comes to establishing a USP, some pubs shift towards gastronomy while others install their own microbreweries. The Green Dragon Inn breathes fire over all of that by housing, somewhat bizarrely, England's longest single-drop waterfall. This is not a joke. Modern health-and-safety dictats being what they are, the 30-metre-high cascade is not actually permitted entrance to the pub and is instead housed within a mystical green grotto out back. It's quite a sight, apparently. William Wordsworth wrote to Samuel Coleridge once about it:

"We walked up to the fall and what I would not give if I could convey to you the images and feelings which were then communicated to me…the enchanted effect produced by this Arabian scene of colour."

You'll no doubt remember that I said, with much less florid ebullience than good old Wordsworth, 'It's quite a sight, apparently'. I say apparently because it was 8:30am and the pub – along with its selfishly private waterfall – was closed.

'What's the point of being an English pub if you're not going to be magically open 24 hours a day?' I complained.

Rob consoled me by scrolling through some photos he'd taken of the waterfall yesterday, accidentally swiping onto a close-up of his swollen big toe that he'd sent to his nurse fiancée. He assured me it was the only swollen body part he'd photographed, and I briefly sicked up in my mouth.

Aside from my silicone-guarded blisters, by this stage of the journey my own feet had the texture and aesthetic appeal of a handbag fashioned in the shadows by a Rumpelstiltskin lookalike (I can describe them in no other way) and I was no longer the tenderfooted greenhorn of Edale.

'Are you doing OK apart from the bloated toe?' I asked.

'Yeah, all good. Yesterday was a cinch. Glad you didn't give up?'

'For now, yes. I reserve the right to change my mind at any point.'

'Me too. Every step forward is a small ******* victory.'

'Well, quite.'

Rob and I steeled ourselves for a protracted slog up to the twerking rump of Great Shunner Fell (the highest point so far at 2,349ft), hoisting our sweat-cured rucksacks and beating manly breasts. We leaned into the gradient, ploughing an upward furrow, the countless and soul-jarring false peaks yoking us with an additional burden – a psychological one – that the existing physical burden carried like its own rucksack. I've experienced anguish in many different forms over my life – I've trodden on Lego, lost a penalty shootout a few times, seen a donkey get hit by a tram – but nothing quite disturbs me in the way getting to the top of something and realising it's actually the middle does.

When we finally verified we were there, the view from the true peak of Great Shunner was worth it though: a rippling sheet of English beauty, freshly laundered, which tucks its distant corners into an unseen mattress; an open letter from God. It's what Celtic theology might call "a thin place", where heaven seems to stoop for an instant and kiss humanity's brow. If I didn't already believe in God then up here I would find it damned difficult not to. Add to that the coffee and biscuits that Rob was preparing, and I'd be running headlong for the nearest altar call.

Great Shunner Fell purportedly translates as 'Big Lookout Hill', which wouldn't win any awards for imagination but gets full marks for not being a lie – another Ronseal place. From here, in every direction fells and hills and scars raise a hand in friendly greeting, or at least that's how it seems in good weather. The high population of cairns marking the path are a clear sign that the climate can be rather pugnacious when it chooses to be.

Below the sturdy flanks of Shunner, the Butter Tubs Pass was worming its way over into Wensleydale. The serrated horizon of the Lake District was visible to the West, while the Pennine Way's highest point, Cross Fell, was vaguely discernible to the North. But I would cross that fell when I came to it and not before.

For now I was musing, and there are certain thoughts that can only occur to oneself high above civilisation. For one thing, it is really rather difficult to feel lonely on top of a lonely hill – the dopamine hit from mastering the climb is marvellous company and something for which I was developing a healthy addiction. For several days now we had been inhabiting this landscape, slowly taking possession of it, leaving indelible tracks on the archive of the ground. I was missing home and the privilege of being comfortable or having a slice of cake at midnight because I felt like it, but I did not miss being inside. I was simply dwelling in the walking.

In *A Philosophy of Walking*, Frederic Gros writes, "In walks that extend over several days, during major expeditions, everything is inverted. 'Outside' is no longer a transition, but the element in which stability exists."

The poison chalice of a long-distance walk, of course, is that you don't get to sit in admiration for very long. You have to walk the view. After a short respite at Rob's hilltop café, we left the summit of Great Shunner and slalomed down a rubble ski slope (far less fun than it sounds) into Thwaite, a cheerfully and ingratiatingly whitewashed village which Rob described as ******* gorgeous when I had thought my description was already standing room only for adverbs. My guidebook was telling me that a thwaite is "a piece of land cleared of woodland for habitation", and also that I really must stop and feast at Kearton Country Hotel and Tea Rooms. Never one to turn down the option of second brunch I deferred to the wisdom of the text… and then took an immediate vow of abstinence when the barmaid informed me that my pint of Diet Coke cost 'just £3.40' – another bizarre adverbial choice. I decided that her price comparison can't have been in the context of other soft drinks, but probably in relation to the cost of buying the entire hotel, or the GDP of China. She was perhaps gearing up to tell me that the Northern Irish Troubles were 'just a 30-year period of ethno-nationalist friendly banter', but I didn't stay around to find out. Rob chose to be less frugal and purchased a pint of Theakstons and a portion of chips, his way of describing the transaction making the perfect Christmas gift for people who love asterisks replacing words.

Thwaite hides itself away in this landscape as though trying to hold out a feeble hand against the irresistible swell of modernity. Little cottages line lanes that jut off from each other almost playfully, and wildflowers that have smuggled their hues between the cracks of dry-stone walling are left undisturbed in their endeavours. According to Mike Harding in his beautifully presented book *Walking the Dales,* the Kearton Hotel was founded by brothers Richard and Cherry Kearton, who amongst other things were pioneers of nature and wildlife photography. Cherry – who judging by his name and that of his brother was their parents' second favourite son – was at one time a popular radio broadcaster but, tragically, he died leaving broadcasting house during the Blitz in 1940. It's tidbits of local knowledge like this that help keep petty things like inflation in perspective.

A pair of leather-clad bikers were perched at the table next to us on the hotel patio, their steel steeds tethered on the road in front. The idiosyncrasies of their dialect gave them away as being from Derbyshire, one of them having 'bin all of a shek' at nearly losing his front wheel that morning and his friend telling him, 'Dunna mither'.

We chatted for a while. They were both from Chesterfield and heading back there that evening (I'm not sure if you know this but travelling by motorbike is much faster than going on foot), and I told them about the preparatory walks I'd done for the Pennine Way around Tapton Golf Course and along Curbar Edge.

'D'ya live in Chezzy too, then?' they asked.

'Up until quite recently, yes.'

'Well, ah bet we'll be 'ome before ya.'

'Only a fool would take that bet,' I replied, watching them mount up. 'Give my regards to Chez Vegas.'

'Tek care.'

They rode off and before too long were just exhaust vapour, an obfuscation of the clear summer air. The echo from their mufflers bounced off hillsides at odd angles like a squash ball for a while, eventually surrendering itself to the valley floor in gracious defeat. Those bikers would cover the 122 miles between Thwaite and Chesterfield in under three hours, and be back in time for oatcakes and a pint or three at the Peacock. Somewhere near their destination was a house and a home, where a new family was writing a fresh chapter over its Magnolia-white walls and filling its margins with laughter and subplots. That's how it should be of course, but you never fully leave a place you have called *home,* I don't think. There's always an echo of some kind left behind.

For me though, and for now, *this* was my home. This blessed plot, this green and pleasant land, was mine. And I dwelled by walking.

CHAPTER 18
GETTING TANNED

The afternoon started with a deceptively gruelling diagonal climb out of Thwaite, where my left knee started to creak like a gibbet in the wind, only quietening down when I applied a generous dose of Ibuprofen gel, the hiking equivalent of giving a teething baby a shot of rum.

'No more until tomorrow,' I told my own knee with some authority. It wasn't that tubes of Ibuprofen are super expensive, but I'd recently bought a pint of Diet Coke and would need to contact Christians Against Poverty before making any further life choices.

The afternoon was warm and peaceful and the long trailside grass swished and hushed amiably… then whipped up from repose when we startled a young rabbit who wasn't expecting visitors. The sky was unilaterally blue, with light pencil clouds washed over in watercolour, and the air held the faint memory of rain but nothing more, as though a policeman had shown it a polaroid and the response was, 'You know, detective, the guy looks familiar but I'm a little hazy on the details.'

On the borders of Thwaite there are lovely meadows of buttercups and cranesbill to walk through and admire, but I'm afraid that's about all I can tell you regarding the plant life in these parts. Unlike the Kearton brothers, my knowledge of naturalism extends to daisies, dandelions and buttercups – to my mind 'The Big Three' of UK flora. To be a professional rambler perhaps I should be able to spot a red helleborine or a spreading bellflower at 100 paces, but I gave up trying to learn the names of flowers at some point in the late 1990s, and I've felt a lot better since.

After his own frustration with guidebooks, Rob had yesterday downloaded an app on his phone with a digital map of the entire Pennine Way, overlaid with a precision line showing the exact route. By connecting the app to his GPS it was now almost impossible for him to get lost, apparently. On the approach to Swaldele, at a fork in the path as I was dowsing right, Rob pointed confidently left up a steep incline and said, 'It's along this way, mate.' My instinct told me this was incorrect and that the surest route was down the bank past one of the many lathe barns in the region.

'Well, Herman, I'll take the high road and you take the low road.'

'And I'll literally be in Scotland before you,' I boasted. 'So long, sucker!'

A sign across a gated track 200 yards hence informed me that, "This is NOT the Pennine Way."

Rob blew me a kiss from 50 feet above, but I refused to catch it. I could imagine the supercilious voice from my rear pouch.

We've been through this before, haven't we, sire?

'Shut it, Alan.'

Using Satnav does feel like cheating, though, doesn't it? The mythical walker of legend had nothing but the sun and the stars to guide his steps, while even Bill Bryson in *A Walk in the Woods* (written in the late 1990s) was blown away by this new-fangled GPS. Strap that to my long-cultivated mistrust of AI in general and fear that at any moment Skynet might go online and start mercilessly liquidating us, and I'm probably fine with analogue methods of walking divination. Equally though, I didn't want to get lost and die in a cave – and I can't say I blame myself – and so on this occasion I would bend a knee to applied statistics and let Rob's phone lead us to death or glory.

For the comedian, it has to be said that the invention of Satnav was a revelation. When I started on the comedy circuit in early 2005 it was still fairly fledgling and distrusted, and you couldn't simply open Google Maps to let it guide you from hearth to stage. In those days – and I feel like a decrepit and toothless crone saying this – I had to literally print off my journey on sheets of A4 paper and read them as I went along at high speed, turning my car into a dual-use office-cum-deathtrap. Then, on the way home after the gig, I would have to read it back-to-front like the Qu'ran in the pitch black, using the car's inner light for long periods, the slightest use of which – as anyone who's ever had a dad knows – is likely to cause an immediate head-on collision. Not all forward momentum is genuine progress, but I'll wind my neck in on the satellite thing.

We became more grubby and less competent as the day went on, plodding into that pungent sweet-saltiness that your body's perfumery creates to advertise its own uncleanliness. And while endurance grows with each day, stamina still depletes throughout it, and we were halting regularly to water down our sweatiness, then moving off quickly to sweat out the water. Rinse and repeat.

Circumnavigating the scree-littered slopes of Kisdon Hill, much to Alan's tacit delight we came upon an unnerving collection of dead rabbits. Whether struck by some epidemic or hunted with an air rifle from the other side of the valley, it wasn't clear, but looking upon death never feels natural, and we walked wincinginly, almost funereally on for a while. The sombre note didn't hang in the air for long fortunately, and a non-monetary reward for my continued 'bonus walking' awaited us in Swaledale:

> "Beautiful Swaledale the land of rest,
> Beautiful Swaledale I love thee the best."
> (Old Yorkshire Ballad)

Swaledale is, to many, the most gorgeous of all the Yorkshire dales: a soul-stirringly elegant valley, lush and steep-sided, with emissary plovers swooping along its lazy river, which Rob described as

******* amazing. I couldn't help but agree. Sheep flecked the hillside like splodges on a careless canvas, while tumbledown mining huts appeared more like sorcerers' hideouts. The river Swale's storyline begins above this valley and sets off on an epic quest of megalomania, as from here it flows east through farmland to merge with the river Ure, after which it becomes the Ouse and, having later merged with the Trent, the Humber. Whether it gets to Grimsby and longs for its once-upon-a-time in this breathtaking vale, we'll never know. But as I said just recently, not all momentum is genuine progress.

The path above Swaledale descends along a root-riveted path to the sleepy woodland hollow at Keld, the most Tolkeinian place on the Way yet, where a fairytale waterfall reassures bone-weary walkers that life isn't just dead rabbits and busted knees.

'Is that Hobbiton by any chance?' I asked a pair of beige-coated ramblers climbing up from the dell, a look of transparent playfulness across my face.

'No, that's Keld,' they replied without recognition or warmth, and carried on.

'If I ever become emperor,' I whispered pointedly to Rob, 'I'll have people like that executed.'

'Maybe that's what happened to the rabbits? Just hadn't read *Lord of the Rings.*'

'It's a working theory, for sure. Shall we stop in the dell for more treats?'

'Obviously we shall.'

Keld is also the location where the noble Pennine Way walker crosses paths with his or her ultimate nemesis, the nefarious Coast-to-Coaster. The Coast to Coast Walk is 100 miles shorter than the Pennine Way – and therefore about 30% easier – and yet these cretins saunter around with the mystifying cockiness of a bay leaf claiming credit for the taste of roast pork. The rivalry between the two groups is both fiercely intense and completely fabricated by me, but the following exchange genuinely happened.

Rob and I settled down by the waterfall with prolific exhalations, exhausted and evaporating, to find a couple of university-aged lads already lounging there like Wildean homosexuals. They smirked patronisingly at us as we continued to deflate.

'You doing the Pennine Way?' one of them grunted. He had all the traits one would look for in a new kitchen – granite jaw, washboard stomach, nice layout etc.

'That's right. How about you?'

'Coast to Coast. Absolutely smashing it, mate.'

'Cool beans,' I replied, and once again they smirked. The human face has 43 different muscles and can muster around 10,000 expressions, but the smirk is the worst and, after 13 miles and smelling like compost, I didn't really appreciate it.

'I've heard Coast to Coast is a piece of p***,' Rob said, taking equal exception to the braggadocio.

'Yes, I've heard it's a piece of cake, too,' I added. 'I don't have any plans for next Sunday, so I might polish the whole thing off before lunch.'

'I might wait until I go fully blind or lose a limb before trying it,' Rob rejoined, and this was now the closest I'd ever come to being involved in gang warfare. The two slovenly Coast-to-Coasters sneered and conferred.

'Well… we heard that the Pennine Way is just for old-aged pensioners who've never quite come to terms with the fact they aren't in *Lord of the Rings*,' the handsome boy quipped.

'Yeah,' the other one added, 'thanks for clarifying what you're doing – I assumed you were going to get yourself valued on the *Antiques Roadshow.*'

'Careful lads,' I shot back. 'It's four o'clock – nearly bath and story time for you, isn't it?'

'Says the guy with a toy bear in his rucksack.'

'He's a fox, he's a bloody fox! And he's not a toy, he's a novelty doorstop from Dunelm Mill – £12.99!'

We were, it seemed, moments away from an intense dance off which would lead – doesn't it always – to a fatal knife fight. But when Rob called them both w****** and the two lads reshaped their facial muscles into apologetic grimaces, Rob and I both realised that we might have overreacted. In my opinion – an opinion I respect and I think everyone should – the bout ended in a tie.

To show there were no hard feelings, one of the young loafers threw an entire packet of Jaffa Cakes our way like a delicious olive branch. I was yet slightly sceptical – Jaffa Cake boxes possess the perfect dimensions for storing a human poo to use in a prank – but I had overthought it again. I said thank you, gave him a chummy thumbs-up, and then asked what was wrong with his strapped-up knee. He explained that he'd twisted it on a descent, but they didn't have any first aid kit because they didn't want extra weight in their rucksacks (translation: they were under 25 and thought they were invincible). I tossed him the rest of my Ibuprofen gel, he said 'Really?', I said 'Yes, really', and then we all fist-bumped as they headed on their way.

You can keep your 1914 Christmas armistices, friend. This was a peace deal of Nobel proportions.

* * *

Finding ourselves, for once, beneath wooded canopy rather than bare sky, Rob and I stretched out under the rustling leaves of the hollow and enjoyed the company of the lovely waterfall. The grass was thick and dark under the shade, the earth felt cool, and I think I even dozed off for a while, roused eventually by the smell of coffee wafting from Rob's not-permitted-in-this-area stove. I propped myself up against bark and drank to his health.

'Sitting under a tree is such an underrated past-time, isn't it?' I said. 'You can see why it happens so often in books.'

'Totally. I always wonder who else might have sat there, you know? In the past, I mean.'

'Absolutely. Perhaps a king hid in these very branches to elude capture. Or a dashing highwayman used it as a cache for stolen trinkets.'

'Yeah, and probably some plummy-mouthed bloke has written a poem here.'

'Oh, there's no doubt about it. I might even write one myself.'

'Well don't read it to me if you do. I hate poems. And plays, too – I hate a play. I forgot Valentine's Day last year, and my girlfriend punished me by taking me to watch Shakespeare. It was s***.'

'Ah, the course of true love…'

'What about it?'

'Never did run smooth. It's from Shakespeare.'

'What did I just say, Herman? What were the last words I just said? Go and walk coast to coast if you're gonna carry on like that.'

'Sorry,' I said.

'And that better not be from Shakespeare either. Here, have more coffee and talk normally.'

'Thank you. And it's the Queen's English* only from now on, I promise.'

(**The Merry Wives of Windsor*, by William Shakepeare)

You can quite feasibly end the day's walk in Keld if you're a camper, and Rob was planning to do just that – ideally hoping to find a farmhouse with a sign that read:

Poets use back door
No exceptions

He relaced his boots and packed up his stove.

'See ya tomorrow, mate. Rabbit stew for tea.'

For me there would be no rabbit stew. Instead, there was a further four miles of searing trudge up onto Stonesdale Moor – the place the chaps at the bus-stop tavern in Malham had warned me about – towards a place regarded by one Pennine Way writer as "hitting the mother lode." Even after my long rest, nap and coffee, the last three miles are always… well, you know by now, and the 'm' on my Ben Sherman shirt decided enough was enough, fraying from its remaining thread and laying to rest in a patch of tawny bog grass. My shirt now read 'HER A', with a single inch of bare fabric sparing me from announcing myself into Tan Hill as the Greek goddess of childbirth.

At East Stonesdale Farm, a man of unworkoutable age and with startlingly flaxen hair was restoring a dry-stone wall. I had never conversed with a dry-stone waller before and the whole scene looked like something from a Constable painting, so I stopped to swig gladly from my water bottle and learn more about his travail.

'Amazing bit of restoration work, there,' I said, assuming it must be.

'Aye…' he replied.

'Is this what you do as a profession?'

'Aye, for a job, like.'

'Wow. Have you been doing it long?'

'Aye.'

'Well, you're certainly very talented from what I can make out. It must be a hard trade to learn?'

'Aye.'

He nodded at this point, which felt like major progress.

'I'm walking the Pennine Way.'

'Oh aye?'

'I am. Just off to stay at the Tan Hill Inn. Do you know it?'

'Oh aye.' Of course he did – it was literally the next building you came to heading north.

'Well, I've had my drink. All the best.'

As expected, he said 'Aye', and I trudged on.

On a lonely hill on the northern edge of the Yorkshire Dales stands a 17th century inn with exposed beams and stone-flagged flooring. After a painful hour of endless moorland and shrieking shin splints, patting my thighs as you would a rosette-winning stallion and plunging deep into perennial bogland, I finally stepped foot inside the world famous Tan Hill Inn: the highest pub in the British Isles. And, as I'm about to explain, arguably the worst. A place where I'd be told a single night's accommodation was 'just £190'.

Just.

* * *

The doorway of the Tan Hill Inn, Britain's highest pub, was a welcome sight. From here the moors stretch out barren and featureless in all directions, a morass of unfolding emptiness, with a hidden army of disused mine shafts ready to take down anyone straying from the official trail.

The climb to the Inn had been interminable, and is still hideous to recall. I had expected it to appear as a faint haze on the horizon then to grow majestically larger with each step, as epic and cultured as Omar Sherif's famous arrival in *Lawrence of Arabia*. By the time I finally saw it, it was barely 100 metres away and my anticipation had been pistol-whipped by the advent of shin splints. But no matter! The Tan Hill Inn was a place that all the Pennine Way guidebooks apparently sought to canonise, cooing over it as though this was 1962 and the pub was a full-colour poster of Peter O'Toole.

I hadn't booked a room for the evening, but the Bank Holiday was practically over and taverns like this always find room for Pennine Way walkers – we are, if you like, their bread and butter.

'Could I book a single room for tonight?' I asked a woman with a clipboard who I assumed worked there, although she could have been doing a survey.

'Certainly, sir… Oh, sorry, we don't have a single room, but we could do you a double? This one has a golden bath.'

I cooed like she was a young Peter O'Toole. 'Sounds OK to me.'

'OK, wonderful. That's just £190 please.'

'Say that again,' I asked, not really wanting her to say it again.

'£190 please. And you get your breakfast for that, too.'

Assuming breakfast wasn't poached Fabergé eggs on toast and sausages that were really just many rubies in a brown sock, this inclusive offer didn't act to soften the blow.

'You must get this all the time, but do you have anything cheaper? I'm walking the Pennine Way.'

'I'm afraid not, sir.'

'I definitely am walking it,' I snapped, before realising that she was referring to the lack of a cheaper room, not just calling me a liar. 'I just want to sleep in a bed for seven hours – I'm not after a season ticket at Hartlepool United.'

My voice was breaking in a way usually reserved for hearing that a childhood pet or uncle had perished.

'This is the best we can do,' she replied, displaying some sympathy and a remedial understanding of superlatives.

I have genuinely owned cars that cost me less than £190, but I didn't have a lot of choice in the matter. Capitalism, it seemed, had finally shown its true colours and it was time to start calling everyone comrade. Maybe I could melt down the bathtub and take it with me? Or firebomb the pub in retribution.

'How much is a pint of Diet Coke?' I asked.

'I'll tell you what, sir, go and take a seat outside and I'll bring you one on the house.'

This was something at least. If I stole most of the cutlery, I might end up breaking even.

The outside seating area was basic but expansive and was bristling with folk drinking in the last of the Bank Holiday sunshine. I sat at a picnic bench with Alan beside me, wryly observing the chemical change in the patrons and waiting for my drink. I had noted a definite change in local accents today. From the 'Ey-ups' of Edale, I had walked through the 'Ow dos' of Yorkshire and was now teetering on 'Haway' territory. There was also the 'Air hairlairs' of Margot and Geoffrey who had just tumbled into the inn looking dishevelled and regal.

You expect to wait five minutes for a drink. On a busy Bank Holiday in a pulsing pub, maybe you're OK with 10 minutes. After

45 minutes, during which time I could have watched half a football match or flown to Jersey, I started to sense I'd been overlooked, although that might just have been the dehydration-induced paranoia. I looked around at the excitable revellers and realised that, in fact, they didn't look excited at all – they all looked irritated. Each table was arm-flapping, neck-craning and mouth-swearing, trying to get the attention of the wispy staff. One family gathering had a tray of drinks delivered to them and cheered like air passengers landing safely after losing both engines to geese.

'Well, Merry Christmas!' one of them toasted. It was the last day of May.

A traumatised waitress galloped past me and I dredged up the final drops of moisture in my throat to ask where my drink was.

'Yes, sir, it's just coming.'

'From where, though?'

A few tables away, a burly man with a Toon Army tattoo had set up pints of Timothy Taylor like bowling pins. He saw my plight, shook his head ruefully and approached me with funereal solemnity, handing me a pint of ale with a 'For your tomorrow, I gave my today' sort of expression.

'I don't like to see people die in front of me,' he said. I wasn't totally sure what he meant so I just said 'Neither do I' and then 'Thank you so much.'

Before the pandemic, Pennine Way walkers were the bread and butter for places like this. Now, it seemed, they were having us for dinner. Geoffrey and Margot sauntered over to sit with me, satisfied smiles on their faces.

'Hello dear!' Margot exclaimed.

'Are you well?' I asked.

'Yes, all good thanks,' Geoffrey said. 'Managed to get a double room for tonight. Only £190 – not too bad really.'

I would let them treat me to dinner, if it ever arrived.

The course of true walking never did run smooth.

Day 9
Tan Hill to Middleton-in-Teesdale
17 miles

"The way to do a great deal is to keep on doing a little. The way to do nothing at all is to be continually resolving that you will do everything."

Charles Spurgeon

"The summer sun was not meant for boys like me. Boys like me belonged to the rain."

Benjamin Alire Sáenz, Aristotle and Dante Discover the Secrets of the Universe

CHAPTER 19

AND PILGRIMS WERE THEY ALL

In early 1993, a Premier League footballer by the name of Alan Cork decided to grow a beard. Cork was playing for Sheffield United at the time and they were about to play in the third round of the FA Cup. Cork vowed not to shave his beard until his team had been knocked out of the competition – something which is always an imminent likelihood when you're Sheffield United. By sheer miracle of luck or some divine prank, United reached the semi-finals, losing 2-1 at Wembley to their arch-rivals Sheffield Wednesday, by which point Alan Cork's beard was so unruly, it looked as though United had suffered a series of last-minute injuries and been forced to field their bus driver in attack.

What starkened the contrast was that Alan Cork was in possession of that singular quality common to a lot of 1980s footballers, that of looking about 40 years older than he actually was. Cork was only 34 at the time, but his beard was so white and his hair so patchy that when he grabbed Sheffield United's equaliser – yes, he actually scored – his celebration brought to mind a demented bear-trapper staggering wildly through the Appalachians. (If you've got time, type "Alan Cork" into a search engine of your choice. I guarantee the first generated image will be from the 1993 FA Cup semi-final.)

Why am I mentioning this? Well, because it was that image which staggered out through the foliage of my memory as I looked in the mirror of the Tan Hill Inn that morning. I had stopped shaving a couple of years previously when my daughter Alice told me I looked like a handsome goblin, but I had since invested in a mid-range beard trimmer to keep everything nicely topiaried. Electric trimmers aren't a necessity when you're spending a fortnight in wild climes, and so my beard growth was currently at the level of 'Junior Wizard' or 'Apprentice Psychopath'.

Who was that fellow though? The one in the mirror. Why didn't he look as I expected him to look? The years had slipped down on him like a mudslide. Who had given him permission to decay in such a gratuitous manner, to have bags under his eyes and grey on his chin?

'What has happened to you?' I asked him. 'How did we get to this point?'

The hardest thing to see, perhaps, is yourself as you actually are.

'You do look quite old today, Daddy,' Alice told me as I gave the girls a virtual tour of the reason they couldn't now go to university.

'Well, I have been trying to tell you, my love. I was at the original table-read for *Macbeth.*'

'Wait... Daddy, wait... is that a golden bath?'

'Yes it is, but don't get too...'

'Daddy, you're a king!'

If I was a king, I was King Duncan at the close of the battle of Elgin, after *Macbeth* has been a bad friend by killing him.

'What will you do today, my darlings?'

'Today, I have decided to make you a celebration stone,' Alice declared.

'A what, pardon?'

'We found some lovely stones in the garden, and Mummy has some paint we can use to decorate them. So I'm going to do one for you.'

'OK, that sounds amazing!'

'What will you do today, Daddy?'

'I will walk, my love. I will walk.'

It was, after all, what I did.

In addition to the three females on the wrong side of a glass screen, I had a new love in my life. Discretion about one's private life is the better part of valour, but sometimes you just need to shout your affection from the rooftops, and I have never felt about anyone the way I now felt about Ibuprofen gel.

40 years of men I had walked this earth. I had glimpsed joy and dined with grief and bathed in grace. But to experience the thrilling, intimate coddle of this topical analgesic was to capture the ineffable and ensnare the ethereal. This was the beloved other for which the bards of old clamoured.

"Vitamin I", as Ibuprofen is known in the walking community, is the opiate of the rambling masses and I couldn't get enough of it. The tube parsimoniously advises against lathering your joints with too much of the stuff because apparently it can have adverse effects; but unless one of those is the desire to pen an ode to viscous paracetamol, I think we're fine. The 16th century English philosopher Francis Bacon thought that the three major inventions of human history were the compass, the printing press and gunpowder. You went too early on that one, Francis. Oh, and you also missed out bacon.

Today was a unique experience on the Pennine Way, in that it started with a short stretch walking downhill. It was the first day of June, the first day of Summer to most people, "and the enjoying of Spring fades as does its blossoming." I had enjoyed a comfortable night's sleep in the Tan Hill Inn and had used the golden bath to bathe, to wash sweaty clothes, and to just sit in imagining myself as Bacchus, Roman god of wine. For £190 I would have also liked complimentary room service from a centaur, but whatever angst I had was diffused by the rhapsodical felicity of Ibuprofen gel as I massaged my hips, knees and shins with it while quoting Keats.

I had asked for a takeaway breakfast from the Inn so I could roll wagons early, and its complete failure to arrive was as predictable as the cop with two weeks left to retirement bleeding out at the end of a movie. Instead, I forced down a full English fry-up and formed a familiar cohort with Rob, Geoffrey and Margot, and we squelched down the bank onto the sheep-swallowing wastes of Sleightholme Moor – a stretch of terrain written and directed by Stephen King. At best it's like walking across a poorly-set trifle. At worst, it's the Pennywise the Clown of landscapes – appears inviting and friendly… then eats you. The Pennine Way weather may have been incredibly lenient with us over the past few days, but nobody hoards anything as well as a moorland stockpiles water. Navigation was also a pain, with only a smattering of ghostly white poles beckoning us on like half-hearted spectres. Nevertheless, the sun was rising in the sky and I was rising along the map, and today I would cross the halfway point.

'You can tell we've had good weather, can't you?' Margot said, rolling up a sleeve. 'My skin has gone from translucent and ghostly to a sort of plain white.'

'Did you buy anything from Hawes in the end?'

'Yes, we did actually,' Geoffrey answered. 'Picked up an old walnut writing bureau, Queen Anne-style, you know?'

'I do not know, no. And where is this bureau?'

'Oh, we've paid for it to be delivered to our house in Bath.'

'I thought you lived in London.'

'We do,' said Margot matter-of-factly, 'but we also have a house in Bath.'

'Ironically, it doesn't have a bath!' Geoffrey bellowed. Nobody laughed but a grouse of some sort was flushed from the bushes.

The Pennine Way is home to a wide range of birds whose names I know but who I wouldn't recognise if they stood next to me at a bar. Here on the northern tundra a whole host of winged avians make their home and, as someone with a limited interest *in* and remedial knowledge *of* naturalism, I had become frustrated at my inability to identify the surrounding wildlife. I wasn't looking to rise to the level of a Mary Anning or a Charles Darwin, but I wanted to at least recognise some of the rich natural taxonomy and not just describe creatures as 'brown' or 'not a pigeon'. To that end I had been jotting down some research notes to use in broadening my knowledge. This sounds like something people only do in GCSE French aural exams, but nevertheless, here's the Andy Kind guide to the birds of Northern England as sketched in my Pennine Way notepad:

Common Snipe: small, stocky wader; a duck with secateurs for a face.

Redshanks: orange beak, not red; looks like a sparrow had a one-night stand with an emu.

Golden Plover: sleek black body with a 1970s-style fur coat.

Lapwing: has the crest of a jousting knight's helmet and says 'peewit' a lot; Newcastle United supporter.

Curlew: miniature pterodactyl, absolutely terrifying.

Red Grouse: a partridge without the pear tree; easily upset.

Black Grouse: a rooster that just came home from boarding school.

Pheasant: a complete moron. Honestly, just a top-of-the-range wally.

Peahen: occasional perverts.

After an hour of plunging and squelching we crossed definitively into County Durham, leaving Yorkshire firmly in our wake. If Yorkshire is indeed God's own county as the locals militantly claim, then for walkers He is truly the vengeful God of stereotype, not the gentle Christ whom I had petitioned to never again make me pay £190 for a night's sleep. We were in the true North of England now though – "proper North" – and I could hear the pennies falling off the pints along the Pennines.

'Speaking of walnuts,' Margot asked, segueing from the topic of the writing desk, 'do you still have that one you were keeping on you in its wrapper? What did you call it – a macguffin?'

I tapped my breast pocket. 'I do indeed. It's safe.'

'Have you worked out why you're walking the Pennine Way yet?' Rob asked.

'I'm getting there,' I replied with a non-committal smile. I was about to divulge some of my inner monologue, but at that moment a vertical disruption in the flat horizon caught my eye, and we found ourselves marching up to a tanned and jovial man sitting Tom Bombadil-like at the side of the path, as though gatekeeping the North East of Britain.

'Are you waiting for a password?' I asked him.

'What's that?' he replied from under the shadow of his wide-brimmed Stetson.

'You're sitting on the border between Yorkshire and County Durham.'

'Am I? Oh, fantastic! Would you like a biscuit?'

'Is that a riddle or a genuine question?'

The gatekeeper held out a pink wafer.

And so I met Chris, an irrepressibly dogged and instantly likeable chap, who worked for the Ministry of Defence and told us between bites of biscuit that he was walking from Land's End to John O'Groats – about five times the distance of the Pennine Way. Having started on the first day of May down at England's most southerly point, he had splashed across Exmoor, struggled up Offa's Dyke and then hoofed it across to Derbyshire, walking for four solid weeks before he even got to Edale.

'I can't afford a fast car and can't grow a ponytail, so this will have to suffice as a midlife crisis,' he said humbly.

Chris' heroic path would merge with my own until the frontier outpost of Byrness, after which the John O'Groats path forks left towards Jedburgh, then ever upwards through the lowlands and highlands to the finish line at the end of the world. Finishing his short power-rest, he held up his fancy GPS like a sonic screwdriver (NB. It made Rob's navigation app look like a treasure map drawn by an imbecile) and I decided in that moment to tuck in behind and let this man slipstream me all the way to Scotland.

When you're walking wounded after a whole week on a national trail, but you're at least feeling resolute and proud of your success, meeting someone who hasn't stopped for a month and doesn't plan to for another month doesn't do a great deal for your self-esteem. Chris' achievement, even thus far, massively outstripped my own in almost every way, and he also seemed like a much nicer person. I decided therefore that I didn't want to write about him unless I could find some incriminating intel that would discredit him in the eyes of moral readers. Rather fortuitously, he did tell me later as we walked alone over Wytham Moor where nobody else could hear or verify this, that he found it funny when animals died and he also invented speed cameras and 'getting stuck behind a tractor'. Let the reader understand.

Even Chris might bend a deferential knee to a chap named George Meegan who, after leaving the British Merchant Navy, walked from the southern tip of South America to the northern tip of North America, a journey of 19,019 miles which took him 2,425 days between 1977-1983. Informally, he is reported to have said, 'There just wasn't anything good on the telly'. More formally, in his book *The Longest Walk* Meegan sums up rather nicely what it is that stirs people to undertake these huge personal challenges in the first place:

"Once the idea seemed to be a real possibility, once I thought I could do it, I had to do it, for I knew that if I didn't, I would be haunted by the omission forever."

Elsewhere, he also captures rather pithily the perverse psychology of a long-distance hiker:

"If I were going uphill, I was relatively happy since I would sooner or later be going downhill. Whereas, if I were going downhill, I wasn't all that happy because I knew I would eventually have to be going uphill."

In 2019, someone used Google Maps to calculate the longest unbroken pilgrimage available to humankind without the need to cross an ocean or take any kind of transport. Stretching 13,910 miles, it runs from Cape Town in South Africa to Magadan in Russia, bisecting 16 countries, six time zones and every season of the calendar year. It hasn't been named yet because it's not technically a trail, and it also (to-date and to the best of my knowledge) hasn't yet been walked – partly because it would take 561 days, walking eight hours a day. But you can absolutely guarantee something: it will be walked, and soon. Because humans are insane.

A rising tide lifts all the boats as the saying goes, and such was the effect of Chris's addendum to our group. For the next few hours, we rolled along, triple-jumping over peat trenches and splashing through puddles, before crossing Frumming Beck – the sort of expression I might use in moments of mild peril – then over Wytham Moor towards God's Bridge which, ironically compared to a lot of the encircling landscape, displayed no discernible signs of the Almighty's handiwork. Here we took a short detour to visit the splendid ruins of Bowes Castle, Henry II's mediaeval bastion built on the site of a Roman fort, which was briefly besieged by King William of Scotland during the Great Revolt of 1174, before Geoffrey, Archbishop of York, arrived with a relief column.

'Haha! Well done, Archbishop Geoffrey,' applauded Geoffrey.

'What's that flag flying above the castle?' Rob asked me quietly. 'Is it Switzerland?'

'English Heritage. Much easier to beat at football.'

Our troop of five crossed Cotherstone Moor and Mickleton Moor, walking in single file and companionable silence. While it still felt like Winter underfoot, in the air Summer had learned her lines and was making her entrance to rapturous applause, dressed in cerulean blue. We heard her happy footsteps pass and followed her across the land, pleased to have her back in the role – for Summertime is always the best of what might be.

At an innocuous and unmarked road bridge over Grassholme in Lunedale, Chris suddenly stopped.

'Guess what?'

'I don't know,' I said, looking curiously at the bridge. 'Trolls?'

'No. You're halfway.'

Really?

'Really?'

'Really.'

'We're halfway!' I called back to Geoffrey.'

'Halfway!' Geoffrey shouted back to Rob.

'Half ******* way!' Rob told Margot, who winced.

Halfway.

* * *

After floating lonely o'er vales and hills, and having reached a point where I thought about individual days of the week as you might remember Christmas as a child, I had done half the walking I would need to do to complete this challenge. At times the hours had crawled by like years. At times my negativity had worn heavy boots, loudly stomping. Your feet contain 25% of all the bones in your body, and in an average day's walking they experience forces totalling hundreds of tonnes, the equivalent of a fully-loaded cement truck. My feet were covering considerably more ground than an average day's walk – but they were still moving forward. And I was going with them.

This was a big hooray for me, but it would have rankled the ancient Greek philosopher, Zeno (one of humanity's neggiest naysayers) who devised a paradox whereby motion was ultimately impossible. As I understand it (and you'd get decent odds that I don't) in order to travel any distance, one must first complete *half* that distance. Whatever the length of journey, before you can get there you must get halfway there; before that, you must travel a quarter of the way there; before that, an eighth etc., resulting in an infinite number of tasks which Zeno saw as impossible. If you ask me, this just sounds like an academic argument for not socialising.

'Fancy coming to the gladiators tonight, Zeno?'

'Sorry, I can't – I'd never make it.'

But I really *was* halfway. However many divisions you cared to split the remaining 139 miles into, they would each be bestest by the simple and rudimentary act of putting one defiant foot in front of the other. Furthermore, unlike our friend Zeno I actually *was* socialising, somehow attracting a community of fellow pilgrims like velcro attracts fluff. My face muscles couldn't quite bench-press a smile, with the realisation that all that pain and gruelling graft so far would need to be done again, only this time in fewer days, over more and bigger hills and with the blisters, shin splints and dodgy knees waiting to be called from their waiting room. Nevertheless, I had reached my Golden Spike.

Some of my preparatory research for the Pennine Way now seemed excessive looking back. I had found an old copy of Joshua Piven's *Worst Case Scenario Survival Handbook* in a charity shop in Bakewell a week before I started walking, and had assimilated it for strategies. While the sections on "How to treat a leg fracture" and "Lighting fires without a match" might still come in handy, fully memorised chapters on "How to escape quicksand" and "Battering a mountain lion to death" seemed erroneous with hindsight.

Chris led the way over Harter Fell, his sharp face and bird-of-prey eyes scanning the land impassively under his hickory-coloured Stetson. Our staggered line clumped on in formation like a mobile Village People (where only Chris had read the memo and dressed as a cowboy; everyone else turning out as ramblers). The wind picked up and raked at us with unmanicured nails at the top of each climb and the mud continued to try and pickpocket our boots in the recesses, but the five of us ventured on in a way Enid Blyton would have been proud of.

At Wythes Hill Farm, about three miles from day's end, when my lungs were broken bellows and we were all bent like dowsing rods seeking out energy, a handwritten sign announced "TUCK SHOP". Sure enough, a sturdy bird box had been reconstituted into a static sweets trolley, with Wispas and Twirls and cans of Sprite and Dr Pepper stuffed in there. Coins cascaded from fingers into the honesty box as we slotted confectionery into pouches and pockets.

'It's like a mirage,' Chris said.

'Devilishly decent of them,' Geoffrey added.

I wasn't that hungry, but it'll be a cold day in hell before I say no to a Crunchie. Besides, I had learned from the shambles of Pen-y-Ghent that, if water was king, sugar was at least a laird. I celebrated our huge calorie windfall by blaring out *YMCA* on loudspeaker as we ascended the last of the day's climbs, goading everyone to join in like the most heinous of wedding DJs. Chris was already in character and Margot predictably threw herself into it. Rob claimed he was too young to have heard of music, while Geoffrey made a nominal contribution, doing the actions from *One Potato, Two Potato, Three Potato, Four.*

'Oh, come on, Geoffrey,' Margot berated him, 'dance like nobody's watching – live every day as though it's your last.'

'I am doing!' Geoffrey snapped at her, losing his focus somewhere between '*Seven Potato*' and '*more*'.

Margot of course was quoting those decorative wooden blocks that people without a proper worldview display on their mantlepiece. I'm relatively happy with the dancing like nobody's watching part, but the living every day as though it's your last seems overly traumatic as mandates go. How would one even begin to cope with waking each morning to the belief that you'll be dead by sundown? Crying over the gaunt faces of my children is how I would spend it – not joining an inane conga line.

The constant peeling shrillness of lapwings and curlews had chaperoned us the whole day. Initially, the peewits and whistled tremolos sounded almost psalmic, a song of shalom sung over you as you enter a new county. After four hours of the same looped harmony though, phrases like 'For frum sake, shut the beck up' were chanted back in chorus and I opted for an alternative playlist. I had been listening to music in small doses along the route, and had learned that you have to be tactical in choosing the right genre. Rap music is too aggressive and riles you up for a fight you can't have, while Country and Western music is too depressing, focussing exclusively – as it seems to – on horses dying in tragic circumstances and people being shot down by the river. Dance is too insistent, Pop is too bubbly, Classical music is rousing and stirring but loses points for not having anything to sing along to. After careful evaluation, then, Folk music is queen when it comes to walking accompaniment. I know it's mainly about prostitutes and how nice it is to be criminally drunk, but the rhythm and cadence just seems to blend with the atmosphere. It is, after all, the music of the countryside. To keep the birdy song at bay and to continue the waning afternoon's party vibe, I decided to let Paul Simon play me into Middleton-in-Teesdale through my airpods. I broke the formation of our quintuplet and let my gait synchronise with whatever tune was playing, an overgrown boy in a bubble of self-reflection.

Middleton-in-Teesdale may not be Graceland, but its single-street community is charming and rife with quirky architecture, the legacy of the now-defunct lead mining industry. The sound of 10 muddy boots tramping along the quiet high street sounded loutish, although nobody batted an eyelid and a woman locking up a haberdashery smiled at us warmly.

'Halfway?' she asked.

'Over halfway,' I affirmed.

From the comfort of my hotel room that evening, I could understand why people would give up here – and plenty do. You have walked nearly 150 miles and trekked across the whole length of Yorkshire. Zeno's paradox notwithstanding, you could quite easily rationalise coming back next year and finishing the other half, blister free. Stopping in Middleton by the banks of the Tees would make for a nice diptych, a pleasantly folded spine to hold two halves of the walk together. And yet...

And yet, that would be too easy. Life is a stream of auctions in which your fear, desire, hope, pain and resolve constantly try to outbid each other for ownership of the next day. For my part, I wanted a shot at redemption – didn't want to end up in a cartoon graveyard.

The old man in the mirror with the salt-and-pepper beard was looking at me again. I removed the Ibuprofen gel from Alan's vice-like grip and held it close to me. I would be carrying on. And I would assume, in the absence of any philosophical defeaters, that tomorrow would not be my last.

And the man in the mirror winked at me.

CHAPTER 20
HAUNTED BY THE OMISSION

That night's dinner in the Teesdale Hotel was special. Tudor beams held everything together and an open fire crackled away. Everyone looked cleansed and rosy-cheeked from hot showers and extended soaks. Wine was ordered, glassed clinked and platters covered the table. Rob was camping again but had joined us for dinner.

I hadn't been eating much during walking hours, bookending my day with two blow-out binges and regretting nothing. Everything tastes better when you feel as though you've earned it, but even on a lazy day a ribeye steak is superlative.

'This is on us!' Geoffrey announced, banging down his spoon like a gavel. 'All of it, drinks and food, whatever you've ordered.'

I assume someone must have protested at this point, but I was busy signalling the barman for another two bottles of Merlot like an injured player calling for a stretcher and was distracted.

Over dinner, Rob wanted to know why Margot and Geoffrey had decided to walk the Pennine Way in the first place; why two wealthy retired people needed to walk through industrial England when there were surely more decadent trips to go on. For the first time I saw Margot's jaw tighten slightly. She creased her brow, not, I don't think, unsure of the answer, but wanting to frame it properly.

'We've done all of that, Rob. We have had all the fancy holidays and posh hotels, and that's all lovely. But... (she took a deep breath) I've just been so fortunate in life. This isn't meant to sound boastful, you know. My parents were always well off so as a girl I never lacked anything, and I've been so lucky to have my lovely Geoffrey.'

'You must have worked very hard as a doctor yourself, though?' I asked.

'Of course I have, of course. But I've never really suffered. I've sat with thousands of people going through the most abject suffering, and I know how to describe that pain and to prescribe medicine as a solution. But I've never had that inward experience of real suffering like so many.'

'And we get all of that on the Pennine Way!' Geoffrey said ironically.

'Oh no, Geoffrey, don't say that, that's not what I'm saying. Goodness, you must think I'm being awfully self-indulgent. All I'm trying to say is that it's nice to feel like you've earned your success. I'm 64 years old. And I've walked 150 miles and I've done it without help. That's all I mean.'

A small round of applause broke out and Margot blushed slightly.

'And I'm 65!' Geoffrey butted in, and we clapped him too because why not?

With our stomachs already nicely distended and testing the flexibility of our clothing, Chris nevertheless chanced to ask, 'Is anyone having pudding?' Everyone, including a young couple at the next table, looked at Geoffrey to check on the terms and conditions of his generosity. His bleary eyes shone with benevolence in the firelight.

'Yes, why not? Why not indeed? Desserts all round!'

'I wonder if this place is haunted,' Margot mused, as the firelight took the strain of the sun's full retreat and the atmosphere indoors changed. She was staring up into the rafters as if a ghost might just be perched there swinging its legs.

'I wouldn't have thought so,' Chris said.

'B*******,' Rob agreed from halfway down his fourth pint.

'It's always Victorian children though, isn't it?' I said. 'It's never a 1970s accountant. I could cope with a ghost if it was a 1970s accountant.'

'When you're dead, you're dead,' interjected a barman clearing plates at the next table.

'No, no,' said Margot testily, 'it can't be that simple. Andy, you're the preacher. Tell us what happens when you die!'

'Shouldn't the doctor be answering that?' I said.

'No, the doctor tells you why you die. The preacher needs to tell you what happens next.'

'Yeah, come on, Herman, nobody's leaving until you tell us what death is like.'

I had burned my pack of theological top trumps a while ago; had learned the hard way that winning arguments rarely wins you souls but often loses you friends. That doesn't mean that I think all opinions are equally valid, even if they are equally available. But I'm not a professional debater, and point-scoring in a game that only you are playing is for children. I just tell stories for a living. And besides, as with anything, you can only lead people where you've been yourself. I have walked through and camped in the valley of the shadow of death, but have not yet crossed to the other side. So what do I know?

I know a man called Tom who was, without doubt, one of the best comedians of his generation. A regular on sitcoms and panel shows and an Edinburgh Festival Award nominee, he did stand up primarily as characters, one of the most renowned of which was a psychic medium. I gigged with Tom many times and we used to live quite near one another so, travel and family permitting, occasionally we would hang out in his kitchen drinking coffee. On one such occasion I probed him gently on his techniques as the stage psychic – I'd been at a couple of shows where the personal information Tom's character was feeding the audience was absolutely mind-blowing.

'Obviously, I understand that you're a showman and you've learned a number of cold-reading and information-baiting techniques….' (he nodded away) 'but am I right in thinking that when all that's taken into account, there's something left over?'

He smiled and nodded. 'Yes, I think so. I wouldn't call myself psychic, and I'm making money from the comedy show, not from the accuracy of the predictions. But sometimes, yeah, I do seem to really know stuff about the people – and I don't know how.'

Something left over.

'That's where I start with the afterlife,' I told the gathered folk. 'When confirmation bias is accounted for and our desire to offset death is ticked off, and when materialism is reduced to its basic parts and we agree that the human brain is vastly powerful and complex, I think there's still something leftover.'

'So, hang on, are ghosts real or not?' Rob demanded. 'I've got to walk back to my tent in the dark and I need a firm ******* answer on this.'

'I'm just saying that life isn't simply confined to the physically observable. Your thoughts aren't your brain; your heart is not your soul. There's something left over. The question is what, why, and where?'

'Well done, Andy, well done!' Margot said, returning the round of applause from earlier. 'Always something leftover, yes, I like that.'

I hadn't won any souls, but nor had I lost any friends, and that wasn't bad for an evening's work. We all scaled the stairs and said goodnight, full to the brim with food, drink and companionship.

"How good one feels when one is full -- how satisfied with ourselves and with the world! People who have tried it, tell me that a clear conscience makes you very happy and contented; but a full stomach does the business quite as well, and is cheaper, and more easily obtained."

Thus spake Jerome K Jerome in *Three Men in a Boat,* the finest of all travel writing books, and a book without which most of the others wouldn't have thought to exist.

I climbed into bed with Alan, the Aloysius to my Sebastian Flyte, the Winston to my Tom Hanks.

'Thanks for being my bodyguard and long-lost pal, Alan.'

But he was already asleep and I was talking to myself again.

It was late. I was warm and cosy and safe. But with something left over.

* * *

The sound of silence was broken at 1am by shouting in the corridor. I'd love to say that I leapt from my bed, grabbed a cutlass from the wall and went to investigate, but I had been dreaming about poaching eggs and was joyfully disorientated. The noise from the corridor crystallised as a domestic argument between the young couple who'd dined at the table next to us. Grabbing one of my walking poles and (not sure why but remember I was sleepy) Alan, I ventured out to see what the commotion was. Chris was already there, and Geoffrey and Margot could both be heard coming along the landing above, Margot exhorting her husband to bring a baseball bat or something.

'I want you out of this ******* room!' the girl was screaming.

'I'm not going anywhere!' the lad bawled back.

'Can you both calm down for a second?' Chris asked. He'd shifted from pacemaker to peacemaker in a matter of hours, although the lad told him to eff off so he wasn't quite the social polyglot we all hoped for.

The girl, looking angry rather than frightened, explained through deep gasping sobs how she'd checked her boyfriend's phone and found illicit messages sent to another girl – and she wanted him gone.

'I've got nowhere to go tonight though, Sarah!'

'Oh, poor you, Damien. Call that ******* ***** then – I'm sure she'll pick you up in Daddy's car.'

I suspected that we were dealing here with a case of a 'slay queen', but it didn't seem like the time to ask for clarification.

Instead, I continued to stand there, ready for any eventuality with my inanimate carbon rod and my stuffed fox. I still wasn't the least well-equipped for battle, mind you. Margot came flourishing down the carpeted stairs carrying a wire coat hanger, followed defiantly by Geoffrey who was holding a shoe.

'What the hell's going on here?!' he slurred through a mixer of sleepiness and French wine. 'Don't you know how late it is?'

'I'm sorry that you've all been woke up,' the young man said, 'I just want to go back to bed and sort this in the morning.'

'No way!' His girlfriend waved both hands. 'No way! You're not coming back in here, and Damien let me make it very clear, we are *never* getting back together.'

'Sarah, please, I haven't done anything…'

'We are never getting back together, and if you ever try to contact me again, I'm calling the police.'

'That sounds harsh, dear,' Margot said gently.

'Andy?' Chris asked from along the landing. 'If I let you have my other twin, would you be OK with this lad sleeping in your room?'

'That's OK with me and Alan,' I responded, trying to keep the mood light but immediately feeling the need to specify that Alan was the chap I was holding – there wasn't another bloke in my room who would need to be negotiated with.

'Thank you,' Damien said.

'But don't think about going into her tonight, young man,' Geoffrey commanded.

'Yes, you lock your door, dear,' Margot told Sarah.

Immediately the door slammed and locked. Everyone else retired or retreated depending on their perspective.

'What were you going to do with one shoe, Geoffrey?' his wife asked as they retook the stairs.

'Oh, I don't know. Hop him to death probably.'

'You're like a big child.'

Chris cleared his stuff off the spare twin bed and I tried to regain my sleep, but couldn't. I could hear spluttering from downstairs through the thin plaster, and the sound of a pillow being pummelled with fists.

'Impossible to know what to say in that situation, isn't it?' Chris said sleepily. I nodded from the shadows in disagreement.

At 1:40am I walked along the landing, creaked down the stairs and knocked on a door.

'Who is it?'

'It's, erm, Andy, one of the people from just now. The one holding the fox.'

'What do you want?'

'I wanted to talk to you.'

'What about?'

'Please…can I just talk to you?'

A door was opened… just a crack.

Day 10
Middleton-in-Teesdale to Dufton
21 miles

William: Oi sir, what are you doing?
Chaucer: Uh… trudging. You know, trudging? To trudge: the slow, weary, depressing yet determined walk of a man who has nothing left in life except the impulse to simply soldier on.
A Knight's Tale

"If it could only be like this always – always summer, always alone, the fruit always ripe and Aloysius in a good temper…"
Evelyn Waugh, Brideshead Revisited

CHAPTER 21
CODDIWOMPLING

I nearly did something on the morning of Day 10 that I hadn't done in ages. I nearly cried.

It wasn't the prospect of the longest leg so far – 21 miles hod-carrying yourself through lead-mining country, to be deposited farther away from Kirk Yetholm than when you had breakfast. Nor was it the fact that my Pen-y-Ghent wounds had been evangelising other parts of my foot and now had a small, missional community of blisters and welts. It wasn't even seeing my daughters' faces over Facetime and realising how much I missed them. No, I nearly cried when I said goodbye to Margot and Geoffrey.

They had always planned to stop here. They were re-entering civilization and, from the sounds of it, would be using their diaspora of properties as stepping stones back to their ancestral seat in London. I met them in the lobby of the Teesdale Hotel after a breakfast of delicious pig meat and poached eggs, Margot's rucksack bulging larger than ever as it rested against the warped 18th century door frame. On the street outside Chris was waiting, eagle-eyed and battle-ready in his wide-brimmed hat. Geoffrey shook my hand with a 'Jolly good show' and then Margot, in sneering disdain of the hotel's Covid guidelines, wrapped me up in a blanket hug.

'You have brightened our lives, Andy.'

A morning dew spontaneously coated my eyes and 'same' was about all I could muster in return. I had never met anyone quite like Geoffrey and Margot – and suspected I never would again. People like that only really exist in 1970s sitcoms.

'We've got something for you, actually,' Margot said, handing me a small folded brown paper bag. 'We found them in an old curiosity shop type place in Hawes. Only very small gestures, but hopefully something to remember us by.'

I slipped my hand inside the paper bag and brought out three pewter badges shaped into words. One said 'Gorgeous', one 'Awesome', and the other 'Beloved'.

'You managed to find my adjectives of choice,' I said.

'Not for you, silly – for your wife and girls. I'm sure all three of them are all three, but they can fight it out amongst themselves for who gets which.'

'You've been so kind to me,' I said, not quite managing to bridle the quaver in my voice. 'Thank you.'

'Thank *you,* dear!'

Margot gave me a final suffocating embrace, Geoffrey ordered her to show some self-restraint, then they scraped their backpacks out through the narrow portico to where a taxi was waiting to chauffeur them to Durham.

'You did check that the driver was registered, didn't you, Geoffrey?'

'No, dear, I asked them to send a murderer. Of course I checked.'

'I bet you'll be glad to get rid of us, won't you, dear?' Margot puffed as she tested the Toyota Prius' suspension with her unfeasible bag. 'Make sure you don't end up like us, won't you!'

For my part, I could see absolutely nothing wrong with ending up like them. Nothing at all. I would miss Geoffrey's indignant blustering and archaic verbiage, Margot's gentle chiding and charming diffidence. Really, I would just miss *them.* They were my friends. Margot pressed her face against the glass like a sad puppy as the Prius slipped noiselessly out of town. I waved until I could no longer see nor hear them.

'Junbi wa deki taka?' Chris asked.

'I beg your pardon?'

'I'm learning Japanese on *Duolingo.* I just asked if you were ready.'

'Oh… enfin, oui, monsieur, j'suis prêt à marcher.'

'I beg your pardon?'

'I just said yes.'

'Thank goodness for that. Off we go then.'

Rob was taking a morning off to level up his Blasphemese on *Duolingo,* so Chris and I found our way to the River Tees (via a couple of bakeries and a chemist) and started walking North West.

I was over halfway. I had a majority share in the walk and had passed with Lower Second Class Honours. But I still had it all to do. Cross Fell, Hadrian's Wall, The Fields of Trenzalore, The Cheviot: it was all there waiting for me. And Day 10 on the Pennine Way is psychological torture for anyone with 'Excelsior' as their battle-cry. Like a trolley with a wonky wheel, the route refuses – rather petulantly, it has to be said – to take you north towards Scotland at any point. By the end of the day, having hiked for 21 gruelling miles, you find yourself nine miles farther away from the finish line than if you'd just taken the crow's route. The reason for this uncharitable detour is High Cup Nick, a colossal glacier-carved abyss which apparently warrants adding Cumbria to the itinerary. But I had become a bit cynical about sightseeing and would have gladly walked along a tunnel of breeze blocks if it meant being closer to completion. The reflected view of my sveltening body was eye candy enough for me.

Over breakfast I had been looking back through some messages. The week before the Pennine Way started my most used emoji had been the *crying with laughter* face, followed by the hands raised in praise and then the small fire. These had now been outstripped and left for dead by the only emoji I had used for the last few days – the monkey with its hands over its eyes. This was especially appropriate now, given that a large globule of Ibuprofen gel had found its way to my mouth during the pre-match warm up, and I spent the first hour of the morning speaking like a forgotten dentist's patient, streams of saliva trickling down my chin like a 3D map of today's walk.

'Fancy a chewy mint?' Chris asked.

'Doh Danks.'

'Is that French?'

'Doh. Abbapofun del.'

He told me to let him know when my mouth was working again and consulted his map – possibly to check whether I'd been landmarked as 'Moron, 6ft'.

There is a lot to be said for not looking too often or too long at a full route map, 3D or otherwise. Studying the whole Pennine Way from the God's eye view has the same reductionist effect as looking at Voyager 1's *Pale Blue Dot.* From that elevation, any sense of progress is negligible as entire days of hard marching and angst appear as nothing more than dispassionate lines on an unfeeling canvas. Much better to zoom in to the tangible and the observable, to know what you're doing today, how long it might take, and what success will look like. Chris was incredibly effective at this. Whereas I had been tending to walk until I felt like a rest or a chat with a local, Chris routinely bitesized his days into four measurable chunks. He would walk for two hours, have a snack and a drink; another two hours followed by a long lunch; 90 minutes after lunch before a short break, and then the final stretch along the home straight to accommodation.

'Win the next duel!' he'd say, and the next duel became the proceeding 120 minutes, *that* hill or *this* morass. I was no longer trying to walk 270 miles – I was trying to walk 3. And it really worked.

On this early June day the English climate unrolled a morning of bounteous splendour as Hawkeye and Numbmouth bounced along the blessedly flat, mercifully straight banks of the Tees, drawn on by the alluring siren calls of the blandly named Low

Force and then (here it comes) High Force waterfalls: unyielding dolerite sills where upland water comes gushing over and out like tantalising secrets in the wrong hands. We made fine progress, striding along the path with the nettles springing hidden traps, and brambles and ragwort and himalayan balsam living in a blended, tangled community.

Given the majesty of High Force in particular, whoever won the naming rights should have been forced into a barrel and rolled over it as punishment. While Low Force is a satisfying 'amuse bouche', High Force is undoubtedly one of the most spectacular waterfalls in Britain and deserves a more regal title. You wouldn't list a Japanese Wagyu ribeye on the menu as simply 'Thick meat', and I think the same principle applies here. The River Tees has been plunging into this gorge for millennia and the rocks it reveals are even older, with origins dating back over 300 million years! It was worthy enough to be painted by Joseph Turner in 1822, and yet nobody thought to call the cascading pair Humilis Vis and Vis Princeps (the far better Latin names, which I happen to know because of the internet).

The trail was fairly well populated on this Wednesday morning. A substantial ramblers' group was out and about, all of them wearing their own branded orange t-shirts with the group's name of "Coddiwomplers" on the back. It's a mediaeval word, apparently, defined as "travelling purposefully towards an as-yet-unknown destination." The name was appropriate. These experienced walkers ambled on as we incised their ranks like hot needles through calloused skin. They were hardly decrepit, and were moving at a decent speed, but it was interesting to note the rhythmic velocity I'd picked up after nine days on the trail. No coddiwompling for me: I knew exactly where I was headed, and I was no longer trundling like a pregnant cow. And yet I wasn't in a hurry, having realised by now that you always get there in time. You may arrive for afternoon tea or a late supper, but there was always time to rest and recuperate, and sleeping was no longer a fitful wrangle with spasming muscles and skeletal anguish.

'Out of the way, Maureen,' the coddiwompling chief declared, 'these men are walking the Pennine Way.'

By now it was just obvious.

I had barely crossed paths with anyone walking the Way from North to South over the past week, but a couple of rangy silhouettes bounding towards us *at the double* pulsed out that uncanny sonar of wayfarers bound for Edale. A husband and wife duo who looked more like brother and sister, they moved in near synchronicity, equine suppleness topped with a bobble hat.

'Are you Pennine Waying it?' they asked cheerily as they reared to a combined halt.

'Yeah, Day 10, going well. And you? Day 7 I assume?'

'Er, no, Day 4 actually. We're hoping to polish it off in eight or nine. Our record to-date is ten, although I broke a toe on that occasion so I'm confident we can go faster this time.'

'Excellent stuff,' I said, yet again forced to reframe my credentials in the light of people simply much more impressive. Both of them somehow managed to look simultaneously emaciated and hyper-fit, as though they had successfully escaped from a series of POW camps and then, for the sheer fun of it, got recaptured to have another crack at it.

'Well, you've got a good day ahead,' said the wife/sister. 'Hopefully the weather holds off on top of Cross Fell tomorrow for you.'

'Yes, fingers crossed,' agreed her husband/brother. 'You really don't want to be up there if it's gloomy. Check the weather forecast before you set off.'

'Will do.'

'Do you have a specific reason for trying to do the Pennine Way?'

Trying to do it? Alan spat from his pouch. *We are doing it, aren't we?*

'Very much so,' I said.

'And what reason is that?'

'My own.'

Feeling slightly patronised, I was keen to impart some equally pertinent advice to these people but it was clear that nothing I had to say would build on their superior nous. Some people just ooze 'Professional Hiker', and this pair looked like they were immune to blisters and would happily drink their own urine to save time.

'Watch out for coddiwomplers,' I said.

'For?'

'For coddiwomplers, farther down the trail. All the best.'

It's the poem Lewis Carroll should have written.

"Beware the coddiwompler, son,
The greying pate, the brittle gait;
Beware the age when wrinkles reign,
So hasten on: don't wait."

The husband and wife siblings reprised their human dressage and Chris and I trudged on.

We stopped for morning break at High Force waterfall and Chris handed me a couple of luxury ginger biscuits which I swapped for the word 'Thanks' – a pretty shrewd trade.

'I don't understand why some folk warn walkers about bad weather,' Chris said. 'It's not as though we're trying to host a garden party which might get rained off.'

I waved an agreeing biscuit at him, and this seems like a good time to include another quote from Jerome K Jerome, who said: "Who wants to be foretold the weather? It is bad enough when it comes, without our having the misery of knowing about it beforehand."

'Imagine completing the Pennine Way in eight days,' I said, thinking back to the annoying centaurs we had just met. During my planning phase back in early May, I had worked on a theory that I might be able to condense the walk into 11 days at a severe push. But people have died of theories, or at least they buckle under the expanding waistline of lived reality, and I decided I would much rather pursue my lifelong dream of staying alive as long as I can. "Don't live every day as if it's your last," as the Prophet writes.

'Eight days is nothing,' Chris said. 'The FKT (Fastest Known Time) for the trail was broken the week before you started.'

'Was it really?'

It really was. Only a matter of days before I stumbled out from Edale, U.S. ultrarunner John Kelly had arrived there from Kirk Yetholm in a record time of 58 hours and 4 minutes – more than three hours faster than the previous record held by Britain's Damian Hall, who had himself beaten Kelly's old record. If it seems as though the record gets smashed every few weeks, before 2020 the FKT for Britain's oldest national trail had stood for 31 years, a time of 65 hours 20 minutes run by Mike Hartley in 1989.

'All of them would have shot past here like a blur,' Chris pointed out. 'They would have decimated those poor coddiwomplers.'

'Indeed. Imagine not being able to sit here with a biscuit and a cup of tea.'

And sit we did, the late morning sun bronzing our skin and the sound of rushing water doing that curious thing that it does to your soul. When nature is smiling on you, all other frowns seem inconsequential for a time.

I sat gazing at the rampant water cascading over its sill with unaudited consistency and unapologetic power. In an act of synergy I let a torrent of thoughts and questions tumble and plunge through my own mind: Was I happy or sad? Gleeful or grieving? Was this an odyssey or an exodus? Actually, I suspected it was all of the above and more. My emotions were pale blue dots viewed through a telescope. Either way, I was going at my own pace. I wasn't going to break any records or get listed in any annals, but you can't measure your own success using someone else's ruler.

'What are you doing?' I asked a robin who had perched next to me and was now hopping about in what I hoped wasn't a cross-species mating ritual. 'Go away, I'm trying to think. Come back at Christmas.' But he wouldn't leave and, after failing to shoo him and deciding against shoeing him, I let him sit next to me and we watched the waterfall together.

CHAPTER 22
ACTA NON VERBA

'I can't believe I'm in County Durham,' Chris exclaimed, shaking a baffled head at High Force waterfall, whose breezy spray was watering us like happy chrysanthemums. He showed me pictures of himself back in Cornwall on Day 1 of his John O'Groats to Land's End expedition, and then demonstrated the dramatic change in his body's geometry by billowing his once-snug trail jacket.

'My metabolism appears to have come out of retirement,' he said with surprised glee. 'My wife had to post me some smaller trousers just before I met you guys.'

Chris was like a hermit crab, leaving his old clothes and crawling along the beach to find jeans that fit. I felt similarly. I hadn't trekked as far as Chris, nor lost as much weight, but I was no longer burping up sick every time I saw my reflection and was past the point where lifting me off the ground would have been viewed as sorcery.

'That's gotta be worth another biscuit, surely!' I said, and Chris obliged me by throwing another ginger treat my way and downing one himself. Long-distance walks invariably take their pound of flesh, and it's nice that some of that is literal.

'In my experience,' Chris mused, 'if you find there's something missing in your life, it's usually a biscuit.'

The good thing about walking all day every day is that you *are* going to lose weight, whatever sort of meals you bookend your trekking with. You can't let that be the reason to give up three weeks of your life, and the telos of my pilgrimage wasn't simply to dewobblyise or to worship at the altar of the no-filter selfie. But this was by far the most success I'd had at slimming down since I ate some poisoned Falafel on Manchester's Curry Mile, and my shrinking form was certainly a welcome by-product of all those ponderous steps.

My body on my 40th birthday had been an oil painting, drenched in grease and left in the baking sun, while the closest I came to playing sport these days was donning a pair of swimming goggles to chop onions. And yes, I know – most Westerners had used the pandemic to build their portfolio of empty calories and it wasn't our fault because what else was there to do? But I had taken it too far, and was one Dominoes deal away from Greenpeace sending someone to drape a wet towel over me.

I had thought it would all be so different – we all did, perhaps? When that first lockdown hit it seemed like the perfect opportunity to focus on downsizing. Within my own context, the wholesale eradication of 95% of my work meant I wouldn't be on the road as much, ordering junk food from motorway services or being treated to dinner by satisfied event organisers. A more stabilised life would allow me the chance to find new rhythms and habits. I would make my own hummus, find a dozen culinary uses for pine nuts. I would finally open that family bag of lentils handed down through the generations because nobody likes lentils.

What I hadn't counted on – what almost nobody had counted on – was the sheer asphyxiating boredom of being imprisoned within your own house with nothing to do but complete Netflix and patrol the fridge. While the first couple of lockdown weeks may have seen me eating as many as six impossible mangoes before breakfast and using the word 'wellness' in every third sentence, by Lockdown 2 I was on a diet of mainly cream. Cream in coffee. Cream on cereal. Cream on toast. I didn't want a coroner's report listing my cause of death simply as "Cream". I didn't want my gravestone to read:

Andrew D W Kind 1980-2021

"Forever in our hearts, in the way that his heart was forever full of cream."

I was once again in danger of seeing my waistline overtake my age, and enough was enough. Once life opened back up like a gullet and it became necessary to leave the house and interact with non-dairy based organisms, I didn't want people coming round and asking why there was an amorphous mound of polyfilla oozing about the house, or to be sitting in a beer garden and hear a precocious child saying to its mother, 'Mummy, look, there's a pig in clothes drinking from a wine glass.'

In an attempt to meet the deadly threat of man-boobs head-on, at the turn of the year I had enrolled into a gymnasium, thinking that a daily dose of gentle callisthenics would be the perfect antidote to my breakfast cream smoothie. It was a noble aim, but alas it was to be short-lived.

To offer some preliminary context for the story I'm about to tell, let me state that I am a heterosexual man. However, as a dedicated aesthete I have always sought to appreciate and affirm beauty wherever I see it – in art, in nature and, in this case, in the body of my fellow man. "Beauty is truth, truth beauty," John Keats wrote, and I agree. And the truth is that there was a chap at my local gym who was absolutely creamy. I've never really had what I think is called a "mancrush" before and so didn't really know what to expect. Nor am I someone who likes to think they will try anything once. There's your context.

This impeccable specimen of masculinity and I apparently shared similar working hours and so would often be found synchronising our gym sessions. By the time of the day in question I had already written about this bloke in my journal and had a dream where I was painting him like the *Venus of Orbino.* And now here we both were, him lifting weights in the big boys section while I was on the treadmill, eyeing him up in the mirror and trying to work out how many right angles his face had. Of course, plenty of men have good physiques, but too often you find that they overshoot Aristotle's "Golden Mean" of sinew and contour, bulking up to the point where their blood vessels show up like ordnance survey maps and you can see the heartbeat in their forehead. Not so this champion. As I was processing all of this I realised that my muse was looking at me, and that my eyes had been loitering on him for what a policeman might call "far too long". Confident at least that 16 years of professional stand-up comedy had chiselled me in the area of social spontaneity, I opened my mouth to say, 'How ya doing, mate, alright are ya?' and instead heard myself saying, 'Your geometrics are impeccable, sir.'

Despite this man's obvious physical capabilities he looked incredibly frightened, and for my part I decided I would like to leave the gym – perhaps the country – and never return. Unfortunately, my potential modes of escape (bicycle, rowing boat, cross-country skis) were all nailed to the floor and thus useless.

'Have a good'un,' my victim said, replacing his iron weight on its hanger and beating a hasty retreat towards the changing rooms. Not wanting to discomfit, and certainly wanting to avoid having my gym membership rescinded because I still had a load of cream to get through, I needed to remedy the situation without delay, and so I followed him into the showers with that in mind. To quote Sean Connery in *The Untouchables,* "How do you think he feels now – better or worse?"

I haven't been back, nor shall I. Not everything, it seems, can be redeemed.

* * *

We trudged on, quickly refinding our rhythm and looking to 'win the next battle' which would take us up to lunch. Cows paid us no heed as they munched at their fields, the overhang of the hills kept us coolly in shadow, and the line of the river removed the always-mildly-present worry of getting lost or trapped.

The River Tees is something of a dark horse. As Mark Wallington points out in *Pennine Walkies,* it's easy to think of the Tees as an industrial waterway, rolling through dockyards to a gaping grey mouth before dumping itself into the inhospitable North Sea. You forget that, like any of its more Instagrammable siblings, it springs from the earth as pure as any newborn. Further east it widens into murky waters and flows through Darlington and Middlesbrough, but upstream it's a playful adolescent, throwing itself over falls for fun. In that way, the Tees from West to East is like a painting that was started by JM Turner and finished by me.

Turning now to some sadder news, and whereas Chris and I had both lost weight, Alan had lost an eye. I wasn't sure how, where or when this had occurred and, bless him, the little trooper hadn't mentioned it. But it looked unnatural.

'You could throw him over the falls and let Peg Powler have him,' Chris suggested.

'You heartless monster!' I rebuked him.

We had been told about Peg Powler that morning in one of the Middleton bakeries, in response to my question about why the gingerbread men arrayed on the counter looked so terrifying.

'Ah, not gingerbread men,' the baker had said with rehearsed relish, 'gingerbread *hag*… Peg Powler.'

In English folklore Peg Powler is a water spirit or grindylow, who inhabits the River Tees and drags children into the shallow depths if they get too close to the edge – a trait she shares with drunken British dads on a foreign holiday. The 19th century folklorist William Henderson described Peg Powler as having green hair and "an insatiable desire for human life" (at which point her story diverges from the standard British father). She is said to use the allure of her hair to waylay people into the river, which is awfully unsporting of her, although personally I would never allow myself to be beckoned by anyone with green hair because they usually want to lecture you on veganism.

The foam or froth which is often seen floating on certain parts of the Tees is called "Peg Powler's cream". A similar creature named Nanny Powler, presumably Peg's grandmother, is said to haunt the River Skerne farther east, and it's nice to see old family businesses still operating in this fractured economy.

The rest of the day was long but uncomplicated, riverside paths handing the baton back to those trusty British moorlands, their long grass and abrupt mud pits, but with two more pots of treasure along the route. The waterfall trilogy was completed by Cauldron Snout, which is said to be the residence of another ghost, The Sitting Lady, a Victorian farm girl who drowned herself when her love affair with a local miner was discovered. This added further weight to my now unassailable argument that all spectres are from Victorian times, but also seemed to be a case of someone literally living every day like it was their last, which made me a bit sad.

But then, if the walker's breath is short after 18 miles of trekking, it really gets cut down to nothing by the abrupt and eye-popping view of High Cup Nick, that stops you in your tracks in the way that realising you were walking around a sleeping dragon might. It was here, with columnar cliffs standing witness and the Lake District looking on jealously from the west, that nature draped us in a near-preternatural silence, as though we were standing in some cosmic courtroom waiting to give testimony. Boulders and rocks stood sentry at the bottom, chaperoning the silver thread of the stream along its middle, and the unfurled horizon reached across the appositely named Vale of Eden, a cloaked sleeve of priestly-white cloud dipping itself in the shimmering valley.

'Wow,' I said.

'Wow,' Chris agreed.

There was only one thing for it: I looked up more Latin words and Chris got the luxury ginger biscuits out. We stood gazing down at the terribly glorious hollow, a giant's skatepark, crunching and chewing and feeling lots. We were a mere filling in a sky and earth sandwich. At the start of the day the Ibuprofen gel had made me unable to speak. Now I could, but I just didn't want to. Sometimes you just have to stand in awe and let nature's marvels receive your stunned but silent punditry.

"Up on High Cup Nick at four o'clock in the afternoon I tasted immortality," Mark Wallington wrote, and there was something in that. It was another *thin place,* a clue to the answer of a question that humanity was too proud to ask, invisible but not hidden in accessible light. Simon Armitage describes it as, "a dizzying vastness full to the brink with nothing but light and air".

Yes, it was both full and empty at the same instant, a sight as rare as astatine and as priceless as francium.

'Wow,' I said again.

'Woah,' replied Chris for variety.

Many things get described as awe-inspiring, but views like this, which are meant to be looked through as much as looked at, really are. Awe, though, is a National Trust property amongst feelings. You can't stay there very long – you can't live there. I sent Margot and Geoffrey some risible photos of the scene (it's not that the camera lies, but it only tells superficial truth) and then, reluctantly and after more photos, we left High Cup Nick to its ineffable majesty, older and more grateful than when we found it.

'I don't think I've ever had that exact sensation before,' Chris said with reverence.

'No, I don't think I have, either. We're not in Kansas anymore, Toto.'

The descent from High Cup Gill is rugged and staccato, and rivulets of brown ale-coloured water bubbled around our squelching boots as we came back down to earth – scree and boulders, sedge and rushes, rough sandstone and smooth limestone, then loose pastures to ease us back from the majestic to the domestic. On each previous day the challenge had been to keep my mind ballasted above my feet and not teleport my thoughts to the finish line. That didn't happen today. I definitely walked the last three miles down to Dufton, but my mind remained there at the top of the High Cup, refilling itself over and over from a spring of thankfulness.

After 21 miles and the customary sweat-wrapped weariness, we entered the village of Dufton and sat briefly on a bench before separating for bed. I dusted myself down like an ancient book found in a tomb, and Chris tipped the dregs of gingerbread biscuits into his reddened face, then doused his Stetson in the remains of his water bottle.

'Another day done,' he said. 'Although I'm not sure if we're the hammer or the anvil.'

'What do you mean?'

'Whether we're beating down at the ground or whether it's beating up at us.'

'Does it matter?' I asked, too tired for common-room philosophy.

'Oh, yes, it matters,' he replied firmly. 'The anvil wears the hammer out eventually, you see.'

'I'll give you my answer at some point over the next six days, then.'

He nodded and chuckled, refitted his Stetson and limped off to pitch his tent on the green.

In my quaint Dufton farmhouse bedroom that evening, with a black and white TV and bed sheets stolen from my grandmother's house in 1981, I avoided obsessing about how tomorrow was regarded as the hardest leg on the Pennine Way. Cross Fell, the highest point in England outside the Lakes, was in front of me, and local farmers had averted eyes or sicked up in their mouths when we asked about it while passing. The sun-burnt slopes of the mountain glowed peach in the dusky light, but I had read and heard and walked enough not to be lulled into false senses of security. Maybe a visit to Peg Powler wasn't the worst idea, after all?

But, no. Tomorrow would worry about itself as it always did. I stretched out on my bed and listened to the sound of a gate bumping gently against its post, and of horses nickering in an outhouse somewhere nearby. Before slipping under the covers I sent off pictures of High Force, Cauldron Snout and High Cup Nick to the girls. I needed to scroll more than normal to find the fitting emoji:

😍😍😍

You can't live in a place of constant awe, but it *is* nice to visit from time to time and High Cup Nick had privileged me with that. It caused me to reflect that, sometimes, the farther away you get from a place the happier it makes you, whereas for all of us I think there are places to which we would always go back, no matter how gruelling the return journey might be.

But it was time for bed.

And also, I decided, before the end of tomorrow, it would be time to be honest.

Day 11
Dufton to Alston, across Cross Fell
21 miles

"Just a spoonful of sugar helps the medicine go down."
Mary Poppins, Mary Poppins

"Summer's lease hath all too short a date."
William Shakespeare, Sonnet 18

CHAPTER 23
IF HE DIES, HE DIES

I had been annoyed at a hat for the last few days.

The sun had been uncharacteristically predatory over the past week and my palantir of a scalp needed covering. In a shop in Hawes I had purchased the only available solution – a garish red baseball cap with NY etched on. Not only did wearing it make me look like the sort of person who wanders around Paris asking where the nearest McDonalds is, but the fact that Hawes was charging £10 for headwear promoting New York City riled me something proper. Some of these tourist places get away with murder (or 'moider' if you're wearing an NYC baseball cap, I suppose) and I couldn't wait to give the hat away and be rid of it. This led me onto another thought worth considering: maybe if the book did really well and I became astronomically famous, I could auction some of my stuff off as artefacts for a tidy profit. I smirked at Alan out of the corner of my eye. He didn't currently have an eye and so was oblivious to my scheming, but, of course, Alan was of profound sentimental value and I would never consider selling him – or certainly not for less than £190.

"There's no easy way to tell you this," my guidebook informed me with a staged fearmongery I could have lived without, "but today is the most brutal day on the Pennine Way." Another writer said, "In anything less than perfect weather, this is a section to strike fear into the hardiest of walkers." Ridiculous behaviour. The guidebook was supposed to caress me to Scotland, not coax me to

Dignitas. With this level of adversarial walking in store, I was listening to the Rocky IV soundtrack to summon the requisite level of resilience and flashbacks.

A squadron of sentinel hills, culminating with Cross Fell, didn't so much lie in wait as stand across the path and leer. Topographically, it's as though the Lake District was fearful of incursions from the East and so sent four of its most vindictive mounds out as rogue scouts. In his book *Walking Home,* Poet Laureate and renowned wordsmith Simon Armitage described Cross Fell as "a truly terrible place" and, less poetically, as "a b***ard". I wanted my morning imagery to be that of fauns skipping down grassy woodland avenues, of cosy tea parties under rocky outcrops – not Beowulf fighting Grendel's mother. The good news was that the weather seemed perfect this morning and the sun was prophesying over itself that today it would live its best life. The bad news was that I would need to wear this stupid blimmin' hat.

As a village, Dufton (roughly 16 miles east of Penrith) seems more charming and softer-edged than other former mining communities in the region, with lawned verges and a village hall at the heart of the pretty settlement.

'Are ye luking forward to ya walk t-day?' the guest house landlady asked me as she delivered the two cafetieres I'd demanded to the breakfast table. Her voice was also soft around the edges, with that musicality of pitch for which we have the Norsemen to thank.

I wasn't that hungry. I had somehow managed to find a takeaway outlet the previous evening that would deliver to the secluded village, and had forced down a curry that had possibly been made many evenings previous to that, including a naan bread – barge-long and brick-hard – which was more like a riot shield than a side order. I don't wish to be crass, but if John Lennon had been carrying that naan bread then he might very well still be alive today. I had still summoned the courage this morning to order a full English breakfast with extra hash browns, and was now fully prepped for a day of back-to-back heart attacks.

'No, I am not looking forward to it,' I replied to the landlady's question. 'Should I be?'

She gave a slight shake of her head.

'If the weatha turns before you's hit the top of Knock Fell, you's can always come back,' she said calmly, pouring cereal into my bowl. 'We had a chap stay with us a few year ago. It were the last place he ever stayed, like.'

'Pardon?'

'Broke his leg falling on Cross Fell, but nebody could get to him in the fog. Died of hypothermia in Penrith Hospital a few days later. I still see him occasionally, like.'

'What do you mean, you still see him?' I asked, in a move I'm sure you would have supported.

'Y'know – his ghost, leaving here in the mornin, takin his last walk, like.'

Like what?! I wanted to ask – like a bloody nightmare? That's the problem with people from the North East – they never finish their similes.

'Any injuries so far?' the lady asked, her short tale of terror apparently back in its crypt. I was looking grimly out of the window, 900 metres towards a thousand yard stare.

'Lots of aches and a few blisters,' I said flatly, 'but I've got some silicone heels which have stopped the friction. With any luck they'll heal fully over the next few days.'

'Aye, time's a great healer,' she said. 'Remember, if it gets rough early on, you's need to come back.'

She disappeared back into the kitchen, leaving me to the unhappiest breakfast I have ever had – and I have had breakfast with Werner. Her story about the poor bloke dying on Cross Fell refused to digest itself as I buckled and strapped up my wares for the day. Also refusing to budge was that idiom she used, the one about time being a great healer. You know, I don't think that's always true. Time works for superficial wounds, both physical and emotional, but for the deeper stuff – for the catastrophic and cataclysmic – time only numbs. It's time *plus* redemption that heals, and often, in order for redemption to happen, 'you's need to come back'.

I bade the landlady goodbye, but didn't sign the guest book because I didn't want to be used in a documentary about ill-fated ramblers. I also didn't say 'Thanks for a lovely stay', for reasons that must be abundantly clear.

'Howdy partner!' Chris greeted me, leaning on an old letter box like a Royal Mail matinee idol. He had camped by the village green in Dufton and looked as happy as a man is liable to when he hasn't been served breakfast by Edgar Allen Poe.

'How was your morning so far?' he asked.

'Terrifying,' I said. 'Yours?'

'Absolutely fine, thanks.'

'Hoo-ray.'

I slipped him a benapkinned hashbrown and we set off once more, dragging the ground away under our measured tread along amenable farm lanes. The Dufton campsite was part-furnished with campers that morning and the place was now hiving with activity, tents going down and stove-smoke going up. The high density of people was apparently down to a cancer research charity, about 60 of whom (mostly retired) were on a sponsored walk across to Windermere. Chris had chatted to some of them, been offered scones and cake and a woman's phone number. The whole group was high on morale and herbal tea, and had morphed sleepy Dufton into a Glastonbury for people who still watched *Taggart*.

Chris had also met a lady on the campsite named Kristine, who was on some kind of bespoke walking tour and was due to meet us on the way up Knock Fell, the first of the evil henchmen to be dispatched.

'How are you finding camping every night?' I asked Chris as we took the first flat mile easily in our stride. 'Is it not utterly uncomfortable?'

'No, it's fine when you get used to it. We must not think of the things we could do with, but only of the things that we can't do without. That's from a book, I think.'

'*Three Men in a Boat* by Jerome K Jerome,' I said.

'Is it? Oh yes, I've read it! Anyway, the camping is fine. I have a bite to eat, hang up my clothes on a little line, and then I stretch out and read or listen to the radio until I doze off. And I do my *Duolingo* of course. It feels very authentic – the noises of night are peculiarly clear, and I try to place as many different animal calls as I can. Plus I couldn't afford six weeks of staying in guest houses – I'm only a civil servant.'

'I'm sure you make more than a comedian,' I said, not meaning to be churlish but actually being exactly that.

'Hmm, perhaps, but there's a little joke at work that M.O.D. definitely doesn't stand for 'Millions of Dollars'.

'Geoffrey would have loved that joke,' I said, and missed him all over again.

But the one thing I didn't miss was camping. I was throwing good money after bad at accommodation, but that little bit of homely comfort promised each morning was good motivation to keep those splintered feet trudging, plus the point of the walk wasn't to prove that I was Bear Grylls. In addition to that, I am a sworn enemy of the tent. I may have sired two children, written several books, dug a really deep hole at the beach once… but I will never fit a tent back into the tiny bag whence it came. As Robert Louis Stephenson quite rightly noted in *Travels With a Donkey in the Cevenne,* "A tent, above all for a solitary traveller, is troublesome to pitch, and troublesome to strike again; and even on the march it forms a conspicuous feature in your baggage."

Tents are for armies and shanty towns – not, by jove, for respectable Englishmen.

I took an instant dislike to Kristine.

She was standing by a kissing gate at the top of a shingle path, sporting a ridiculous straw boater that one might wear at an annual regatta but certainly nowhere else, and the first thing she did was to tell me I was late. I have arrived late for many things in my life – for coffee meetups, for work, for being the hero – but my excuse on this occasion was that I'd never met her and had no idea who the flipping heck she was. None of this, however, seemed to pass muster with Kristine. She had the look and demeanour of a Victorian Nanny on holiday, refused to let Chris and I have a short breather at the gate, and she tutted at me four times within the first 20 minutes of our acquaintance, most notably when I burped atop a stile and then congratulated myself.

'Goodness, do you do that at home?'

'If I want to, yes.'

She tutted again and told me I was ill-mannered, in response to which I made it my life's goal to break wind violently in her face. All other life ambitions – including, if necessary, finishing the Pennine Way – would be furloughed in the meantime.

In lieu of a rest, the three of us started that slow, methodical, funicular climb that sheer slopes require. The hardest day of the Pennine Way was afoot. This would have been a good reason to not say anything and conserve one's energy but, instead, the hills were alive with the sound of Kristine. She wanted to know why I was wearing a hat with NY on if I hadn't been to New York. She also wanted to know why I hadn't booked all my accommodation yet, why I'd chosen to have a tattoo, and lots of other things that you might answer over coffee but not while you're in the process of climbing to 1,100 metres with *Eye of the Tiger* on an internal loop. Then she kept talking about a walking group she was part of, all the walks they'd been on, all the board games they'd played, all the flavoured teas they had tasted. They sounded like Jean Paul Sartre's portrayal of hell.

'Shut the hell up, Nanny McPhee,' I felt like saying.

'Be quiet please, Mary Poppins,' I actually said. This drew a tut and bonus harrumph from Kristine, who spent the rest of the morning walking with Chris, leaving me to my well-fitting cap and fits-like-a-glove misanthropy. If she carried on like this, I told Alan,

I would unsheathe the remainder of last night's granite naan bread and send her sledging back down towards Dufton on it.

I could see it looming in the distance ahead of me with its angular features: the Capulet to my Montagu; the Ivan Drago to my Balboa; the Kristine to my me. Cross Fell.

'Don't think about it yet – just win the next battle,' I said to myself, tightening my shoulder straps by half an inch. I dug my heels viciously into the ground and started to scale the leering hillsides, stabbing the peat with prick after prick of pronging legwork. The thud of my boots was the opening bassline to a tune I knew, whilst the burn in my thighs felt familiar, almost amicable. After 20 minutes I passed the cairn of Knock Old Man and crested Knock Fell to stop and catch my breath… to discover that I hadn't actually dropped it. I turned to see Chris and Kristine way down the slope, then looked about furtively as though searching for the teleporter which had brought me here.

That's odd, I thought.

The village of Dufton grew smaller and smaller as I climbed higher and higher on stress-tested legs. The next stage up to Great Dun Fell along the highest road in Britain flew by like a training montage, my shadow stretching out long against the hillside. There's a radome up on Great Dun, a futuristic ball-like weather station which holds multiple all-England titles for 'Most Foggy Days', 'Highest Wind Speed' and 'Most Prolonged Frost.' The annual mean temperature here is only 4 degrees, but the weather today was placid and warm and hushed, as though Great Dun Fell had been visited in the night by three spirits and decided that, why, today was Christmas Day. My breathing was rapid but not ragged, and the sweat streaming from my brow was cooling in the breeze.

'Is this going to any harder?' I taunted Little Dun Fell in front of me, and then, 'Is that really the best you've got to offer?' from that same peak once I'd jabbed and pounded my way to its summit. I was three hills down and ready for another. The ground was steak and my boots were testing forks, and it was delicious. This was very strange. This was… easy?

But soon the weather would deteriorate as it did in all the books. Soon the clouds would fold in, the horizon would disapparate and mist would descend with ritualistic solemnity, out of which Cross Fell would appear to crush me in a fake Russian accent. The experts say that the weather up here can be so antediluvian, human evolution is defenceless against it – not only your internal compass but your gyroscope, altimeter and chronometer all go haywire and try to dissolve back into primordial soup.

What exacerbates the climate is the route itself. Legend has it that the hill was originally named Fiend's Fell and was said to be a hotbed of demons. Augustine of Canterbury climbed up here sometime during the 6th century and sorted them all out fortunately, although in his haste to imitate the verse in *Luke 10* where "even the demons obey us", he neglected the earlier scriptural request of *Mark 1* to "make a straight path for the Lord" – because whilst the climate was feeling generous, navigating the successive slopes was like trying to solve a puzzle set by a maniac, with pathways beginning in earnest but reneging on their quest before they got very far. There are cairns a-plenty, but this is no join-the-dots book for infants. If the direction was uncertain in this crystal clear weather, I had no idea how people successfully navigated the fells when the fog rolled in. And of course, tragically, not everyone does.

But the clouds didn't descend. The rain was held back. The wind floated like a butterfly but never stung. Chris and Kristine arrived at the highest point on the Pennine Way to find me shadow boxing, strutting around and, most bizarrely of all, enjoying myself.

'I could do that again!' I announced.

'Ain't gonna be no rematch,' Chris spluttered through bites of sandwich.

I was triumphant, exultant. I loved my New York baseball cap – my lucky cap! Even Kristine's offer of a spoonful of linseed oil couldn't dampen my spirits. The stormcrows and doombringers had lied to me, or rather the climate tombola had rolled and tumbled and drawn out my winning ticket. Scrooge had been redeemed.

I texted Phil from the Pennine Way's highest point:

"You know what, mate, it might not always be getting worse."

Indeed, the only thing getting worse was the state of my Ben Sherman shirt. Last time I updated you on it was back at the Tan Hill Inn, at which stage the S, M and N had seceded. I had left Dufton that morning with four letters still clinging to life, but the A had struggled with the altitude and fainted, leaving less than half the original lineup. The whole shirt would need to be given a lethal injection once this walk was over, but I smiled at having initialled Cross Fell with my calling card.

Other walkers reaching the summit from myriad directions came and greeted us like new arrivals at the gates of heaven. The Helm Wind, the only named wind in Britain and the vengeful scourge of many a good walker, brushed our cheeks as mere bluster. How often did this rare occurrence happen, I wondered. How often did walkers reach this place unscathed and unworried? We were like V.I.P.s, gifted with a view and a rest when others had arrived here just happy to still be alive. It was as though we had broken into a museum at night and were creeping with gleeful freedom around its forbidden corridors. I might only have been on top of the Pennine Way, but I felt as though I were staring down at the whole world like an astronaut. All those hills, fields, rivers, farmhouses – all were ours, mastered by our ascent.

The only downside to the *carte blanche* view was that I could see what was to come. To the North, some of the Pennines' most bleak and formidable hills sat schemingly under cloud, and there at the edge of the horizon, grouped in conspiratorial plot, were the Cheviots – the final destination.

Look on my works, ye mighty…

A stone-cross shelter on top of Cross Fell, homage to the banishing of Augustine's fiends, was a place to have lunch and give thanks. Alan had his photo taken with a number of different walkers, one of whom tempered my *joie de vivre* by asking if his dog could have a sniff and a play. Kristine tutted at the man, which was seemingly her default response to anything mildly unsanitary.

'So where did you buy this cap if you've never been to America?' she asked me while eating cold porridge.

'I don't know why you keep asking me about my cap,' I replied, annoyed that she hadn't toppled into a lead mine, 'but I got it from Hawes.'

Kristine looked thoughtful and then suddenly gasped with some kind of inverted laughter.

'Oh, you silly man!' she said.

'What?' I asked. 'What are you laughing for?'

She proceeded with her breathless chuckling.

'Tell me why you are laughing, Kristine. Kristine, why are you laughing at me?'

She put down her tupperware porridge and the camping fork she was using to eat it.

'You got it in Hawes, you say?'

'Yes.'

'NY?'

'Please come to the point,' I said, still very much planning to unleash my own Helm Wind into her pious features.

'Not New York then, is it? Hawes is in North Yorkshire. That's what the NY stands for.

'Oh,' I said. 'Oh yes, so it is.'

'That's so funny,' she said. 'I shall remember that one.'

'Be sure to tell your walking group all about that,' Chris suggested, in a smirking act of abject betrayal.

'Oh yes, don't worry, I'm going to.'

Kristine was now rummaging through her rucksack and I was half-expecting her to draw out a standing lamp or an impossible vase, but instead she revealed a small cellophane bag.

'I bought something the other day, you know... this lovely badge. I don't buy a lot of mementos and it was quite dear, but I just had a sense that I *should* buy it.'

She opened the pouch and pulled out a circle of beautifully woven fabric with exhilarating flame-red stitching, which read: 'I climbed Pen-y-Ghent.' I shuddered at the memory of that grim leviathan, that eater of hopes.

'What a rip-off,' I said, remembering full well the hiked price of the souvenir.

'Well, it's worth what someone is willing to pay, isn't it?' Kristine replied, 'And as I said, I just felt as though I should buy it.'

Having had my fill of Kristine and of canteen water, I rose to my feet and strolled round to one of the cruciform windbreak's other cubicles to relieve myself. I studied the angles (if you're going to urinate outside, you really can't make yourself a hostage to wind flow), found what I considered to be a perfect trajectory, unbuttoned my hiking trousers and just went berserk, really enjoying it, graffitiing the stonework with abstract designs and wild patterns… only for Kristine to come marching round the cairn to ask me what I was doing.

'What does it look like I'm doing?!' I asked, trying to hold onto both my dignity and my willy.

'You can't do that here!' she barked, and if there's one thing that helps when you're trying to go to the toilet, it's being shouted at.

'What do you want me to do – hold it in?!'

She broke the all-England record for number of tuts in a minute and eventually – much later than I would have scheduled – went back to her forking porridge.

CHAPTER 24
A SAVAGE ENOUGH PILGRIMAGE

Time may not be the great healer, as the Dufton landlady had quipped, but it *is* a great assistant manager to effort, bridging as it does the suspension of disbelief between the dream and the reality. Whatever journey you're on, if you can maintain that "long obedience in the same direction" that Nietzsche talked about, time will do its bit and ensure to tick off your strides one second at a time. And in order to walk a very long way over very long days, that's really all you need. Yes, you need to have prepared properly – Old Man Chronos has never been an ally to the malingerer – and you need the right gear and to know roughly where you're going and probably a bit of luck with weather and injuries. But after that, all you need is time. Not even all the time in the world – *just enough.*

I remember living in London back in 2004 and going to watch a show at the Covent Garden Comedy Club. The line-up was insanely good and included a guy named Addy van der Borgh, who blew me away with his material and whimsical style. 'I could never do something to that level,' I thought as I sat beguiled and aghast by the stagemanship (NB. I had tried comedy a couple of times at that point and been unmitigatedly awful). I left Covent Garden that night having had a brilliant time, feeling totally depressed and trying to work out an alternative thoroughfare to self-actualisation. But I was looking too far ahead when I should have been focussing on my next step, which was simply being less terrible than the last time I went on stage. Less than two years later I was making a living from comedy, and within five I was compeering the Covent Garden Comedy Club with Addy van der Borgh headlining. Time passes, but if you don't just let it pass you by – if you climb aboard and start shovelling coal – it's not exactly that "anything is possible", but you do start to loosen Hopelessness's stranglehold on your life. As F. Scott Fitzgerald wrote in *The Crack Up,* "one should…be able to see that things are hopeless and yet be determined to make them otherwise."

In a technical sense, from the summit of Cross Fell it was all downhill from here. In a more literal sense, the seven-mile slog along and down the purgatory surface of the Corpse Road to Garrigill would pummel all that triumphalism out of me. Like a lot of places in these parts the road's name is chillingly literal – it was used in days gone by to carry corpses from outlying villages for burial in consecrated ground.

Just below Cross Fell we came to a place called Greg's Hut, a mountain bothy and a place that would have seemed like Rivendell or Camelot had the weather stayed true to form. On the outside the hut is painted yellow and lime green, deliberately luminous so as to be found in the fog, whilst inside are two rooms, one which apparently used to be a blacksmith's forge, the other containing a basic sleeping platform, the sort of bedroom a sly tourist page might describe as "charmingly rustic". The hut itself was erected at the peak of Britain's lead mining industry – miners would leave their families on a Monday morning and stay here each night until home time on Friday. Lead mining in Britain had been birthed, reached adolescence, retired and died in these hills. 2,000 men, stoic and sinewy, used to be employed on the surrounding fells and a constant cacophony of iron mating with stone rippled down the hillsides to the formerly prosperous villages. All that is left now is piles of rubble and dark forbidding holes, the wind whistling through the hollows as if calling out to the miners to start work. But they won't be returning.

We mooched around inside for a bit, soaking in the history of the place, straining to hear all those imprinted voices that have stained the slatted walls. For good or ill, a number of them have been transcribed in the guest book, which read like a harrowing greetings card or the *Book of Mazarbul.* Here are some of the lowlights:

"I've walked this road 20 times in the last 40 years, and I ain't seen sleet like this. The only thing stopping me from staying here is that I need to find my dog." – Derek Salter.

"I haven't a single clue why I chose walking as the cure for my midlife crisis. I should have just committed suicide like my wife suggested." – R. Monton.

"I'm in my 50s and I didn't expect to be on an 18-30s holiday, but that's what has transpired. 30 of us started from Kirk Yetholm – 18 are left." – Chris Granger, Stow.

"I. Just. Want. To. Go. Home." – Mary Chestnut.

Whatever literal truth there was to some of these entries, the emotional angst dripped from every page. Kristine was at my shoulder and sucked all the air from the room with one of her abrupt gasping chuckles.

'Look at that one!' she said, practically delirious, pointing to a scrawled hand in black ink:

"We cannot get out. The end comes soon. We hear the drums in the deep… they are coming…"

'It's from *Lord of the Rings*,' I said flatly.

'Yes, I know, that's why I'm mentioning it. Isn't it funny!'

'Shouldn't you be tutting at the impertinence of it?' I asked.

'No, I think it's rather clever, don't you?'

I absolutely did think it both funny and clever, so I said, 'If you like that sort of thing.' Which I did. Chris punched me lightly on the arm in an attempt to knock some of the Kristine-directed belligerence out of me. Then he wrote his own entry:

"Looking for a man named John O'Groats. Will keep going until I find him, but this has been a savage enough pilgrimage so far."

'Come on, now,' said Kristine, 'we've still got half the day's walking to do, and I don't want to be late.'

'Late for what?' I asked.

'For getting there,' she replied, and stepped briskly out of Greg's Hut.

The descent along the Corpse Road is impressively desolate. This ground has been subjected to repeated freezing and thawing since the Ice Age, and I don't wish to be rude but it shows. Nothing really lives here except moss, and even that looks mildly homeless. The oxidised rocks, the colour of dried blood, bear tacit witness to how this land was sacrificed to the god of Industry.

The path curves round the back of the fells that we'd walked all that morning then takes the cadaverous walker across Long Man Hill and Pikeman Hill, ever moving, never progressing, like enchanted things in a nightmare. The pebble and cinder track is brutish and hard-boiled like a Raymond Chandler novel. From a distance it might look like the Yellow Brick Road, but there was to be no singing or skipping or holding of hands. That afternoon was the only time since Chris and I had met that we failed to maintain the rhythm of two-hour stretches without a break. Even with my silicone heels the incessant crunching impact on the loutish track sent debilitating quivers through my legs and body, a dripping tap torture, Cross Fell's cynical off-the-ball foul. Chris stopped every so often claiming to examine rumours of fluorspar, the bluish mineral left as a legacy of the lead mining – but really, like me, I think he was just plain knackered.

It didn't matter. Days ago I had been floored by the upper cuts of Pen-y-Ghent. Now, I had crested the apex of the Way and I was thriving! There were even whispers of redemption along the road: disused quarries upholstered by rainwater and now appearing as oasis pools in the landscape. And despite Kristine's punctilious fussing, we weren't actually late. You never really are when you're walking, nor are you early – you arrive precisely when you mean to. Punctuality is the virtue of the tedious.

'I haven't asked you about your fox,' Kristine said as we entered Garrigill, a pretty and pretty grey village, slightly ghostly perhaps, with a post office and pub which have been inoculated against modernisation.

Having developed a hair-trigger reflex for correcting people about how Alan identified, I was all set to berate her, but didn't need to because she had surprisingly named him a-right.

'A sort of mascot, is he, I suppose? A link to home and family or something?'

'Yes. Yes, that's exactly what he is. Thank you.'

'Do you still have his other eye?' she enquired.

'No, sadly. It's lying in a marsh somewhere I imagine.'

'Would you like me to sew a new one on for him? I like to embroider before bed – that's why I don't want to be late, you see, or the light fades too much – but I'm sure I could rummage around in my kit for something appropriate.'

Chris looked over at me with anticipation, but also with a hint of prescriptive peacemaking in his eye.

'Erm… yes, well, if you don't mind, I'm sure Alan would be very grateful for the surgery.'

'Well, precisely,' Kristine said. 'With NHS waiting times being what they are, it's better to go private.'

An implosion of air marked another of Kristine's idiosyncratic laughs, and, very much against my own wishes, I found myself laughing with her.

'I'm not sure I can do very much about your t-shirt, though,' she said. 'It looks to be on its last legs.'

'Aren't we all?' said Chris.

And Kristine laughed again.

The final four miles of Day 11 followed a woodland riverside path along the River South Tyne, never straying more than a couple of contours from the river itself, which is amiable and gossipy, a lined margin to help keep your scrawling step in line. It was a stretch of path that would seem idyllic if walked in isolation, but for our trio any aesthetic pleasure fell like a pebble into the shallows after the barbarism of the Corpse Road. A heron patrolled the bank, watchful and wary, then flew off towards

Alston to ask them to put a brew on and change the keg. Once at Alston, Chris and Kristine diverted on the edge of town in search of available camping space, while I located the Angel Inn, drank a Guinness, took a nap, had a shower, rang the girls, drank another Guinness, and let my psychology recalibrate as I looked forward to supper. We may not have won all the individual duels over those 21 miles, but we had picked up the day's gauntlet, ridden into the merry lists of combat and staggered out eight hours later as tourney winners.

In a final act of defiant underscoring, I opened my guidebook to the page where the map of Cross Fell even now tried to rear up from the paper. With black ink I scratched my own indelible cruciform symbol over its fiendish, forlorn heights – and smiled.

"I don't know how to tell you this… but I beat you, you b******."

Thanks be to God.

* * *

It was too nice an evening to be indoors. We were sitting in the churchyard under an old-fashioned streetlamp, Kristine and I, staring up into the blanket sky's luminous mauve. I was breathing self-consciously, noticing the way the cold air catches the warm heat leaving your body and sweeps it back into your nostrils. Chris had briefly reappeared for a cocoa nightcap but was now deep in *Duolingo* and would soon be deeper in sleep.

Night, from her phantom palace, reigned in stillness. An owl swept overhead, offering a nighttime benediction. Kristine was knitting, click-clacking her way through a pair of gloves for her niece; Alan was in gowns at her side, waiting bravely for his operation. I had my Swiss Army knife in my hand and was whittling sticks into chips, making nothing.

'It was a lady from my walking group who got me into knitting and embroidery, you know?' Kristine said without looking up.

'Quite a few of us do it now, and sometimes we share our designs with one another, although it's a bit embarrassing because I'm not very proficient.' She gave a small chuckle.

'Why are you doing this walk on your own, then?' I asked her, the bright stream of light from the lamp encircling her busy brow.

'Why are *you* walking the Pennine Way on *your* own?' she responded, still not raising her gaze. 'You didn't start out with Chris, and I don't know many married men who would be given such a licence. You must have a generous wife.'

'Yes, she's lovely,' I replied.

'Anyway, you seem much more relaxed than when I met you this morning. I think you enjoyed today very much.'

'You don't have to guess – you can just ask whether I did. And yes, overall, I did enjoy it.'

'That's good, then,' she said. 'It's nice that your demeanour finally matches your tattoo.'

'What do you mean?'

'εὐαγγέλιον. The Good News, the Gospel.'

'Er, yes, that's right. Do you speak Greek, then?'

She rummaged in her Mary Poppins bag and handed me a card for the walking group she kept going on about. I was apparently face to face with the deputy chair of The Christian Walking Association. I smiled detachedly, my thoughts somewhere else.

'I walk because I like it,' she said, head lowered back to her knitting. 'But also because it spring-cleans your soul. Do you not find that?'

'I suppose so,' I said.

'It really does, Andy, and you must surely have learned that. We live in a world obsessed with cries of sex and money. I'm 50 years old and I've never really had either, and so I come into nature because I recognise that voice. Nature doesn't judge you or discredit you. It doesn't tell you that you'll never find a husband, never have children. Humans do that, but hills don't – rivers don't. And the only voice I really need giving me feedback is God's. I've had some really rotten things said about me in my life, but out here it's easy to hear His whisper clearly above all that din. Whatever anyone else says about me, God spoke first.'

In that moment, all my residual antipathy towards Kristine melted away and was replaced with pure-cut affection, with an almost Dickensian outpouring of goodwill.

We so often get it wrong when we observe from a distance. The night sky is not black through a telescope, and human beings are not superficial plateaus of easy analysis, but rather a soulscape of contour lines that comprise both valleys and peaks, that are as much forged by freeze-thawing and erosion as any ancient hillside: once-flowing rivers choked with sediment, or desolate quarries refilled with living water.

Kristine was not who I thought she was, and I regretted lowering my gavel too soon in judgement. But nor was I quite the man she thought me, either. In fact, I wasn't half the man any of my walking companions had been led to believe. And I decided, finally, to change that.

'I'm not,' I said to her across the darkness.

'You're not what?'

'Married. I'm not married. I used to be, but I'm not anymore.'

She put down her knitting and looked at me. Was I perhaps still waiting for the tut to rebuke my little white lie? It never came. Instead, she nodded and pointed a knitting needle at my chest.

'Is that why you're walking the Pennine Way on your own, then?' she asked.

I looked down at the remains of my Ben Sherman t-shirt, and smiled.

'Yes,' I said. 'For HER. For *them.*'

Day 12
Alston to Hadrian's Wall
17 miles

"I am poured out like water, and all my bones are out of joint:
my heart is like wax; it is melted in the midst of my bowels."
Psalm 22

"Never give up. Today is hard, tomorrow will be worse,
but the day after tomorrow will be sunshine."
Jack Ma

CHAPTER 25
PEREGRINUS
(DON'T STOP, MOVE IT BABY)

I didn't want to get out of bed. Yesterday's 21 miles across wicked fells and down the Corpse Road's walk of shame was the longest distance I'd ever travelled on foot in one day. By the end of tomorrow that record would have been broken again, and I would not be celebrating. My shoulders were clamped in a phantom pack sensation, and I felt like I was wearing a coat three sizes too small – a munchkin's coat – while my legs were archipelagos of spasming muscles and twitching nerves. I also had a headache and a sore throat and was in the running to be the next Patron Saint of Hypochondria. The soft cotton sheets of the Alston Inn's double bed, the rising simmer of the bedside kettle, the benign chirpiness of early morning cartoons from the TV: all of them knitted together a swaddling blanket of maternal cosiness, the sort Kristine would have been proud of. I should quite like to stay in this place for a while longer, please and thank you. "Ah! how delicious it is to turn over and go to sleep again: 'Just for five minutes.' Is there any human being, I wonder, besides the hero of a Sunday-school 'tale for boys', whoever gets up willingly?" Jerome K. Jerome (obviously).

Having crossed the highest peak of the trail and with only five days remaining, perhaps in theory it seemed all-but-assured that I would complete the whole walk. But you only have to look at salmon to know that not all journeys end well. Endings are much harder than beginnings, and nothing is inevitable when your body is continually asked to stretch itself beyond comfortable boundaries. Simon Armitage never finished the Pennine Way. Bill Bryson walked only a portion of the Appalachian Trail. I just wouldn't want you to lose that sense of jeopardy at this point.

Human beings love stories (good ones, at least) because they safely lay out for us beginnings, middles and ends, in that order and in their proper time. But an ending is not the same as completion. The end of the race is not always the finish line, but simply that place on the track where the runner decides to stop, or that skidmarked patch of tarmac where the crash happened. The end of a novel is, likewise, just that point in the story where the author says: 'Enough now'. What we want is not just an ending but for something to finish *well,* to be resolved and reconciled. A proper resolution is when the end point of something matches the finishing line you had marked on your own map (whether figurative or literal). With the Pennine Way, that's Kirk Yetholm (or Edale). With a marriage: that's death… and maybe not even then.

What makes all covenants so sacred is that, unlike a walk, unlike a book or a film – unlike life itself even – they promise no ending. Parents who have lost a child prematurely do not stop loving her, nor do they simply love the memory of her, but rather their love remains intact like a fly preserved in amber; a living relic.

Covenants are not the same as contracts. Contracts, being written on paper, can be torn up. Covenants, being written on living hearts, beat on as eternal story. As Dylan Thomas wrote, "Though lovers be lost, love shall not; And death shall have no dominion."

But sometimes the story gets jumbled up. Or sometimes you misread it, or try to make it say and mean something it never did, in a flagrant act of eisegesis. In writing the Harry Potter saga, J.K. Rowling gave us an epic tale of friendship where love is self-sacrificial and not self-serving, where main characters have to die for life to win. And yet a whole generation of readers left Hogwarts with the idea that Rowling's main message was somehow, "Your feelings are magical".

Feelings are not magical. They are – certainly – authentic and descriptive and functional; but also, so often, deceptive and treacherous. Feelings are not *pre*scriptive – they tell you where you are but not where you should be – and they should not, in my opinion, be trusted as lead scouts on life's undulating journey. The zeitgeist seems to cry out, "Follow your heart." The problem is that your heart isn't known for its map-reading abilities. Walk with it, yes, listen to it and listen well. But don't let it set the course when Reason and Will and Conscience have vastly more expertise across certain terrains. They may not be as fun on the mountaintops, but they know how to navigate the valleys when your idol-factory of a heart is lying at the wayside, broken from his impetuous sally of self-love. And we don't need a cartographer to tell us that the surface area of a valley floor is much greater than that of a mountain peak.

Because sometimes you wake up to realise that you have taken the wrong path. You stumble upon the reality that you made a covenant with the wrong thing; that the great love of your life is, in fact, *you*. Your heart has deceived you and you open the morning papers to find that Death indeed sits on the throne, His dominion stretching out as far as the eye can see. You have misread the story. You tried to make it say something it didn't.

It's so easy to do – part of what Francis Spufford calls "That Human Propensity to **** Things Up". We believe what we want to believe, see what we want to see, make spine-shivering errors and then do them again. We forget where we began and take for granted the ending, and lose our footing in a suffocated middle, the swaddling cloth that once held and comforted us now in bloody tatters on the muddy, broken ground.

But still you have a choice – even then. Anyone who has experienced the ending of a marriage by a decision that was not their own knows all too well that grief which scorches everything it touches, that undermines your stability and leaves the landscape of your future barren and lifeless; that raking paralysis which makes even baby steps impossible. The worst thing about grief is that you can't sidestep it or walk around it – you just have to go through it. Deny it and it will come out in other ways. It seeps into places you don't notice. But you still have a choice, and it's the choice that faces every one of us at times of great trial and torment: Despair or Hope. Despair, as Evelyn Waugh said, is the only great evil in the world. And Hope is the greatest, perhaps only, weapon against it.

Hope is not wishful thinking or confirmation bias. Hope is that choice to believe that Love *will* win in the end; that the narrative arc of the universe, though it takes a route directly through the grave, bends upwards towards Redemption. Hope is the voice that whispers in the ear of the paralysed man: "Your sins are forgiven – *get up and walk.*"

It's difficult to make any progress when you feel like even the ground beneath you is tumbling away, but ultimately you must try, and try again, and again and again – one step at a time, one foot in front of the other, left boot then right. Nobody avoids the darkest valleys if you walk for long enough, but Hope is a signpost on a map that was previously uncharted. The signpost might only be an acorn, but you know what acorns tend to do, don't you?

The ancient idea of the Peregrinus (pilgrim) was not one who is heading somewhere, but essentially one who is *not at home where he is walking,* who is an exile wherever he treads, who walks seeking intercession and is purified by the suffering. As Frederic Gros says, "Internal transformation remains the pilgrim's mystical ideal: he hopes to be absolutely altered on his return".

That's why I had chosen to walk; to hoist my rucksack of guilt and pain and shame and make plodding progress through the Slough of Despond, Difficulty Hill and the Wicked Gate: to become Peregrinus. For months I had been something in a bottle, something kept alive in a laboratory, not a real man but forgotten bits of one; a tune stopped short without the expected chords to close it. Now I was voting with my feet, leaving empty places in favour of big open ones, swapping the life of the nomad for that of the pilgrim, feeling that purifying pain. Better to walk perpendicularly than to go round in circles.

I didn't want a wandering life. Nor was I walking *away*. I was walking to get somewhere, to get *back*, through the valleys and the shadows to a town called Redemption. And I wasn't carrying a relic – I *was* one. I didn't need to find myself for I knew exactly who I was, nor was I lost for I knew exactly *where* I was and where I wanted to be. Through all of it and in all of it, I was just trying to walk *home*. I had made myself a prisoner of Hope, and Hope is never mere even when it is meagre.

And, for me, Hope lived in the hills.

* * *

The Angel Inn, Alston, was my favourite accommodation on the Pennine Way to-date. It didn't have a golden bath, but then I hadn't needed to put my children on Ebay to afford it. Oh! and the owner hadn't delayed my bedtime ablutions by doing a massive poo, so by any barometer it was well ahead of the curve.

Gareth, the newly installed publican, was celebrating his 40th birthday in the lounge bar that morning and was enjoying a breakfast of smoked salmon and Lambrini as I slinkied my way down the stairs for breakfast, 90's dance music blaring out from the establishment's retro jukebox.

'Breakfast is on the house this morning!' Gareth gushed.

'I've already pre-paid it though,' I said, utterly crestfallen.

'Oh… well how about a pint, then?'

'No thanks,' I replied, 'not when I'm on duty. But bottomless coffee would be great.'

'That can be arranged!'

Gareth docked a huge trawler-sized cafetiere into my harbour and then, because I'd asked for bottomless coffee and because he was drinking alcohol before 9am, he showed me his entire bottom.

'Many happy returns!' I said. It was that or have him arrested. I was just happy that neither Kristine nor Margot nor, for that matter, Werner were present for the screening.

The early morning rave continued, plenty of big and little fish and more than a few cardboard boxes being unpacked as Gareth danced his forties into being like some Native American medicine man. I acknowledged from where I was now vogueing behind a Cumberland sausage that I was also double the age I wanted to be and, as such, I felt it was incumbent upon me to douse the flames of his hopes that life begins at 40. In response to his resolution to 'have more adventures', I pointed out that about 11% of life in your forties is spent staring aghast at bizarrely long hairs which have sprouted from various parts on your body. You also waste a lot of time trying to put keys onto keyrings. "Would I lie to you baby, would I lie to you?" Charles and Eddie backed me up from the jukebox.

'Are you sure you don't want a pint?' he asked. 'Go on, it's m'birthday.'

Gareth was due to be on a flight to Magaluf by the end of the day and I couldn't afford in any sense to join him, so I accepted half a pint of Westmoreland ale as compromise and convinced myself it was just fancy gravy. A few minutes later Mary Poppins floated down from her cloud on the first floor, tutted at Gareth's dancing, tutted twice at my full pint of ale (I lied when I said it was just a half) and asked whether some lighter, more tranquil music would be possible while she ate her Eggs Royale. Gareth asked whether she would like a birthday pint, and she tutted to herself so many times it sounded like she had entered – although not come close to winning – the Christian Amateur Beatboxing Pageant. Kristine did however orchestrate a rather rousing rendition of "Happy Birthday to Gareth", with hymnal undertones and cutlery-percussion accompaniment. Then she told me we were going to be late and, with the surprise party pooped and Gareth left to sing both male and female parts of *Rhythm is a Dancer,* within 10 minutes we were back on the road.

It hadn't rained for over a week. Dawn had mounted her lovely chair again and the hail-battered walk I took over Saddleworth Moor on Day 2 now seemed like something from an alternate timeline. Chris was waiting for us down by the South Tynedale railway line, so Kristine and I took a short walk through the pretty town of Alston, England's highest market town, with steep cobbled streets and 18th century buildings adding to its character.

'Are you ready to see the patient?' she asked gravely.

'How is he, doctor?'

Kristine smiled and pulled Alan from behind her back.

'I couldn't find a bead for the eye, I'm afraid, but I did the best I could,' she said.

And what a job she had done! In place of a blind spot, Alan now had a shining silver button for his second, replacement eye. It made him look a bit like a cyborg, but that wasn't necessarily a bad thing.

'He looks ever so handsome,' I said, clutching him to my chest. 'And now he can enjoy Hadrian's Wall in all its glory.'

Kristine looked pleased with herself. She spun me round and stuffed Alan back into his pouch, then opened the top of my rucksack and placed the folded Ben Sherman t-shirt into it (she had insisted I let her have a crack at trying to salvage the remaining letters, and she had washed it in her sink and scented it with lavender salts).

Chris was already two energy bars deep by the time we met him, a result, he said, of choosing to camp in a land possessed by nettles, getting stung to the hilt and then being unable to sleep. His midnight feast of insomnia had, however, seen him devise a cunning plan for today's opening section, which he now drew from his pocket along with a third energy bar.

'This railway track isn't the official Pennine Way, but if we walk straight down it for a few miles we'll splice back onto the trail, and we won't have had to go uphill and down dale. It's the same distance in footfall and we won't miss anything in terms of views. What do you think?'

'Sounds fine to me.' Kristine said.

'You're the brains of this operation, Chris,' I added.

'I hope that doesn't make you the looks,' he replied.

'No, no. I'm more the collapsed lung or the burst appendix.'

What happened next? Kristine tutted. Then the three pilgrims, with their long staffs, voluminous cloaks and mendicant pouches stained by long travel, set out once more.

Chris and I were heading for Hadrian's Wall, where Rob, who had apparently walked deep into the night and stolen a march on his allies, would rejoin the legion. It would be great to hook up with him and his foul mouth again, and we had already had a phone conversation that morning in which gigantic plans were made for dinner and drinks.

'Just don't make fun of me when you see me,' he had said during the call.

'About what?'

'You'll find out soon enough.'

I was intrigued.

Kristine was leaving us at lunchtime to jump back into a chalk drawing and dance with some half-dressed penguins, and I had those short intervening hours to think of a way to thank her for Alan's revival.

The morning's progress was remarkably swift as we headed down the former railway line now designated as the South Tyne Trail. There was no fog on the Tyne this morning though and zero navigational difficulties, and we incised the soft underbelly of Northumberland past the defunct but well-preserved signal box at the wonderfully named Slaggyford, a place absolutely crying out to be used in an ITV period drama where Martin Clunes dies in the war (NB. I don't mind which war, just as long as it happens). There's a Hornby Model Railway feel to this whole stretch actually, an ethereal days-gone-by wistfulness as the cloistered landscape chugs gently by. While loitering in the sidings at Slaggyford, enough time for Chris to eat a ludicrous fifth energy bar, we crossed paths with a duo attempting the Pennine walk from Kirk

Yetholm to Edale, who came shunting and swaying down the track towards us. It already seemed like they had bitten off more than they could chew – the lady looked like a L'Oreal model in peril, while the young chap's expression hung from his face like molten rubber. They stopped with us a while to let off some steam, already taking steps towards talking themselves into early defeat, but we reassured them that it was quite doable if they didn't think or feel too far ahead.

'How did you two meet?' I asked the L'Oreal woman, whose real name was Linda.

'He popped out of my tummy,' she replied.

'Like *Alien?*'

'Like I gave birth to him.'

I knew that, really.

'How about you?' she asked, and I was quick to point out that I hadn't given birth to her son.

The mother-son couple's reason for walking was a very sweet one. Jez was heading off to Thailand for two years that summer and they wanted to undertake an epic quest together that would lodge in their memories while they were apart.

'That's very special,' said Kristine.

'Yes,' said the mum, 'he's still my little boy really, even if he is a grown man now, and I will miss him a lot. You never stop parenting your children, do you?'

'I wouldn't really know,' Kristine replied.

Linda rubbed her son's arm chummily, and he looked at his mum with grudging fondness.

'Fancy some Fruit Pastilles, Jez?' I asked, lobbing him a pack. Jez, whose face was now looking slightly less warped from torque, accepted the gift gratefully.

'What's been the highlight of your walks so far?' Linda asked us with an interested, wary smile.

'That night I got a good night's sleep,' Chris said. 'And High Cup Nick, I suppose.'

'The breakfasts,' I added, without a sliver of irony. 'Also, Malham Tarn, High Cup Nick.'

'I think being with friends is the best part,' Kristine said. 'Just being together with people you like. And so that's a way for you both to think about it, maybe? Stick together and you'll always be in the best bit.'

Linda nodded enthusiastically. Jez looked a little embarrassed by the whole thing, but I could tell he was listening.

'Just don't wait for it to be fun,' I said.

'Couldn't agree more,' Chris added. 'Endurance over enjoyment.'

'Sorry if we haven't put you more at ease,' Kristine concluded.

'It's probably what we needed to hear,' Jez said. 'Isn't it, Mum?'

With Jez's face fully de-rouged and Linda full of fresh bounce and body, they struggled to their feet and lurched back into motion.

I would meet Linda again as it turned out, by complete chance. She came to an event I was performing at later that year and it took her a while to recognise the less hirsute, more sanitised version of me, but we had a lovely chat at the end of my gig. She told me that Jez was happily settled in Thailand and that he had joined a mountaineering club. Oh, and they did make it all the way to Edale in the end. It took them 22 days, but they did it. And what's wrong with that? Why not, given the glorious chance, spend 22 unbroken days in the company of those you care about the most? Outside of the Spine Race there are no prizes given along the Pennine Way for speed or velocity, and slowness of motion only adds to the immersiveness. In his book *Slowness,* Milan Kundera wrote, "Where have they gone, the amblers of yesteryear? Where have they gone, those loafing heroes of folk song, those vagabonds who roam from one mill to another and bed down under the stars?" Or, as that other renowned wordsmith Marge Simpson said, "Slow and steady wins the race."

My friend Kristine left us at lunchtime, at the place where the South Tyne Railway reconnects with the official trail.

'Right, time to say goodbye,' she said with a smile. 'End of the line, literally.'

'Thanks for your company,' Chris said, who by this point had eaten so many energy bars that his eyes looked like they'd been to Woodstock.

'Yes, likewise,' Kristine replied. 'I try to do something like this on my own annually, so maybe we could all collaborate on a hike next year.'

'Groovy, man,' Chris may or may not have said.

'Goodbye, Andy. Goodbye, Alan.'

'Wait, please,' I said, walking purposefully over to Kristine as she donned her bergen. I removed the garish red baseball cap from my head, and slotted it loosely onto hers.

'What's this for?' she asked.

'NY,' I said. Not New York, and not North Yorkshire either. *Next Year.'*

She tutted and gave me a hug. I whispered something, she nodded, and then she was gone.

The wind had changed, after all.

* * *

Chris and I walked through the clear afternoon in amiable silence, measuring the length of the land with unrivalled legs, enjoying the weather, storing up these sunny memories for the long crepuscular winter evenings. By hiking standards, a lot of Day 12 is just fairly dull, a blank entry in a thesaurus, like listening to a rice cake give a TED Talk on the colour beige. My page of notes for this section is the least populated of all the days on the Pennine Way, the most notable jotting being that I (and I quote) "saw a bull with a huge bull's willy." I'm not sure what other type of willy I was expecting a bull to have, but I'd been distracted during my writing time by the grim discovery of a singularly unassailable eyebrow hair and had lost concentration. Still, if walking is slow food in a fast food culture then the absence of any high drama was a simple-but-tasty plate of serenity on toast, with a cup of kindness perched on the side.

The Pennines halt their northern march before the Pennine walker does. There's the arable muck of Hartley Burn floodplain and Blenkinsopp Common, and then the official Pennine Chain lowers you from its shoulder like the *BFG* and points a lingering finger towards Caledonia (NB. Technically the walk should be entitled the Pennine and Cheviot Way, but it's not). We crested Black Hill, half expecting to see George R.R. Martin's colossal wall of ice looming large above us, but instead the village of Greenhead crouched comely in its place, waiting to offer us comforts not permitted to members of the Night's Watch. While Chris took the King's Road into Greenhead, I chanced my hand at a little short cut… and ended up skydiving down a vertical hill of slick grass onto a main road, narrowly avoiding an onrushing camper van and its fear-stricken driver. Those last 200 metres were the only taxing part of the entire day, but as we've already discussed, beginnings are much easier than endings.

It's another of those legs where you could quite easily rationalise falling off the wagon. By sundown you've reached Hadrian's Wall, the world famous "No Entry" sign pinned across the North of England. You've crossed into Northumberland and watched the last Pennine take a ride back along the rail track to join Gareth's evening birthday celebrations. The ungloved wind from Caledonia promises that not everything is done and dusted, and for those walkers who have hit the wall figuratively, hitting the Wall literally might seem like a good excuse to go home.

But not for me. Today had been the dullest day; tomorrow would be the longest. But I was potentially only four sleeps away from the best.

And after 18 months of deathly pandemic, I was in growing danger of having a near-life experience.

CHAPTER 26
PALATE CLEANSER

Pay attention.

If you haven't ever tried homemade chips with a truffle oil and parmesan coating, you are letting everyone – yourself, your family, me, even Alan – down. Gather round yon hearth, ma wee bairn, and I shall tell ye a tale.

The Greenhead Hotel looks so innocuous. They don't welcome you in with a knowing smile or a prophetic wink. The section of the menu which reads "Hand Cut Chips with Truffle Oil and Parmesan" isn't underlined and circled with aggressive asterisks and arrows pointing to it. The staff don't swoon with disbelief or vomit with rage if you order something else from the board, nor does a spectral crusader materialise to inform you with chilling certainty that 'You chose poorly'. When I said, 'May I try the truffle oil and parmesan chips?' from my comfortable seat, no klaxon sounded; no balloons fell from the ceiling; no cheerleaders skipped out with pom-poms to chant my name one letter at a time. Without pomp or ceremony, the young lad just said, 'Of course, of course… and to drink?'

I've never seen restraint like it.

When the food arrived, I sensed nothing. Monks did not accompany the tray carrying wistful candles, and no word – not a single word one – was spoken in Latin. I was halfway through telling Chris how I never order soup because drinking a chicken is not something I've ever felt the need to accomplish… when the taste that launched a thousand ships washed over me unprompted – and how!

It was Woodstock for the tastebuds, Concorde for the tongue. My mouth was on a once-in-a-lifetime safari and had just seen a pride of lions in a pitched battle against some unicorns. Chips with Truffle Oil and Parmesan, that's all it was. So simply named and so modestly presented. Yet this taste was an ancient magic: buried with Tutankhamun, cached with the Dead Sea Scrolls, a leviathan of flavour rising from the murky depths.

The Epicureans sought ataraxia. Buddhists seek nirvana. The Apostle Paul resolved to know nothing except Christ crucified.

I agree with Paul, but he never tried these chips.

Certain seismic events over the course of my life have stayed indelibly with me. The birth of my daughters was wonderful, as was that time Stephen Fry stood next to me at a urinal and I saw his willy and said, 'Do you think there'll be more Blackadders?'

Well, these chips were up there.

Once I'd finished with the chips and pocketed their wire basket to keep as a relic, then when I'd put it back on the table after Chris had said, 'Not sure you can do that' and the young serving boy said, 'Please don't do that, sir,' I sat with my flabbers well and truly ghasted at the idea that I might want to see the desserts board.

'Who's the chef?' I demanded.

'Er… Alf, he's retiring in a couple of months.'

Alf. A fine name: Anglo-Saxon and true. I wanted to meet him… to thank him… to sketch him while he bathed and splashed in shallow waters. I wanted to tell him that he must never retire and never die – to grab him by the shoulders and say, 'Do you hear me, Alf?! You must never die!!!'

And yet one day, I knew in my heart, Alf *would* die, and I needed to cherish the moments we still had left. And so I would order two more baskets of chips with truffle oil and parmesan, and no I didn't want another burger as well or any more sauces, and yes it was fine if Chris ordered dessert now because I still might have a bowl of custard or something later on.

Healthy food might be good for the conscience. Some food is just good for the soul. To this day, if you arranged 20 truffle oil chips in a circle like standing stones, there's a strong chance it would summon me instantly into your kitchen.

You will need to buy some Gaviscon, though. I will say that.

Day 13
Hadrian's Wall to Bellingham
22 miles

"The only easy day was yesterday"
Unofficial motto of the U.S. Navy Seals.

"What is grief if not love persevering?"
Vision in Wandavision

CHAPTER 27

WALKING DIARY OF A NOBODY

'Only four days left, my loves!' I told my girls over a glitchy Facetime call.

'Do you remember the dinosaurs, Daddy?' Alice asked, picking up our old game of how old and decrepit I was.

'Yes, love, I was on first name terms with all of them.'

'Have your legs falled off, Daddy?' Heidi then asked.

'I'm keeping them on with plasticine, darling. Are you both having a nice time and looking after each other and Mummy?'

'Yesssss,' they chorused. 'And will you bring us presents?'

'I already have them,' I said with a smile, and that was really all they needed to hear.

'Good luck, Daddy… we love youuuu.'

'I love you Alice, I love you Heidi, I love you…'

'You love *me?*' Chris asked, appearing at my shoulder. I told him we were just good friends and he seemed relieved.

We were finally getting there. I had assigned the four-day route march from Middleton-in-Teesdale to Bellingham the title of "The Four Horseman". Those four days contained the two longest stages of the Pennine Way, plus the hardest and the dullest. After today's 22 miles the Horsemen would all have been unsaddled and the daily distance would reduce to 15 miles, then 14, then 13, then 20-yard shuttle runs between fridge and settee.

The guidebooks all heralded the 40-mile stretch after Bellingham (pronounced Bellin-jam) as the home strait. Just three mornings more then to wake up in unfamiliar beds, to treat blisters and lather on Ibuprofen gel like a pervert. To heft, heave, tramp and trudge. If I found the right breach in Hadrian's Wall and made it over the bare wasteland to Wark Forest beyond, I sensed I would finish the Pennine Way. My legs, those noble servants of the will, were certainly creaking, but in the pleasing way that an old bookcase does. And at least I hadn't needed any plasticine. It was scheduled to be another scorching day and I felt that promise hanging prophetically in the Northumbrian air as I walked down the guest house's gravel drive, a precocious young sheepdog doing sprint training through ox-eye daisies in an adjacent field. I suspected I might feel the lack of my NY baseball cap today, but I wouldn't be the one most in need of modest head-covering as we'll find out in, oh, no more than a trice.

Having lost all sense of money's intrinsic worth since Tan Hill, and without having the energy or inclination to check the current strength of the pound, I had paid an extra £10 for a packed lunch to be provided by the guest house, the constituents of which I found lined up neatly on a Persian footstool by the front door – a ham sandwich, small bottle of orange juice, a banana which I left because bananas are gross, and a packet of crisps with a European name like 'Klaps'. A handwritten Post-it note, curled up at the edges, had "Enjoy!!!" written on it. Three exclamation marks seemed excessive for a packet of bootlegged Doritos, but I wrote "Thanks for everything!!!!" underneath and felt as though I'd made my point. The room had been comfortable after all, the sheets sweet-smelling and my night's sleep undisturbed. The hosts (a relocated southern couple sick of London, the male of whom kept calling me Adrian for some reason) were nowhere to be seen or found as I surfaced, so I stowed away my schoolboy's lunch, donned my boots, hoisted my pack, added a ghastly fifth exclamation mark to the Post-it note, and clipped on my Alan as usual. Then our tiny but battle-hardened cohort sallied forth once more.

Rob was back. He had pootled along on his own for the last few days, 'famping' as he called it, and you shouldn't need more than a moment to work out which two words Rob had selected for that compound noun. He had been due to join us for dinner the previous night but had mysteriously pulled out due to 'unforeseen circumstances', depriving *us* of his company and *himself* of those chips I think I mentioned. Around 8:30am, Chris and I were perched on a mossy dry-stone wall just north of Greenhead, scanning the route map and predicting potential rest points, the sprinting sheepdog audible behind a hedge, when Rob came plodding down the track towards us, a look of great imprecation on his face. The 'unforeseen circumstances' became steadily unmissable as he approached.

It's common, isn't it, after a prolonged absence, to see a friend and notice a difference in their appearance. It's usually an extra wrinkle or a rumour of grey in the beard, but in my experience almost never that their hair has changed abruptly from brown to fire-engine red, which I'm desperately sorry to say is what had happened to Rob.

'You look different,' I told him, with as much gentleness as I could muster.

'Don't f****** ask,' he replied.

'You don't want me to ask why your hair is now suddenly and entirely red?'

'Well done, Herman, you've got it.'

'OK... Can I ask a different question though?'

'What?'

'*How is it* that your hair is now suddenly and entirely red?'

Rob's tale was a dark one, and I lay it out here to the best of my memory.

Two nights prior, Rob had taken a bus to Penrith in search of a civilised sit-down meal for the evening. On reaching the Lake District town and realising that it would now be too late to return to the trail via public transport, our hero sought accommodation locally. While enjoying a large steak and a warm ale in one of the town's lower-market establishments, he asked the waitress serving him whether she knew of any cheap lodgings nearby, at which her eyes apparently glimmered like a witch and she told him that he could stay at her house… on the proviso that he let her practise her hairdressing skills on him. (NB. One must assume that waitressing was only an interim measure for the young woman.) Rob, stoic fiancé and ardent self-flatterer that he was, made her promise in speech and then – for some reason – in writing that there would be nothing sexual involved (and here I've sanitised the verbiage for younger readers), to which she responded that she lived with her boyfriend and that Rob wasn't her type in any way. According to eyewitness testimony, the woman said 'in any way' about three times in the restaurant, then a further four times on the way home, although scholars on the subject argue that it may have been considerably more than this. However, in addition to the promise of a warm bed the waitress offered to knock 10% off Rob's steak bill, which served to calm the storm of his scepticism and soothe any feelings of low-level rejection.

Later that evening, having been introduced to the young woman's boyfriend whose hair looked, and I'm quoting here, "pretty normal – a few split ends but nothing to worry about really", and having been informed that the module she was studying at "f****** Hairdresser University or something" was colouring, Rob found himself in something of a social cul-de-sac: he needed a bed and under no circumstances wished to pay back the remaining 10% of his meal. And so, reluctant but displaying incredible bravery, he let a complete stranger with a bag of scissors have her wicked way with him. Suffice it to say, in the vein of all the great fables, it did not go well *in any way*. Despite the comfortable lodging Rob slept fitfully that night, suffering occasional night terrors in which he imagined his hair all ablaze. He also awoke in the morning to find his pillow stained deeply with red and, before his memory of the previous night took hold, assumed he had severed an artery in his neck and was now bleeding to death. Here the account ends.

'I'm not sure I've ever been happier,' I said as Rob drew his tale to a close.

'I've tried to wash it out, but I'm worried it's permanent. I might just shave my head like you.'

'I would like that very much,' I replied.

'What will you tell your fiancée?' Chris asked, scratching his own head through instinct and relief.

'Dunno. I think I might just have to end it at this point. She deserves better.'

'Well, we'll support you in whatever you decide,' I said.

Rob could see that I was having such a wonderful time looking at his hair – it was in my Top 10 views of the walk so far, without a doubt.

'Please don't spend the day ripping me over it,' he continued. 'I'm embarrassed enough already. I didn't come for food last night because I didn't want people to see me. Let's just go.'

I wanted very much to honour his plea for clemency, but the brochure hadn't mentioned this surprise addition to the entertainment listing.

'I'm ready to go, Rob,' I said, pointing at his noggin, 'but I'm just waiting for this traffic light to turn green.'

'OK, quite funny,' he said. 'Enough now.'

'Tall buildings could hire you to stand on their roof and planes wouldn't fly into them,' I followed up, unable to help myself. I was hitting quantity over quality for sure, but you've just got to have fun with it.

'Please p*** off,' Rob responded.

Then Chris said, 'I know you're renowned for turning the air *blue*, Rob, but this is ridiculous.'

I didn't say anything at the time because I didn't want to upset the fellow, but later that morning I took Chris off to one side and asked him what the hell he thought that was.

Along with Not-Wuthering-Heights from Day 4, the first half of Day 13's walking is about as touristy as you can get on the Pennine Way. Within minutes of leaving Greenhead the trail ushered us towards a 12th century ruin with the slightly inflated name of Thirlwall Castle, built in the 1330s using stones pilfered from Hadrian's Wall. Like a lot of places in these parts a mythology has grown up around it, but not a very good one. As the legend has it, Baron John Thirlwall returned from the Crusades with extravagant spoils, chief of which was a banqueting table of solid and scintillating gold. The table was guarded, or chaperoned or something, by a hideous dwarf – and we don't know whether he was the artisan or whether he just got thrown in as part of the bundle. Jealous of the Baron's wealth however, and seemingly not deterred by the marked ugliness of the dwarf, a band of roving Scots assaulted the Castle from the north under the raven-black blanket of night, killing most of the inhabitants in search of the treasure. Not wanting to yield the golden table, the hideous dwarf – and I'm sure you've guessed his next move because it's such an obvious solution – threw it down a well, jumping in after it and magically sealing the shaft behind him. With that level of magic, you might think the dwarf could have conjured up some better defences for the brutally murdered family, but maybe being referred to exclusively as "hideous dwarf" had gotten too much for the chap. And obviously, according to the lore both dwarf and table remain there still, the spell only reversible by the only son of a widow – although it doesn't say whose widow, or why him specifically.

I told you it wasn't a very good legend, but in fairness to people from the 12th century they didn't have the same access to creative writing courses that we do. And perhaps a few hundred years from now, in a draughty house outside Penrith on a raven-black night, small children will gather round a fire to hear the legend of The Burning Man, who passed, with fiery brow and hellish speech, along Hadrian's Wall one summer day long ago, searching for his lost love, the fair lady Vinegar Rinse. I do hope so.

What isn't not very good is Hadrian's Wall. In fact it's magnificent. It might not be visible from space in the way that the Great Wall of China or that bull's penis from south of Greenhead are, but it's a real treat nonetheless, evoking mytho-historic scenes that dance and joust in your imagination and distract you to some degree from the gruelling undulations of the wall itself. We joined it at Walltown Craggs, beginning a hefty 8-mile stretch along its best-preserved segment, the Whin Sill arcing and curving away ahead of us, baring its teeth at any encroaching Scots.

It was a baking hot Saturday, the heat pressing down on the open ground like a winepress, and the day-walkers were legion, ambling along in benign swarms with their hampers and their flip-flops, breaking our rhythm and stride with their undisciplined leisure, nipping at our heels with their ebullience. I hadn't been around this many people for nearly 18 months and it was otherworldly, like an uncanny sci-fi movie where people communed in an atmosphere I recognised but couldn't quite place. Still, we made good progress. Along the length of the wall the Romans built milecastles, and even the vague remains of some of these acted as pleasant progress trackers. Up and down we went, down and up, imagining ourselves on patrol, faces red from effort and sun-bleach, boots coated with the cinders of scorched mud, campaign veterans etching our own history over the thousands who trod before us. By this stage we were double centurions of the Way: Rob and I had walked over 200 miles, while Chris had done over twice that. "Only the die-hards and oddballs get this far," one newspaper article had said, and we felt proud to own either or both of those titles.

Chris became upset during this section, and I'm the first to admit it was at least partly my fault. He had sidled up to me while Rob was lagging in the rear, to say, 'He needs to cover that hair up – he looks like a supervillain.'

Chris was quite correct: the sort of cartoon bad guy who nobody has heard of and yet action figures of which you can find languishing in sodden boxes at midweek markets, that have lost all their clothes and always cost a pound.

Then Chris said, 'I've heard of keeping it under your cap, but this is ridiculous.'

By this stage I was completely worn out from Chris's inane 'I've heard of X but this is ridiculous' motif, could bear it no longer and so, already goaded by the suffocating presence of day-trippers, I really was quite unkind, telling him in no uncertain terms that the 'I've heard of X but this is ridiculous' joke structure, albeit popular among comedians in the late 80s and early 90s, was now considered facile and hackneyed on the circuit and that he really must stop it immediately. He was naturally embarrassed, said he was just trying to join in, that he was more of an actor, and that he really was very sorry. Obviously, I relented and apologised, told him that we might still salvage something from the day and that he mustn't dwell on it. But he was pretty distraught by this point.

At Whinshields Cragg we stopped to take on water. The peroxide-bleached grass of the encompassing fields was crackling in a shallow fry, while Rob, his hair the colour of embarrassment, had been garnering a good number of curious looks from other walkers along the wall – one couple even asked if they could sponsor him for whatever stunt his ludicrous head was in aid of. He said yes, and found himself £5 better off, planning to spend the ill-gotten earnings on a big disposable razor. I offered him a packet of Klaps for £2, but he had obviously been perusing the Nasdaq and told me to p*** off again.

'You do look different, though,' I said to him as we sat in the cooling shadows of the Cragg. 'And I don't just mean the hair. You look older maybe, or perhaps that you seem more at home in your features. I'm not sure what I mean, really'.

I'm still not sure what I meant entirely, other than this perhaps: that it's possible to feel sometimes as though you're simply a tenant in your own body, leasing it for 70 years or so until the landlord kicks you out and changes the locks. A sort of psychic dysphoria, I suppose, where you feel more like your shadow than your actual *self*. But then there's something about sustained pilgrimage, about binding those spirits of lethargy and torpor which hold dominion in domesticity, that sees you take ownership over yourself again (or for the first time), that raises enough moral capital to purchase the freehold of your being, and that sews you, like Peter Pan, back onto your shadow. Lewis Carrol's concept of the Caucus Race in *Alice in Wonderland,* in which "you have to run as fast as you can to stay in the same place", is the experience of a growing number of people today I would have thought. Bowing out of that race, even for a time, certainly slows the pace of life, but it somehow allows for greater perspective on the question of *who* and *where* you want to be and why you were running in the first place. And that's progress in itself. It's definitely how I was feeling anyway, and how Rob appeared to me, infernal hair notwithstanding.

'You look different too, Herman,' Rob said. 'Happier.'

'Chips, my friend. Chips,' I replied.

'Do I look different?' Chris asked Rob, who gave him a quick glance.

'You look more tired.'

'Ah yes. Nettles, my friend. Nettles.'

The intertwining of legend and historicity around Hadrian's Wall peaks when you reach the hollow of Sycamore Gap and the famous tree seen in 1991's *Robin Hood: Prince of Thieves,* where Kevin Costner and Morgan Freeman fight it out for the prize of 'Least Effort Put Into Attempting a Foreign Accent', and both win.

That tree, overshadowing conqueror of the ruins of empire, had become almost as emblematic of northern hardiness as the wall itself over time, and not just because of Hollywood's influence. I say "had", because more recently of course the tree was cut down – "the chainsaw yawned, then breezed through hundreds of years of weather and kings and wars" (*The Holy Land*, Simon Armitage) – depriving the toppled skyline of its herald in a fit of wanton destruction.

But it's interesting what happens to martyrs. Maybe this is just wishful thinking, but it's possible that the act of being struck down might serve to knight the old dead tree with even stronger motif power: history becomes legend, legend becomes myth, and myth oftentimes tells the most powerful tale. In her poem *Sycamore Gap*,

Zoe Mitchell imagines a conversation between the tree and the wall in a grudging but enduring union:

> "I am a survivor, said the tree to the wall;
> I host the resurrection of each turning season."
> …
> "I stand alone, replied the wall."

And now, sadly, it always will. Because no commitment to endurance can survive something like a chainsaw. No resurrection is possible from that kind of absolutist decree. As the Armitage poem says, "There's a gap now in the Gap, where your face fits."

I didn't know any of this at the time, of course. I was just looking at the tree in awe, picking bits of Klaps from my teeth, as if we had all the time in the world.

CHAPTER 28

SOMETHING THERE IS THAT DOESN'T LOVE A WALL

The wall went ever on and on. And so, seemingly, did the number of tourists and part-timers splintering our progress.

A young girl with blonde hair was sitting in her dad's lap eating a sandwich, her brother racing around and shouting loudly for 'Reinforcements!' Another father was standing on top of the wall pointing out landmarks to his kids, while the mum fretted over their safety and told them to drink some water. Children were racing around screaming, families were laughing and playing, and all of them were getting in my way. Consequently, my enjoyment of the glorious wall was rapidly beginning to crumble. More on that in a second, but first a quick update on Rob. Fed up from looking like a flaming brand on legs and being accused of such (by me, but not just by me) he had drenched a beanie hat in water and was now wearing it under the sun's disdainful smirk, his face now exactly the same colour as his hair as he perspired at death-defying levels.

'I just need to wear it until we reach the forest,' he said repeatedly as a kind of mantra. With his predicament, Chris's distress at being told off and what was about to happen to me, we were all struggling a bit.

Back to what I was saying about my crumbling enjoyment of the wall, and how its vestigial magic was waning. And I think it has something to do with that lovely German word *Sehnsucht* – the longing or desire for something seemingly out of reach. I talked about *awe* when we were back at High Cup Nick, didn't I, and how it's a place that humans just can't stay for very long, a National Trust property of the emotions. Well, I'm circling back to that here.

Everyone experiences "magic". It starts as a young child when we listen to fairy stories and when we visit Santa's Grotto for the first time. It doesn't matter to us then that we're actually in Debenhams, that Father Christmas is an unemployed actor in a £2.99 costume or that Mum thinks she recognises him from an episode of *Casualty* – the magic of it is all that matters. That initial, inchoate wonder takes hold of us, and we take hold of it. When we get a little older, we begin to incarnate those stories ourselves, replaying them in local woods and spare bedrooms, reinvigorating them and making them real. It's what J.R.R.Tolkein called "the realisation of imagined wonder" – the inherent magic of those stories renders the incredible *credible*… for a little while.

But then over time it gets drummed out of us. We get called fantasists or daydreamers for holding on to such childish notions. We continue to perceive more than our senses can discover, but decide perhaps that it's impractical to continue our search for what cannot be empirically verified or scientifically proven. And so, fairy tales and magic and myth just get lumped together as 'fiction'; as something for children. We choose the reliability of pure matter over the stories that really matter.

But we never really lose that longing. It may be stolen from us, and we may become dull to it, but we don't ever lose it. "The world is full of magic things," wrote W.B. Yeats, "patiently waiting for our senses to grow sharper."

Matter, according to Quantum Physicist Bernard D'Espagnat, is simply "a veiled reality," while Arthur Machen in *The Great God Pan* wrote, "There is a real world, but it is beyond this glamour and this vision."

Perhaps there is a place where our senses will no longer be numb to long exposures of awe and wonder. I see no reason why there shouldn't be. Thirst can be quenched because there really are drinks. Darkness can be extinguished because there really is light. Maybe that longing we all have for a world beyond the physical isn't just some weird quirk of evolution. Maybe things like awe, wonder, beauty and myth simply flash open the curtain or pierce the veil. Maybe they are what Peter Kreeft called "doors in the walls of the world", acorn signposts to a far border town somewhere. And maybe, some day, we'll be old enough to start reading fairy tales again.

But it was not this day. The heat of the sun, the constant chirpiness of the tourists, the endless swelling and slumping of the ground: all of that demystified the magic of the place and turned it for me into a stubborn insensate barrier between where I was and where I wanted to be. I could still see the skill of the ancient craftsmanship and the magnitude of the surrounding pastures, but I stopped caring to see them – could bear it no longer. The wall ultimately became for me the epitome of the Covid experience: tracking and tracing a series of unflattened curves, trying to cross a threshold so close but so impenetrable, with the constantly thwarted hope that the end was just over the next rise, just down the next slope. Walking is really just a mobile self-isolation, a fluid extension of lockdown in terms of how detached you are from other people's lives. To arrive here after a fortnight on the journey I had largely needed to swap feelings for function, to let expediency bleach me of sentimentality. High Cup Nick and Malham Tarn and Cross Fell had flashed open the curtains for a while, but they had been closed soon enough in favour of a functional objectivity.

So, I'm not sure how much the continuous miles under a summer fire warped my emotional shield. Or whether the flights of fancy into chivalry and Hollywood had chiselled at my defensive wall. Or whether three weeks restricted to low-resolution Facetimes with my daughters had simply battered my weapons of self-preservation into blunted pulps. But the sight of all this familial conviviality speared me deep in the spirit, and punctured something that had been hitherto meticulously well-guarded.

Half a mile shy of Rapishaw Gap, where the path breaks left and leaves Roman Britain in its wake, I spotted a young lamb trapped on one side of a wall with its parent on the flipside, neither knowing how to reach the other and both of them calling out in distress. And I found myself simply unable to cope with that.

'How can we help them?' I asked a bystander, who was watching the scene sympathetically.

'It's illegal to manhandle them,' he informed me flatly.

The bleating got more desperate.

'We should open the gate down there,' I said.

'All gates need to be closed.'

'Then we lift the lamb over the wall.'

'We're not allowed.'

'They're in distress though.'

'Nothing we can do ab…'

'Can't you see that it wants to get to its child, you bloody idiot? Can't you see that – are you blind?!!'

The bystander backed away with his hands raised in submission, although Rob had jogged over and taken his hat off so it might have been that which caused the retreat. Chris came towards me, placed his hand on my shoulder and led me away down the hill, apologising to the man on my behalf. The bleating continued for as long as we were in earshot, and for who knows how long after that. But it wasn't my problem apparently.

Rob led the way into the forest, her gentle scents of pine and moisture swallowing us up, and soundproofing the cries of despair.

* * *

I chose to walk on my own for a couple of hours after that. Rob and Chris strode on together ahead of me, occasionally looking back to check I was still there, still moving forward. I was. The Pennine Way had chosen the perfect time for a change of scene.

For we were now in the great border forests, and the transformation of atmosphere was as complete as it was dramatic. Suddenly the crowds and the moorlands were gone. Suddenly it was dark and cool and secluded, the forest throned upon shadows. All was silent.

A light breeze gossipped lazily with the leaves. Our footsteps lost their power as we stepped over the springy pliant turf, the trees beckoning us out of the summer heat and into calm communion.

> "I enter here with furrowed brow and heavy-burdened heart;
> But little unseen hands are softly pressed
> Upon the frowns, and little unseen hands
> Tug at the burdens till they all are gone."
> *Amos Russell Wells, The Comfort of the Woods*

It was one like world handing over to the next, a revolving stage, and before long the turgid slog along Hadrian's Wall seemed remote, a thing that happened yesterday or last week or to someone else. Along the happy, peaceful forest paths we tracked, the subtle fragrances like incense, the woodland murmurs like a hymn. Nascent storylines and potential adventures threaded between the branches with each step and each new view. A faun flashed through the trees to the left and vanished. A squirrel darted away down a track, daring me to follow. On another day it might just have appeared a banal, characterless man-made forest; but for me, on this day, truly I had entered the land of Faerie.

We dipped in and out of the trees, over clumps of wood sorrel and ground-ivy, with mountain bike paths and logging roads intersecting in a sporadic cross-hatching. The Forestry Commission treats these synthetic forests with the same entitled hegemony that a teenager treats his parents' house, and between the tranquil stretches of welcoming woodland there were areas of grim desolation, bald spots in the weave, as though we had arrived in the immediate wake of some tragic sylvan purge. Logs lay in slaughtered mounds, severed branches stretched morbid twigs towards forlorn trunks, and a huge wagon came crashing past us, kicking up dust and bark shrapnel and forcing us to shield our faces. And rising above the spires of the trees, like some huge leviathan emerging from an ocean of timber, were the Cheviots. They may yet prove to be the great wronger of rights.

'It's a tough one today, isn't it?' Chris mused, as we sat eating our afternoon snack on a trio of hewn stumps that a previous walking group had clearly arranged for posterity. 'Harder than woodpecker lips.'

'I don't think I've experienced as many reversals of spirit in one day,' I agreed.

'I've never felt glumly exhilarated before,' Rob added. He was topless, his t-shirt a miasma of sweat and stickiness. He heaved it into a nearby copse and took a fresh one from his bergen. 'Only three days left – won't need it now.'

'What if an animal gets trapped in it?' Chris asked him.

'It's breathable,' Rob replied.

'Oh, that's fine then.'

The reversals of spirit and mood continued. We emerged from the woods at last and into a land of pastoral farms and sleepy homesteads. The sun was still high in the sky and the land lay prostrate beneath it, pummelled senseless by the unequivocal heat, with streams reduced to a trickle and fly-infested cow pats dried to Klaps. At least the woodland reprieve had prevented us from completely frazzling, but I could feel by touching the back of my neck that the sun had held me too long under the grill.

I hadn't packed any suntan lotion for the trip because I'm an Englishman, and you get used to the sun being that dad in a movie who always says he's coming to the violin recital but never quite makes it because of traffic or terrorists. Preparing for sunburn in the UK is like preparing for a lottery win – there's always a chance it could happen, but to act as though it actually will makes you look cretinous and psychotic.

It really was quite the day. Having traversed an ancient wall and a magical man-made forest, we were now invasively back in civilization, crossing private land and trespassing – seemingly – through people's back gardens, with wild foxgloves and tended rose bushes living side-by-side in an amenable truce.

At one farm (I think it was named Horneystead) a sign signalling refreshments necessitated an unscheduled stop. Chris would normally not have allowed this, breaking as it did with his disciplined two-hour stretches routine, but the presence of a couple of deck chairs, their faded rainbow seats bristling in the light breeze, was too good to turn down.

'I think we deserve it,' he said, lowering himself cautiously into one.

'I hope they have ice-creams,' Rob said. 'I would murder for a Calippo. I mean, I would literally kill a man.'

They didn't have ice-cream fortunately, but a ramshackle cold-store did have a kettle, an array of church biscuits (the Big Three – Bourbons, Custard Creams and plain Digestives) and a surprisingly well-stocked fridge.

'Don't have a beer,' Chris suggested, 'there's still plenty of yardage to cover before Bellingham.'

Rob and I agreed with that wisdom, and both had a beer, stowing an extra can each into side pockets and leaving a generous tip.

'I thought I said not to have beer,' Chris protested.

'This is for Alan,' I told him, popping the lid.

'This one, too,' Rob added, downing his in one.

'I think Alan might have a drinking problem,' Chris said, closing his eyes to the sun and to us.

The last three miles were as you'd expect them to be – the worst – with our collective resilience waning fast. A line of ash trees led us out onto a tarmacked road, then parallel to Black Burn and across Houxty Burn we wheezed, our feet tired, our bones decalcifying, three pairs of boots squeaking from dehydration and a one-size-fits-all anxiety. The relay station atop Shitlington Cragg (not a spelling mistake) signalled the final climb of the afternoon, and then it was down through the contours, past Shitlington Hall (yes, really) and on into Bellingham itself, with the sudden scream of rush-hour traffic adding yet another aspect to the day's multi-sensory experience.

Rob, beanie hat refitted now that we were back among the humans, was staying in the village and tramped off to find a place for dinner and a place that sold blades. That evening he would shave his head completely and for the first time ever, and return to us in the morning looking like he'd been punished by the Dutch resistance for fraternising with the Nazis.

Chris and I were overnighting at a guest house just off the local B-road and we found it easily enough – the Pennine Way basically led straight up the drive. A retired woman (who must have told me her name, but I didn't write it down or try hard enough to remember it) welcomed us to the place, which looked like a converted boarding school or a glammed-up military barracks, in the way that the '&' symbol on your keyboard is just '+' in a ball gown. The guest house sat on some decent acreage, lots of it wild and overgrown, and the host told us she lived alone at the single detached house on the site.

'So let me know if you have *any* problems,' she told us.

'I'm not sure my Dad was ever proud of me,' Chris said earnestly.

'I just mean if you need an extra towel,' the woman said kindly. 'But would you like to talk about it? I used to be a counsellor before I retired.'

'I was just joking,' Chris replied with a smile.

'Oh, well, you know where I am.' She patted him on the arm and hurried off to tend to another guest. There were a good number of tenants milling about, nipping in and out of shower blocks and shuttling stuff between rooms, but none of them looked happy or sad enough to have walked the line that we had followed today.

'Any new injuries?' Chris enquired, after we had collapsed onto the functional-but-comfortable beds in our twin room.

'No physical ones, no,' I replied, and he nodded.

‘A savage enough pilgrimage, hey?’

‘Savage enough,’ I agreed.

‘But it looks like you’ll definitely finish it now, though.’

‘It looks that way, yes. The Four Horseman have all been unsaddled – just need to keep my nerve and my footing for a while longer. And you’re 22 miles closer to John O’Groats.’

‘And with the whole of Scotland still standing against me,’ Chris said, massaging his leg. ‘Plus, my knee is killing me.’

The signs of wear and tear were showing everywhere. My rucksack had been subject to multiple snags through the branches of the otherwise beneficent Wark Forest, and the constant pounding on dry ground had caused the toe of my right boot to detach from its base a little. I would need to do something about that, and Chris might need a new knee, but they were tomorrow problems.

‘If you don’t mind,’ Chris said, stripping down to his underwear, ‘I’m going to have a shower and take things a little Oriental.’

He meant *Duolingo*, but I wish he’d been clearer about that earlier because it would have shortened the awkward, leaden silence which followed.

‘Don’t forget to go for your counselling session,’ I said, distractedly trying to find a spot of carpet with some phone signal. ‘All included in the price, presumably.’

‘Probably not, hey,’ he replied, considering his next words carefully. ‘I’ve heard of getting your money’s worth, but that – *that* – would be ridiculous.’

‘OK, fine, you can have that one,’ I said. ‘A rule of three and a call-back. Nicely played, sir.’ I looked Chris directly in the eye and slow-clapped him into the bathroom.

I also needed a shower, probably several back-to-back, to rid myself of those wet and dry odours of far-travelling. I groaned off my bed, picked Alan up from where he was lying spread-eagled with exhaustion, grabbed the famous Ben Sherman t-shirt which Kristine had folded into my pack, and wandered off to find the shower block. We would need to order a takeaway, too, with our muscles now sunk in a morass of lactic acid and the odds of making the short walk into the village not even worth the bet. The quad onto which all the lodges faced seemed like the best space for some phone reception. I opened up the recent calls list and pressed the top one for "My Girls". It failed to connect. I tried to ring three times but each time, after a whirring and stammering, the "Call Failed" icon flashed up on the screen. I typed out a text telling them I'd ring them later, but it came back as "Message Not Sent". I gritted my teeth and walked off towards the showers.

Somewhere on the hillside above me, a sheep bleated.

CHAPTER 29

WINE IN WHISKEY GLASSES

When I looked up, I hadn't expected to see a woman standing in the window. She was looking down at me curiously, as a counsellor might, but she didn't wave or smile and perhaps she didn't see me. But then she left the window where she had been framed and made a slow descent to find me.

The door to the single house swung open and she came out into the garden where I was sitting with a pencil and a pad – which had sentences that couldn't quite couple with other sentences, which was annoying – and she sat down quite close to me and brought an over-full carafe of wine in to land on the wood, with two whiskey glasses inscribed with "To the happy couple" and a date on them.

'Wine in whiskey glasses?' I asked, and she said she didn't know the difference and shrugged as though she didn't care, though I think she might have done. But I stopped writing, and we started talking together as the early evening of the early summer, which makes everything pleasant and makes everyone feel safe, enshrined us.

She was maybe 20 years older than me, recently widowed as it turned out, and it showed in her face and in the way she walked. I was recently divorced – had been forever, it seemed – and perhaps that showed in my face too, although I didn't talk about it unless someone asked, and even then, not very far or very deep.

'The garden is always growing,' she said, flourishing a hand. 'I can't keep up with it.'

It was more like a meadow than a garden, and it was wild and quite wondrous as most of Northumberland is, a good place to sit and write stories about new things and old things; things that grew wild or got tended to so they didn't.

'Would you like a cigarette?' she asked, and I said I didn't smoke, which hadn't always been true and I think she caught that somewhere in my expression.

'You may if you like,' she said, pouring us both another glass of whiskey-wine, which was cheap and past its best but it was there and it was free. And so I did have a cigarette, but only one, and then another one after that, watching the smoke drift wherever it wanted and then disappear into somewhere or nowhere. And we talked for a long time under the setting of the sun, the shadows creeping like soft hands over patches of warm grass and up the trunks of trees, and darkness welling up in the corners of the world. And she told me about how the garden used to be when he was still here, and complained about the Japanese Knotweed, saying, 'It kills gardens, as you know', when I didn't know that at all.

And I told her about the story I was writing, and how I couldn't find the right ending and I was using too many adverbs which were killing it.

'Like Japanese Knotweed,' she said, and I laughed at that. It was just nice to have a conversation that wasn't about walking, and so I kept it up as long as I could, watering it with questions and more wine. In the morning before I left I would help her move a table, and I would tell her how I had started writing another story and it had Japanese Knotweed in it, and she would say 'Thank you' without exclamation marks.

But for now we sat in the meadow-garden, the two of us, and drank our wine and smoked our cigarettes, and talked like people who haven't lost their husbands and still have their wives. And she told me what starlings sound like, though I've since forgotten, and

I told her about my books and she listened even though she hadn't asked.

But then the light started to decay and the sky darkened and she said, 'I'm going up to bed now. Don't stay up too late.' And I said I wouldn't, but that I might sit here a little longer and let the edge of night sharpen my pencil. So she took a match and lit the small table lantern for me, and then she went back inside and the blackness submerged everything and the lantern was powerless.

And the woman at the window looked out towards me from the fond light of her bedroom, but she wouldn't have seen me, I don't think. And then she closed her curtains which had been open for a while, and it was as though she wasn't there either.

And I'm sorry that I've forgotten her name.

* * *

I walked back to my room, where Chris would now be snoring and dreaming of home. It was still too hot, the sun's legacy abiding, and a young mother (I remember her name was Samantha) was rummaging around in the boot of her car, looking for something to quell the sound of a baby crying inside one of the lodges.

'Anything I can help with?' I asked, confident that I couldn't.

She hadn't heard me coming and looked a bit shocked, but relaxed when she saw my bare feet and Gonzo from *The Muppets* pyjamas.

'No, no – thank you though. Our little boy wants his toy, but I think we've forgotten to pack it.'

'Oh no, disaster,' I said with real sympathy, well aware of the fall-out from misplacing a favourite teddy.

'The car is usually full of stuffed toys,' she continued, 'but my partner must have had a clear-out before we came away.'

'Have you tried whiskey?' I asked.

'For him or for us?' Samantha replied, her head deep in a footwell. 'I just need him to stop crying – we don't want to be *those* parents, keeping everyone awake.'

'I don't think the sound is that obvious,' I said, lying – it sounded like someone was practising necromancy in there. 'Sorry I can't help more.'

'Well, not unless you carry a cuddly badger around with you, no.'

'No, sorry, I… *Unless…*'

I had made the word 'unless' sound unnecessarily creepy and she asked, 'Unless what?' with understandable caution.

'Unless… unless wait there a minute and I'll be back.'

'Erm, OK?'

With great haste but less speed I went back to the room. I returned, as you will have predicted, with the finest stuffed fox to ever walk the Pennine Way.

'You could try this,' I said, holding Alan out to her like a commemorative sword. Samantha didn't look that convinced or grateful, but decided it was better than nothing. For the next few minutes I stood outside, pacing around, hoping to hear the sound of a baby not crying, like a cruel 1940s father in a maternity ward. To say that the baby was totally soothed would be fanciful fiction, but there did seem to be a reduction in the levels of distress. Samantha came back out into the floodlit car park to give me the good news.

'He looks intrigued rather than pleased, but it's taken his attention away from crying for a bit.'

'That's a relief,' I said.

'Can I ask? Is it actually a doorstop?'

'Indeed he is. £12.99 from Dunelm Mill. His name is Alan.'

'Well, thanks to Alan. We'll obviously give him back to you in the morning. Thanks to you, too – you're a HERO.'

I laughed incredulously. 'I am a long way from being that, Samantha.'

'That's not what your t-shirt claims,' she said.

‘Eh? Oh no, this just says HER…’

But it didn’t. Not anymore. Looking down at my post-shower change of clothing and the t-shirt that was ready to be thrown away, I saw that where there had been empty space there was now something else: a badge. A circle of beautifully woven fabric and exhilarating flame-red stitching displayed the words ‘I climbed Pen-y-Ghent’ in fine bold lettering. She had sewn it in perfect alignment with the other letters, just after the ‘R’.

‘My goodness, she…’

‘Did you not know about that?’ Samantha asked.

‘No,’ I said. ‘Someone else put it there. But I’m glad you told me. Goodnight.’

After the longest of days, finally I went to bed. And I would sleep well that night. But not before I had lifted my eyes to the clouds with a baffled smile and a shake of the head.

‘God bless you, Mary Poppins,’ I said.

God bless you.

Day 14
Bellingham to Byrness
15 miles

"When on my country walks I go,
I never am alone:
Though whom 't were pleasure then to know
Are gone, and you are gone;
From every side discourses flow."
Herbert P. Horne, Amico Suo

"Blessed are they who feel like pilgrims and strangers in this life, and whose best things are all to come."
J. C. Ryle

CHAPTER 30
TRAVEL-STAINED BEGGARS

It was 7:45am and my eyelids were determined to stay shut for a few minutes longer. They would ideally have liked to declare their own bank holiday and stay closed for the whole day, but the insistent pinging from my bedside table threw wide their shutters and declared the morning open for business. Whether through a shift in the weather or a delinquent satellite showing up for work after its doctor's note expired, a window of phone signal had abruptly opened up and messages were now diving down into Bellingham like seagulls on chips. And all of them were from Margot:

"How are you getting on, dear?"

"Nearly there?"

"We miss you."

"Is this the right number for you, Andy?"

"Hope you're ok!"

'Can you throw that phone against a wall, please?' Chris asked grouchily from his bed. 'And how are you so popular? I've got signal too but nobody has texted me.'

'It's just Margot,' I said. 'Every single one of those messages is from Margot.'

I was too muggy-eyed to be texting, but the haranguing needed to stop before Margot made Geoffrey finance a search party.

"Hello Margot," I typed back. "We are still alive and getting there. 15 moles today…" (Send)

"...Moles..." (Send)

"...Molested..." (Send)

It's my view that all communication of any kind should be illegalised before two cups of coffee, and the preceding only adds weight to my case. Almost instantly the phone rang.

'Hi Margot,' I bleared.

'What have you been doing, Andy? Those poor moles!'

I explained to her that I meant miles, and that no moles had been molested in the making of this trip – nor would they be.

'Well, thank goodness for that, dear,' she replied. 'I thought you might have succumbed to something. How are you?'

'Well enough, thank you. We're in Bellingham – off to our final accommodation tonight.'

'Oh yes, that's right. Haven't you done well? And Geoffrey says hello, don't you Geoffrey?'

'Don't I what?' I could hear Geoffrey from a different wing of their house.

'You say hello to Andy – I've told you I was calling him. (She lowered her voice conspiratorially) ...He's not in a good way, Andy. He's had awful diarrhoea since we got back.'

Geoffrey was shouting something now.

'I'm sorry to hear that,' I replied.

'The doctor needs a doctor, as we often say. And how are your lovely wife and girls, anyway? You must be so excited to see them soon, and you will remember to give them those badges we bought you, won't you?'

'Of course. I haven't forgotten.'

'Lovely. Well, we just wanted to check in. Glad you're all OK. We're heading back to London today, and you must come down to visit us when you can – and bring the family!'

'That sounds like a lovely idea,' I said.

'Goodbye then, dear. And all our love to Chris and Rob.'

She hung up before Geoffrey could complain about his love being dished out willy-nilly via an intermediary.

'What's the news?' Chris asked.

'Geoffrey's got the runs,' I said.

'Wow, lucky man. I can barely walk.'

Neither could I. But I had only had 40 miles of it left to do – a final three days to carry around this mobile hermitage – and I was determined not to be waylaid now. I was starting to dream of a life after this. Of lounging on a settee for hours in front of films, only rising to urinate and sometimes not even then. Of browsing the musty shelves in those old second-hand bookshops, where the owner is mad and decrepit and nobody knows how he or it survives but they both somehow do. Of going out to dinner in a pair of trousers with fewer than nine pockets. Of not smelling permanently and ever-so-slightly of sheep droppings.

Soon. I could visualise the finish line. I'd come close to breaking on a few occasions and yesterday had been the hardest day physically and emotionally, but the mercies of hope and rest are new each morning, and here I was singing Enya in the shower.

Confidence is a weird thing – you go up the stairs but down in the lift. But a sports team that wins 14 matches on the bounce expects to win the next one, and it was like that for me. I was the most aching I had ever been, and I was invincible.

There was a moment of slight paranoia that morning when from the other side of the bathroom door it sounded like Chris was putting a curse on me, but when I leapt out to confront him he was simply finishing his Japanese homework, and what I mistook for a hex was merely a handy phrase enquiring where to find a museum.

Alan's sudden face at the window then provided a genuine jump scare, as Samantha knocked and entered (having checked our willy-nillies were first under wraps), bringing her baby son to say thank you for last night's rescue operation.

'It wasn't a total success,' she said. 'But we're going home this evening, so I think we got away with it.' She handed me a pack of chocolate-covered rice cakes as a reward. 'Sorry it's not very fancy.'

'On the contrary,' I replied. 'For walkers, this is a feast.'

Samantha departed happily, taking her son with her – who hadn't actually said thank you at all, but who started crying again the moment they left without Alan. Babies: will their reign of terror never end?

'I didn't realise Alan had been making friends,' Chris said.

'There's a lot you don't know about Alan,' I replied, opening the rice cakes.

'Hitotsu chōdai, please.'

'I don't know what that means.'

'I said I would like one of those.'

I claimed I still didn't understand and ate both the rice cakes in front of him.

I was at 85% completion. The Four Horsemen had been defeated and the longest and dullest days were behind us. In fitting tribute, our serendipitous trinity would be joined today by Kevin, a softly spoken Boltonian who the newly-shaven-headed Rob had met on his campsite. Chris and I rolled waggons into Bellingham while the village was still putting its shoes and socks on, and met the pair at St. Cuthbert's Church for the antepenultimate leg of the walk.

Sitting on the banks of the North Tyne, Bellingham is a beautiful village – the kind of place that some Americans think all of England still looks like – with ivy-adorned stone cottages sitting around every corner and the sound of waterfalls just out of sight. The presence of St. Cuthbert's Church and St. Cuthbert's Well mark the fact that you're now in the realm of the Patron Saint of Northumbria, the "Wonder Worker of Britain" and arguably the most popular British saint prior to the death of Thomas a-Becket. While it's likely that at least some of the miracles and dream appearances attributed to Cuthbert have been enhanced or invented over time, what can't be in doubt is that his ministry of reconciliation across the North East during the 7th century served to unify a later sense of *Englishness* between Saxon Wessex and the Dane-populated North – and largely due to the following account.

One day, early in the reign of King Alfred, who was stranded in the marshes around Athelney having been driven out of Wessex by the invading Norsemen, it is said that the king found a road-weary traveller standing at the door of the house in which he had taken refuge. Not having much to spare, Alfred nevertheless offered the man bread and wine… only to find later that the whole loaf had reappeared in the pantry. That night, the travel-stained beggar appeared to Alfred in a dream, only this time in a bishop's vestments and with golden rings on his fingers. He said that he was St. Cuthbert of Lindisfarne, and told Alfred to rise early in the morning and wind his great horn three times. By three o'clock in the afternoon, the figure said, 500 men would have rallied to his banner, and in one week Alfred would have all England for his realm.

And so it happened. Three times Alfred blew his great horn, and seemingly from nowhere 500 warlike men gathered to his side. A week later the army of the Danish leader Guthrum was driven off in dismay at Edington, and Alfred regained his kingdom.

I'm 85% convinced that it's apocryphal, but as I have previously noted, the way we tell stories has power. History may well be written by the winners, but other stories are written by the losers: to give them a second chance at winning, or at least to mitigate the loss. Certainly, the idea of a travel-stained beggar in need of food was something we could all identify with. Our guest house didn't serve breakfast and there were no shops where we were headed, so we converged on the no-fuss, no-frills Bellingham bakery to 'carboload'.

Kevin, the incoming addition to our merry band, wasn't strictly a Pennine Wayer and seemed uncertain where he had come from or where he wanted to end up. He had been made redundant from his job as a car salesman a week prior, and so he was 'just walking'. And good for him. He was affable and easy-going and had several tattoos along his arms, one of which just said 'Kevin'.

'What's the significance of that one?' I asked, pointing at a menacingly coiled dragon on his left arm.

'In the Orient, a dragon symbolises supernatural power,' he replied. 'Hidden knowledge and untamed chaos and the like.'

'Interesting,' I said. 'And this tattoo on your other arm?'

'That's my name. Kevin.'

'I see. Nice to meet you, Kevin.'

I scraped my bergen into the bakery and bought a pork pie that, in the local dialect, was called a 'Geordie Pie', and also splashed out on something called a 'Geordie Pasty' – the flagrantly usurping names hinting that Wessex-Norsemen relations had re-deteriorated somewhat over the last thousand years. It was 'nae bother' for Rob though, who appeared to have bought one of everything and was now finding space for it all in his rucksack.

'Do you think it'll rain today,' he asked, rummaging around.

'Perhaps,' said the woman baker. 'It's June.'

'Kevin,' said Kevin, holding up his arm.

I stored the sham pastie in my rucksack for lunchtime, then ate it straightaway like James Bond and went back inside to buy three more, followed by Gaviscon from the pharmacy next door. Chris opened a pack of energy tablets and I asked if I could have one to gee me up for the morning's walk.

'Sorry,' he said, 'I only speak Japanese.'

'You're speaking English now though, aren't you?'

'I don't know what you're saying, I'm afraid.'

'Oh. Touché.'

We climbed out of the North Tyne valley before heartburn set in and onto moorlands of lush, knee-deep heather, set amid a landscape that was so serene and so self-assured. Gone were the Devil's Dykes and Bleaklows and Black Hills of the early days, replaced by Deer Play and Padon Hill and Sugartop Farm, almost onomatopoeic in their pleasantry. There was something in the air that hinted at a downturn in the weather, but I hadn't seen rain for a week and the hailstorm outside Diggle seemed like a lifetime ago. (NB. I was tempted to say that the weather had been 'nothing short of miraculous', but it *had* been short of miraculous – it had just been really nice weather.) The pages of the various walking guides had been stuffed with dire warnings of capricious climates and murky, impenetrable morasses, but the only drop I'd felt in the past seven days turned out to be a lapwing weeing on me out of spite, while the foreboding bogs had been baked into springy earth trampolines, cushioning and reprieving my feet between horrendous stretches of Corpse Road and gravel path. From waterproof everythings and soaking-wet spirits early on, my raincoat had spent the last week stuffed at the bottom of my bergen – a joy only slightly diminished by the discovery of a mangled banana in the pocket of it that morning. Never eat fruit, is the lesson.

Today's destination was Kielder Forest and its frontier village of Byrness – the final settlement before Kirk Yetholm. Studying the maps back in Edale, Kielder had assumed a mystical quality – a magic faraway wood whose canopy was the gateway to Scotland and the end of the quest. I would see it later that day. We trudged on as always, over concrete slabs and wooden planks and past grouse butts, our conversation levels more liberal than usual and with an undercurrent of ticking anticipation. For once I was enjoying the view whilst walking it, unbuckling the straps of self-preservation and caution a little and giving my hopes room to breathe. I stopped to read a painted stone, sitting on top of a small cairn of gathered rocks, which read, "In memory of Thomas Hillingthwaite, who loved this part of the country but who won't, now, return." The final line of a sweet story that most people would never read.

The steep ascent towards Redesdale Forest took the wind out of us and was loathe to give it back, but it was a dolly compared to Jacob's Ladder or Tan Hill. The Pennine Way is like a barium meal for your claim to endurance: each day you leave your comfort zone and set off in search of a new one, and everything in between just has to be dealt with. What you need is an imperturbable lack of surprise and the chiselled art of patience – and preferably, of course, boots that aren't flapping wildly at the gums. Mine were, sadly, or at least one of them was, the toe and the sole now at complete odds with each other and sending up comical clown-like slapping sounds every time my right foot touched the ground. I had said yesterday that it was a problem for future me, but now I was future me and I had done absolutely nothing about it. Where was Kristine when you actually needed her?

On the outskirts of Redesdale, we met a rare traveller going against the grain and doing the walk North to South. He came down the slope towards us and I could tell instinctively that he would need to lighten his pack if he wanted to finish the walk, and that his expression would need substantially more flint before he reached Cross Fell and the Pen-who-must-not-be-named. He stopped to talk to us, glad of the rest, and he looked like the guy in a zombie movie who has been fatally bitten but is trying to keep it a secret because he wants to see his family one last time. His ability to be both hugely unprepared and grossly overweight displayed a real tenacity of ignorance – he was the sort of man, perhaps, who'd chosen to walk the Pennine Way having once been blackberry picking and concluding as a result that he could survive alone in the wild.

'I'm just a raw recruit, not a veteran like you guys,' he said coyly over a Geordie pasty, which I had broken into chunks and was sharing out like communion bread. 'Any tips?'

'Keep your chin up,' said Chris.

'One foot in front of the other,' Rob added.

'The pain *is* the healing,' I offered.

'Pardon?' he asked.

'Chin up, one foot in front of the other,' I said.

'Oh, OK great. Cheers, fellas. Best keep going, eh?'

'He won't make it,' Chris said, after the poor bloke had lolloped off towards Bellingham waving martyrdom like a chequered flag.

'Not a f****** hope in hell,' Rob agreed.

'He ate a lot of pasty,' Kevin said.

'Hmmmm,' I added wisely. 'Hmmmm.'

Redesdale Forest is actually pretty rubbish if you don't mind me saying: a dull, homogeneous army of pines planted in well-drilled regiments, much of which had been obliterated by the Forestry Commission's need for furniture. And it was here, after much hesitation and flirtation, that the rain finally began to fall – and with incredible force – like the person who turns up late to the staff Christmas do and downs shot after shot of whatever is cheapest, just to catch up.

But who cared?! Certainly not us. We unstowed our raincoats, zipped ourselves up, and strode through the decimated coniferous city like the veterans we had become. The rain might be biblical, but accordingly I would forgive it. I turned my face to the sky and opened my mouth, letting the pounding droplets spring clean my weary features.

'Do you want this banana, Alan?' I asked, opening a pocket.

No thank you, sire, it looks like roadkill, I imagined him saying.

When, a few hours later, we finally crossed the river Rede and entered Kielder Forest itself, it was a different story. By this point the rain had ceased as abruptly as it had begun, the sun dispersing the clouds and deciding there would be no further silliness, thank you very much. But the air had that wonderful vigour now that follows rainfall – the cuddle after the tears – and the trees caught and compressed it and fed it into our grateful, willing nostrils.

'Do we need to talk about your shaven head?' Chris asked Rob over the current bout of pasties.

'Not if you don't want to go swimming in the river,' Rob said, as aggressively as any man can when he has puff pastry around his mouth.

'I'll leave it, then,' Chris demurred. 'I've done my cardio for the day.'

'We do need to talk about Kevin, though,' I said, coming to a sudden halt. 'As in… where is he?'

The three of us stopped and looked about ourselves with mild concern.

'Oh blimey, you're right,' Chris said. 'I'd forgotten he was with us.'

'When did either of you last see him?'

None of us could quite remember. This was negligent to say the least. We had been so used to walking as a trio that the complete disappearance of another human being had gone completely unnoticed. 'Kevin?' we shouted, 'Kevin?', and then 'KEVIN?!', but to no avail. One minute he had been with us, the next he was gone. He hadn't said goodbye, hadn't notified us of his absence. He had just decided, presumably, to go in a different direction.

'Perhaps he'll appear to us in a dream like St. Cuthbert,' I suggested.

'I think he just didn't f****** like us,' Rob said. 'Or was getting p***** off with the sound of your clown shoes, Herman.'

'I couldn't blame him.'

'Imagine not even knowing he'd vanished, though,' Chris said guiltily. 'We'd make terrible detectives, wouldn't we?'

We all agreed, and I bit sagely into another Geordie pasty.

We never saw Kevin again, and I still don't have the foggiest idea what happened to him. My only consolation is that, in the event where he'd possibly taken a fall and suffered temporary amnesia, his tattooed arm would have offered at least some clue as to his identity. I have taken real solace from that, I can tell you.

* * *

Aside from Kevin's group shunning, the only thing that rankled me slightly amid all the pantomiming on Day 14 happened because of what someone *didn't* say. Three miles short of Byrness, with all the pasties devoured and my clown boot taking performative hubris to new levels, a lady walking her labrador along a logging track smiled as we passed her.

'Afternoon!' I said. '250 miles down, nearly there.'

I was waiting for her to look impressed, to ask dumbfounded if we were walking the *whole* of the Pennine Way, and then to overwhelm us with praise and perhaps some small trinkets when we said, 'Verily, Madame'.

'OK,' she said instead.

OK? Was that it? Was that all she could muster? I hadn't slogged from Derbyshire through all terrains and every weather just to be told that it was OK! Back in Edale (before I met Jon at the church) a lad serving in the Penny Pot café couldn't begin to fathom all those miles of walking over hills, while people we met and passed early on the journey were astonished, appreciative, applauding. Now here we were close to the finish line, and it was suddenly only OK?

'Can you believe that?' I asked Rob and Chris, scratching my lusty beard with irritation. 'No "Well done", no "Would you autograph my dog for me?"' I was pretty vexed.

'When you live by the Scottish border,' Rob said, 'reaching the Scottish border isn't that impressive.'

'She probably sees people like us every day,' Chris added with a light shrug. 'No big deal.'

And that was probably fair, wasn't it? No matter how unlikely or improbable something seems, if you observe it on a regular basis then it becomes ordinary and even normative. That woman never met the thousands of people who take the road of good intentions from Edale and end up in hell. She never strolled past the gibbering wrecks who get Pennine Wayed on Day 3 and are medevaced back to base camp. She only met the victors. Whatever trauma and anguish grips you mid-walk, it has largely subsided by this stage – the pain has been negotiated with, the fear has been assuaged. It is no longer visible. It reminds me of the anthropic principle – the hypothesis that we can only say a life-permitting universe is unlikely because we are alive in the universe to say it. So it is with the Pennine Way: the higher you go, the less impressed people are because, naturally, if you hadn't done it then you wouldn't be there for them to damn you with faint praise. Still, I thought we deserved better.

Terse natives notwithstanding, entering Kielder Forest was like slipping into Lothlorien. Whatever fabulistic or mythic idea I had conceived of it over the upleading days, my *Sehnsucht* was decisively satisfied on arrival. And for the first time on the entire Pennine Way, the last three miles were actually the best: the warm moisture of resin; the lapping of the stream; the brief sighting of a stag crossing the path. Smoke rising listlessly above the trees to the right told us we were soon to enter Byrness, while a carpet of pine needles chaperoned our tiny band, bequeathing the last of their scent and naming us as sole benefactors. Rob and I became giddy, drunk on woodland toxins and adrenaline, snapping inane selfies and taking David Attenborough-style videos of Alan with accompanying commentary.

'And there he is, Alanus Rex. Never before has this species been seen in the wild this far north. A rare sight indeed.'

Everything we could imagine seemed real. We were envisaging the Forest View Inn, only a mile away now, as a kind of mythological tavern. A buxom wench with elven ears would serve us buttered mead, while a sly goblin-type fellow plucked at a lyre in the corner before being arrested by hooded men and sent off for execution. We were old enough to start reading fairy stories again.

The reality of the accommodation was more mundane – how could it not be? – the Forest View Inn being nothing more than three terraced houses from the old logging community knocked together. But it was still havenous, and there *was* beer on arrival and a range of dinner options, and a fitting welcome from Oli and Laura (the new owners). *They* at least understood the momentousness of a travel-stained beggar reaching their front door.

'I'll show you the rooms when you're ready,' Oli said, 'but let me get you a drink first. And there's a drying room for your boots and wet clothes over there. Take a seat in the garden and I'll be back in a sec, and relax – you've all earned it.'

We peeled off our boots and stuffed them with newspaper, then strutted about the garden for a bit, posturing with obscene levels of masculinity, before reclining on the patio chairs and drinking beer as if we were being paid to advertise it. Laura was busy preparing chicken fajitas (the married couple alternated the chef duties) so Oli returned and sat with us in the sunshine, drawing out our excitement, massaging our inflated egos, asking the right questions and letting us answer them. I texted Margot, Vino, Phil, Jon and Kristine with a blanket message: "Five o'clock and all's well. Byrness reached. Two days and counting!"

"Well done!" came the blanket response.

"Don't mess it up now, Kindy!" Vino typed in addition.

The fat lady hadn't yet sung. The Cheviots awaited, their "snowy summits old in story" (Tennyson), and three of the hardest climbs along the whole route were still to be tackled. But for now my smile would need to be surgically removed. The very thing that had seemed so fraught with frightful problems a fortnight ago was now merely a minor chore, a task on a to-do list.

The American writer, John Cheever, wrote in his journals that he was homesick for places he had never been. He had obviously never walked across the Yorkshire Dales, stood atop Malham Cove or downed a pint of ale on the edge of Kielder Forest. I had though, and as I sat in the fug of my own fumes, watching what looked like an eagle soar languidly overhead, and with a malty beer still halfway up its glass, a remarkable thought occurred to me…

I would be very sad when all this was over.

Day 15
Byrness to Windy Gyle
14 miles

"Though nothing can bring back the hour
Of splendor in the grass, of glory in the flower;
We will grieve not, rather find
Strength in what remains behind…"
William Wordsworth, Splendour in the Grass

"Never say goodbye because goodbye means going away and
going away means forgetting."
J.M. Barrie, Peter Pan

CHAPTER 31
RHAPSODY ON A WINDY DAY

In front of me stretched a taut tightrope along the loneliest peaks in the least populated part of England. Somewhere over yonder the hills were kilted with tartan and the mountain streams ran with malt. Through the chill morning air I could smell Scotland, but the cloud formation of battleship grey suggested it wasn't planning to make me feel that welcome, laddy.

I had slept badly. Not because the bed in my double room wasn't comfortable – because it was, very – but because the Dopamine which had flooded my system at the end of yesterday had decided to party through the night unabated and hadn't invited Melatonin along. I wasn't feeling stressed as such (that party pooper Cortisol wasn't on the guest list, either) but I did feel strangely hungover and lethargic. I needed to invite the Endorphin family over for breakfast, and ask them to bring Oxytocin round for a cuddle while they were at it. Alan was still face down and fast asleep on the other side of the double, so I padded down to breakfast in my socks to find my friends.

Today would be a day of goodbyes; of severing those little soul ties that had been soldered by synchronised steps and shared struggle. Next to 'sorry' and (for Americans certainly) 'Worcestershire', goodbye is perhaps the hardest word to say – and I was not looking forward to saying it to anyone.

The dining room was full, the Forest View Inn sizzling with walkers ready to shunt off at various compass points, everyone enjoying sausage and coffee and comradeship, a mixed grill of excitement and nerves reminiscent of a Hogwarts end-of-term feast.

Rob and Chris were seated by the window with an American couple in their fifties named Glenn and Madeline, and I squeezed in to join them with standard English beg pardons. The pair were travelling from John O'Groats to Land's End by motorhome (which really annoyed Chris), tangentialising whenever the urge took them or to visit the places from which their forebears had originated.

'It's been like coming back to the Motherland,' Glenn said with affection. 'We loved Cornwall, obviously, and Dartmoor was swell. Bath was something else – probably our favorite place – and, boy, too many places to mention.'

'And Hebden Bridge, hun,' Madeline put in.

'Man, Hebden Bridge! The lid's off the cookie jar there, huh?'

'It certainly is,' I said, nodding vigorously both in agreement and to shake the image of Werner's tiny penis which was once again plastered across my mind's eye.

'And you guys have walked everything we've driven, is that right?' Madeline asked.

'Just him,' I said, pointing at Chris. 'Rob and I only started at Edale.'

'Well, that's *quite* good,' Glenn said.

It was fortunate that I'm friendly with enough Americans to know that when they say 'quite good', they don't mean it in the way British people do – as in, 'not very good at all' – but in the way we might still say 'quite wonderful'. Our achievement was better than quite good, thank you. Better than just OK, stupid lady with her stupid labrador and stupid anthropic principle.

Oli and Laura were shuttling around tending to the myriad breakfasters, refilling hot plates and replenishing milk jugs, the Florence Nightingales of the hospitality world. There simply wasn't anywhere else to stay indoors for miles around, and the new hosts didn't want to be culpable of letting people depart without at least a full stomach.

'What was that strange meal you had in Warsesstershire, hun?' Madeline then asked her husband between mouthfuls of scrambled egg. She was dressed in shades of summer green, while Glenn looked like he was ready to hunt big game from the back of a Jeep.

'A plough man, I think it was,' he said. 'Really odd, just bread and loose cheese and onions in vinegar.'

'It's pronounced Ploughmuns,' I said, not wishing to patronise. 'And Wusstershuh.'

'It just looked like leftovers, though,' Glenn persisted. 'Who would want that?'

I tried to explain that you don't eat a Ploughman's because of its constituent parts – you eat it because it makes you feel like a farmer in a Thomas Hardy novel, which is a good enough reason for doing anything. A Ploughman's, very much like honest English trifle, is a *gestalt* food – the overall effect is greater than the sum of its parts. Glenn wasn't buying it, but then I don't really buy baseball or taking the 'o' out of humour, so let's agree to disagree.

Just before 9am, a motley crew of hikers and bikers gathered for photos outside the inn, with plenty of handshaking and faretheewelling and a gratuitous *Auld Lang Syne* for good measure. Who wouldn't take a cup of kindness yet, after all? A few yards away sat the A68, the last road I would cross before the finish line, with just the occasional car scooting even-temperedly along it.

'Can you imagine being hit by a lorry as you crossed?' Rob asked. Unlike me, he wouldn't be returning to the Forest View that evening and so had smuggled out a bewildering six extra sausages in a massive napkin. 'To get this far, cross the last road and then *squish?*'

'Of course I can imagine it,' I said. 'That would be just like me.'

We were both trying to avoid the elephant in the room, who was standing behind us in his wide-brimmed Stetson, ready to leave.

'OK, chaps,' he said sadly. 'I'm afraid that the fellowship must now split.'

I turned reluctantly about, clasped Chris by the shoulders and looked him in the eye.

'I don't want you to go.'

He smiled. 'It's been fun, hasn't it?'

'No it ******* hasn't,' Rob said. 'but it's been *good.*'

'Indeed,' Chris replied. 'West Highland Way next year sometime, perhaps? Get the band back together.'

I nodded and sighed. This was tough. I had heard of parting being such sweet sorrow… but this was ridiculous. The man in the Stetson slung his pack and walked off into the sunrise. The eidolic mist rising from the early morning forest framed his departure with angelic liminality.

He wouldn't make it all the way to John O'Groats – not in one go, anyway. A sprained ankle just shy of Fort William (1,000 miles in) barricaded his path of glory temporarily, but he would return to the trail in the autumn and polish off the remainder. I would miss my genial, irrepressible mountain goat of a friend. Of all the wayfarers I had met on the path, he had helped me most of all.

I would also need to do my own navigation now that I couldn't tailgate Chris, but then I was a big boy now I supposed. The fresh notch into which my belt was slotted however hinted that I was actually a much smaller boy around the midriff. This was splendid news, and would ensure that when people started talking about 'the elephant in the room' I might become less defensive.

'And then there were two,' Rob said stolidly. 'You got everything you need?'

'Think so, yeah,' I replied. 'Shall we?'

I had come so far across a spectrum of meanings – not least the literal 230 miles of seismic yomping up the map. Yes, it was only walking, but given that back in January my New Year's resolution had been to 'try more chutneys', it all felt quite momentous. Not bad for someone who spent the first Covid lockdown method-acting the grandparents from *Charlie and the Chocolate Factory.*

I was headed for Windy Gyle, a hill about halfway between Byrness and Kirk Yetholm, whose peak I would reach sometime in the early afternoon and there divert from the Way down to Trow's Farm, where Oli's Land Rover would be waiting to shuttle me back to Byrness for the evening. It meant that I had been able to leave some spare clothes back in the room, along with my saturated notebook, redundant guidebook and the gift badges from Margot and Geoffrey. I had also planned to give Alan the day off, but Rob wanted to have a chance to say goodbye to him when the time came. Nonetheless, my DLX Twin Peak 45 bergen felt light and bouncy as we set off, with just a full water bottle, spare t-shirt, change of socks and novelty doorstop for tenants.

The day ahead was freighted with anticipation. Alfred Wainwright, in his pioneering *Pennine Way Companion,* called the walk between Byrness and Kirk Yetholm, "the longest and loneliest of all… no amount of pre-study can anticipate the rigours of this walk. (It is) Damned long (and) Damned hard."

So it proved. We left the sap-on-tap forest of Kielder and began an immediate vertical clamber up towards the rocky outcrop of Byrness Hill, chest-high bracken lashing out at us while disciplined ranks of spruce and pine stood watching in taciturn vigil. Yesterday's rainfall was still making its way to ground level, turning the bank into a sludgy waterslide which saw both of us slip around like Sisyphus playing Snakes and Ladders.

I don't know why I couldn't have stayed in bed, sire, Alan berated me.

The hill seemed to harbour some malign intent, some vestige of long-forgotten need for vengeance. Even after a fortnight of doing nothing but what we were doing, the exertion of a sheer climb immediately after breakfast came at a price, and I stopped just beneath the peak of Byrness Hill to vomit. Wainwright wasn't wrong when he wrote, "the Pennine Way offers you the experience of a lifetime, which is not to say that it offers you continuous enjoyment. It is a tough, bruising walk and the compensations are few."

You can *never* truly relax on an expedition like this, not if you want the narrative arc to ultimately curve upwards towards a happy ending. Nature is neutral – neither hero nor villain – but it certainly isn't there to help you, and it has played the unwitting antagonist in many a walker's quest.

At the crest of Byrness Hill, we stopped to catch our breath and saw what writer Mark Wallington described as "the b**tard Cheviots", our destination and final foe, fully uncloaked. Catcleugh reservoir was visible back down the hill and looked like a much more enjoyable day out, but we had front-row tickets for the Cheviots and they were neither refundable nor transferable. Featureless and androgynous those hills looked – but not, I knew from experience, indomitable. Every hill is climbable if you make sure your next step is always in front of the last one. And thus, we trudged on.

Most of Day 15 is essentially an elongated border walk, as you tread the dotted line between England and Scotland following a ubiquitous fence line along the tesselating hills, Northumberland National Park laconically to your right and the Promised Land tantalisingly to the left. The sky was huge, the clouds oppressive and the facts of summer sketchy, but we found our rhythm and kept it up, our crunching boots a *basso continuo,* each step a rooting in shallow soil and immediate departure to pastures new. We had grown used to the monotony of the long marches and, like monks, that monotony had become serenity for us. The sacrament of the everyday imparts all long-distance walkers with a sense of divine grace.

"To be silent the whole day, see no newspaper, hear no radio, listen to no gossip, be thoroughly and completely indifferent to the fate of the world is the finest medicine a man can give himself."

Henry Miller, The Colossus of Maroussi.

We chatted if we felt like it, listened to music if we chose to, but always dragged the undulating landscape steadily beneath our soles. The blisters I had picked up on Day 6 were nothing more than blemishes now, Margot's silicone heels having performed stellar work in neutralising their inherent threat, while my hamstring seemed to have forgotten that it had ruptured a matter of months ago – and I was grateful for that. 600 muscles and 206 bones in the human body and all mine were still just about functioning. Indeed, the only real casualty of the walk had been Rob's hair, but we still weren't talking about that apparently.

'How will you get home?' I asked Rob during morning break. Like his spartan hairline we hadn't dared mention such things until now, but even a leg break at this point would probably mean having to reach Kirk Yetholm for extraction. Whether by foot or on the back of a stretcher, we would cross the finish line from here.

'I'll get a bus to Kelso,' he began, 'then another one to Edinburgh probably, then a train. My fiancée is gonna meet me there and we'll have a couple of days getting drunk on whiskey before we head back to Nottingham.'

'That sounds perfect', I said, chuckling.

'******* right. Can't wait to see her. Might need to buy a wig first – she still doesn't know about hairmegeddon. What about you?'

I smiled. The stowaway walnut was out of its wrapper and I was caressing it between finger and thumb.

'Well, I'm not totally sure because it's not guaranteed yet. But maybe…'

'Maybe what?'

Maybe, I was going to say, *my family might come and pick me up.* It wasn't definite, and I certainly hadn't asked for or expected it, but the girls had mooted and got excited about the idea on the phone a few nights ago and said they would talk to Mummy. I hadn't followed it up, had even suggested to them that their mum might not be able to manage that, and I was fairly certain it wouldn't materialise. But maybe…

'Can't you just message and confirm either way?' Rob asked.

'Not really, no,' I said. 'We don't talk at the moment unless it's about arrangements for the girls, so….' My sentence tumbled down the hill into the valley, unfinished.

Rob rubbed his head.

'When was the last time you and she had a proper chat?'

I scanned the horizon for an answer, finding nothing but bare hills.

'I don't really know, mate. Quite a while. Communication is just so flipping hard after divorce – there's a lot of subtext, a lot of pain. I can't remember the last time we sat down together.'

Rob was splitting his attention between me and a Cumberland sausage, but he seemed to be listening.

'Would you want to sit down and talk with her, though?' he asked, opening a sachet of ketchup from his zipper.

'Of course I would. I would like a lot of things to happen, but yes, that's definitely one of them.'

'Can I ask another question, then?'

'You can.'

'Have you done this walk to get her attention? To… to make a statement in place of having a conversation?'

The surrounding hills encircled us like a Witenagemot, a council of wise elders, their crownless heads bowed in dignified silence with Rob's own bald peak at the centre. I smiled at my friend, at his salient question, then rested my face on my palm and shrugged.

'I don't know, Rob… maybe, yes… partly, probably… I don't know.'

I probably did know – I just hadn't quite articulated it in that way. But it *was* true.

The last time I tried to walk Pennine Way we were still married. After five gruelling days of attrition following minimal preparation, I had needed to be picked up from Malham, wounded, beaten and pathetic. It was, at that time, yet another thing I had totally mismanaged; another thing I had failed to properly commit to, failed to properly understand. I didn't have the endurance for even those things I wanted the most, and it was, if I'm brutally honest, *just like me.*

But I write stories for a living, and I know that stories can be rewritten. Maybe I was stuck in a Panglossian delusion, but I believed that things could be different – that *I* could be different. That I could circumnavigate my tendencies, *stay on the map,* be present and diligent, long-suffering and attentive – a Ship of Theseus, so refurbished by weather and storms that it's no longer what it used to be. Divorce is like a soldier dying in peacetime, like a non-terminal cancer, but I believe that narrative arcs, like hills, can go upwards as well as downwards; that imagination is superior to knowledge; that myth is more potent than history; that hope outranks experience. I believed that we might yet, she and I, travel through Hades and come out at Elysium or at least the Fields of Asphodel. That the Ginnungagap might yet be breached, that the gates of hell need not prevail – not this time. Even after all this time. And I believed that we may yet be sentenced to redemption.

I had looked into the morass of my own morality… and I had chosen a path out of it. It hadn't been a loveless marriage – simply mis-administered, the love injected into the wrong vein. But the physician had healed himself, or tried to, and he was desperate to share his findings. My footsteps were my vows renewed. In lieu of words, I was letting my feet do the talking. In place of a conversation I was indeed, as Rob pointed out, releasing a definitive statement, my very own *decree absolute.*

'I think if I could talk to her,' I said, 'maybe I could help her see that I'm not the king's jester I used to be.'

'And a drive back from Scotland together would give you that chance.'

'It would.'

'Let's crack on, then,' Rob said, finishing his sausage and jumping to his feet. 'They can't pick you up if you don't get there, can they? Sun's coming out at last.'

And so it was.

CHAPTER 32
RAJUL ALQIAMA

We picked up pace. The clouds above the Cheviots dissipated and our old friend Mr Blue Sky came out to watch the invasion from the royal box. Ravens Knowe and Coquet Head beckoned and bid us on, duckboards conveyor-belted us, hillsides tattooed with heather tramlined the path. The old Roman fort at Chew Green offered a potential detour but we demurred on the basis that the Romans have been dead for ages, had their season in the sun, and this was ours. Thunder cannonaded from distant valleys but the barrage never reached us. The wind went before us, heralding our passage, coercing the grass to bend and bow and scrape. *These men deserve respect,* I imagined the wind articulating, although its actual sound was more like a ghost sitting on a cold toilet seat.

I forgot to say, too, that my boot was no longer smacking its lips like a buffoon. Oli from the Forest View had given it what for with a tube of Gorilla glue, and Jeeves and Carson (the names I had given my boots, remember) were now both grunting and squeaking with respectable discretion. Not another soul was visible across the whole panorama, whilst practically the only man-made thing we saw all day was the fenceline – without which, it must be said, navigation would have been a nightmare, the route switchbacking up and down and zigzagging in and out like a drunken Ceilidh.

Presently, Rob checked the route map on his phone's walking app – and stopped.

'Passport please?'

'Sorry?'

'Failte *gu* ******* Alba.'

'Do you need to be sick?' I asked.

'Not really. We've just entered Scotland!'

'Ohhhhhh, failte gu ******* Alba,' I said. 'Right, I'm with you.'

Winston Churchill once said, "Of all the small nations of this earth, perhaps only the ancient Greeks surpass the Scots in their contribution to mankind."

I'm sure that's true, and yet the guardian of the Celtic realm, Scotland's Checkpoint Charlie, was just a narrow gate on its hinge. No signpost or momentous delineation, no banner with "English Beware" scrawled on it in lamb's blood – just a narrow gate, left open, for anyone who wanted to come in. Duly, we spent a good couple of minutes jumping back and forth across the border like scamps, then Rob did a massive wee back into England for reasons only known to himself, and we carried on.

Lamb Hill was next, then Beefstand Hill. All very meaty, all very slabby, all going according to plan. But "the best laid schemes o' mice an' men gang aft agley" as the Scottish bard Robert Burns said, and when I misjudged an uneven slab on Mozie Law and went tumbling into the heather with a cry of pain and a jolted knee, I feared the worst.

Not now, surely – not when I was so close.

I sat anxiously in the brush and ferns for a few minutes, hardly moving, gingerly bending and rubbing the knee, looking fretfully up at Rob who returned the favour.

'How does it feel?' he asked, after I had drowned my right leg in Ibuprofen gel as though it were holy oil.

'I think it's OK,' I said cautiously. 'I don't think I've pulled anything – it just really stings.'

I got to my feet and started pacing carefully up and down. I couldn't decide whether the wincing I made with every step was genuine pain or simply paranoia.

'Do you think you can make it?' Rob asked. He retrieved my rucksack from its grave and gave Alan a brush-down.

'I shall have to,' I said, with a resolve to rouse the spirits of every Englishman.

'Try running on it.'

'Absolutely not!'

I hadn't run any of the 500,000 steps on the Pennine Way so far, and by God's good grace I had no intention of starting here.

I reattached my bergen and carried on, only slower now, taking my time over those renewed vows, each tentative step a prayer, a staccato psalmody of lament and hope. Whatever views were there to behold over the next couple of hills were missed as I fixated on my feet, limping psychosomatically, obsessed now with every slight disparity at ground level and how to avoid it. Consequently, when around 2pm I suggested brewing up in a sheltered cairn atop the next ridge before ploughing on, Rob's response surprised me.

'No need, mate. That's Windy Gyle. That's the end of your day.'

'Really?'

'Really,' he said with a grin.

I gave a shout of praise – and saw it snatched away as soon as it left my lips, for there's a reason why the destination isn't just called 'Gyle'. The wind up on that hill is mocking and malevolent, an evil genie released from its lamp. That final, steep, thigh-searing climb was like all the events from *Gladiators* rolled into one as we battled against the gale with a curse and an oath, careening about like flimsy pleasure boats caught in a swell. Eventually we reached it, lumbering over Russell's Cairn and collapsing ignobly into its central hollow. The wind continued to smack and whip against the bare rock, wolf-whistling and name-calling. The shelter protected us from its force but not from its taunting disdain. "The moon holds no grudge," T.S. Eliot wrote. But the wind holds plenty.

We divested ourselves of every encumbrance and stretched out tired legs, propping our backs against angular granite. The cairn, which has been a lookout spot since Bronze Age times, supposedly gets its name from a chap named Lord Russell who was slain by the Scots in 1585. From here, if you can find the wherewithal to stand up, the North Sea is visible to the West while extensive views of the surrounding area blah blah blah blah blah. No – the sight of my stationary legs and decumbent pack was enough of a view for me.

'I think this calls for a smoke,' Rob said, drawing out a battered tin from his inside pocket. 'I'm not really a smoker, but I saw a little pipe in Hawes and thought it might be a nice way to mark the end of our time together.'

I smiled and nodded. He crouched over the tobacco tin, stuffed some appropriately named "Spirit of Scotland" into the pipe's bowl, and after several thwarted attempts he somehow managed to light it. We sat there for a steady hour, Bronze-Age men in modern clothing, smoking our victory pipe, sheltering for comfort beneath its blanket of embers.

'We *did* it, didn't we?' my travelling companion said as he laid the tobacco ashes to rest. 'We actually did do it.'

'Just about,' I replied, glancing warily at my knee. 'How do you feel?'

He tapped the pipe against a rock and looked pensive. 'I never quite believed I would finish it, Andy. It's a dream come true, I think. You?'

'You obviously have more pleasant dreams than I do,' I said. For me, a dream come true would be a sabre-toothed tiger chasing me through sand or 9th century Vikings pillaging my family home. I was quite content for those things to stay in the subconscious, thank you.

'It feels momentous,' I said instead, as Rob got to his feet.

'Cheers to that. Do you want me to wait for you at the bothy tomorrow? I really don't mind hanging around.'

Rob was going to camp that night at the final refuge hut on the trail – a strange thing, like a beach house delivered to the wrong address and subsequently abandoned – and then make a morning descent into Kirk Yetholm like rainwater after a storm.

'Thank you,' I said. 'But no. I'd like to cross that finish line on my own tomorrow. I have a lot to think about.'

'I understand,' he said phlegmatically. I noticed that he hadn't sworn since we reached the top of Windy Gyle.

'Thanks for the pipe, though. And for the listening ear. And for everything in between, Rob.'

'You're not gonna ******* cry are you?' he said, in a startling return to form.

'I'm not. I might have forgotten how.'

I held out my hand, and he took it and shook it.

'All the best, Herman. Take good care of Alan.'

'You have my word. And all the best for your marriage, dear boy.'

'Same to you, mate.'

My friend headed off along the path on his own, and I watched him shrink to miniature in the afternoon shadow.

Half-past three, my phone said. I had two hours to reach my extraction point at Trow's Farm, a 20-minute byline down the hill, from where Oli would bumble me back to the Forest View for a second night at the inn. I had time to doze, to write, to send self-satisfied texts from my elevated perch. To prepare for how this might end.

I sat beneath the parapet of Russell's Cairn with my notebook, the imposing Cheviot Mountain – the Pennine Way's final twist of the knife – winking a feeble eye from the horizon. Words shivered onto the page whilst the brutality of the gale shook the shelter as a madman shakes a geranium. But there are certain scenes that mere prose struggles to capture, and I quickly closed the book on my clunky jottings and chose to sit in silence. Painters and poets are needed at altitude – not joke writers.

Then from seemingly nowhere a skylark arrived to hover above me, surfing resiliently on the monstrous wind, unfazed by the brazen apathy of the landscape, singing her unassailable song. I was alone on a grassy hillside under a blue sky and there were birds singing. And so, with no-one around to cower or cringe and nobody to write a scathing review… I decided to sing with them.

* * *

Half-past five, the clock said. Oli was driving me back to Byrness along bumpy roads through land owned by the M.O.D, trying to overtake a man on a tractor with a dog riding shotgun.

'How did you find today?' he asked.

'OK, actually. The boot held up under the glue, thanks. I could do with an icepack for my knee, though – almost suffered a career-threatening injury at one point.'

'We'll see you right. Burgers for tea, too. And I've got another beer for you to try.'

'You're a fine fellow,' I said, closing my eyes with satisfaction… then opening them with panic as Oli veered aggressively past Tractor Ted.

The Forest View Inn wasn't nearly as packed that night as the previous evening, with the only other people I spoke to being a small group of Liverpudlian writers who had come away to the borderlands for inspiration. They were sitting in the garden with tonics and sodas as I unloaded from the Land Rover, and they waved at me cheerily. I joined them for a while, slightly overwhelmed by their enthusiasm and energy levels. They were talking about ruined novels, their own and others they had read, and when I joined the conversation a man in a Trilby was waning lyrical about *Huckleberry Finn,* decrying it for its abrupt and ambiguous ending. Another member of the group had just read *The Handmaid's Tale*, and was now in counselling.

'I see you've been walking?' said a lady in tweed, displaying the searing observational skills you find in top-level authors.

'It's a long story,' I said with a smile.

'Well, we've got the time if you have?'

'Ah, but it's not quite finished yet. And plus I need a shower.'

'Well, rather you than us,' the chap in the Trilby quipped, receiving approving nods as feedback. 'You don't have to move from your arse when you're writing.'

'True, but it's much harder to go the wrong way when you're walking. Someone else has drafted the synopsis out for you.'

'Ah, but with writing you can always edit if it goes wrong. Can you do that with a walk? No.'

'Fair enough.'

'Can we read you some of our work later?' the tweed lady asked.

'If I'm still awake,' I said, and went upstairs to wash.

It felt odd not having Rob and Chris knocking about the place. There were no expletives emanating from open doorways, no Japanese phrases before bed, no giddy rambling on the subject of a day's giddy rambling. I didn't like it. I would go and sit with the writing group after dinner and happily listen to their tales, but the anticipation of tomorrow's final march felt muted and anticlimactic without the expectant faces of my friends. Excitement is always better appreciated when drawn on the page of other people.

And then, in an event that I would very much like to edit, but simply can't, I got a message from the South.

In olden times it would have been dramatic: a crisp telegram, urgently delivered on horseback, brought fluttering into the drawing room by a lachrymose butler, then hastily read and dropped dolefully into the fire.

But this was just a ping on a screen.

It said that she was sorry. Sorry, but she had only just heard about the girls' idea of them meeting me at the finish line and that it wasn't going to be possible now. *She was sorry* (it wasn't anyone's fault), hoped I would get back OK, and the girls were looking forward to seeing me soon, best wishes and good luck.

'Is everything all right, sir?' my butler would have said in olden times.

'Yes, quite all right, thank you. Just had a spot of rotten news from back home. Would you prepare my carriage?'

'Certainly, sir.'

Something in me, some voice or instinct, told me that I should cry; that this would be the perfect time for weeping and screaming and raging into the night. But still I didn't. I deleted the message, threw my phone on the bed, opened a fresh beer and went to locate the company of writers. I found them in the garden, as irrepressible as before, with laughter fomented and their tonics and sodas upgraded to spirits.

'I need to hear a good story,' I said.

'Ah, well we can help you with that, young man,' the lady in tweed said confidently. 'Come and pull up a pew.'

So I sat with the storytellers, and we stayed out under the stars for hours, telling tales.

Day 15 was over, and it had been a day of goodbyes. But I wasn't quite finished.

There was still one more to go.

* * *

There's this one story about a pilgrim that was passed down by the old desert fathers.

This pilgrim set off from Jerusalem around the time of the Crusades and walked alone into the wilderness to spread the good news. He rose each morning at dawn and walked until dusk, or until his feet were tired. He passed many travellers, heard their stories and shared his, slept in caves and drank from streams. He took no pride in his appearance nor his achievements for they were few; he had no supernatural virtue save for endurance. He drew strength from God, and comfort from the fact that he was upright.

In the second year of his pilgrimage, under the shadow of a mountain peak he found a camp of nomads who offered to take him in. They asked if he was a nomad too, but he said that he was not – he was just a pilgrim. For many weeks he stayed in that camp amongst the nomads, and he heard their stories and shared his, sleeping in tents and drinking from wineskins. He taught them about the wonderful things he had seen on his journey, and preached to them about resurrection and redemption. The nomads had no concept of such things, they told him: how could it be that something dead could be raised once more to life?

They laughed at the pilgrim and his teaching, but they gave him the name *Rajul Alqiama,* which means 'the resurrection man'.

One scorching day under a red sun, riders were seen on the horizon. Their armour was burnished and their swords were straight, like the road that passes between life to death. Dust clouds rose as they approached the camp on their horses, to scout for men and women and weapons and riches. Seeing them advance, the nomads grabbed their spears and clasped their shields, blowing their horns and praying to their gods.

Rajul Alqiama, the pilgrim, ran about the camp and tried to bring calm; tried to talk the nomad chiefs out of a battle. But the nomad chiefs wanted a battle. They would defend their camp and scream their war cry, and they would not be beaten for their Gods were with them.

The nomads turned on the pilgrim then and beat him with sticks, shouting to each other that he must be a spy from the riders' camp; a wolf in sheep's clothing. They were too clever to be fooled, they told him.

The High Chief approached the pilgrim and struck him across the face, and banished him from their midst, sending him back into the wilderness.

Heavy with grief and longing, Rajul Alqiama picked up his staff and a skin of wine. He left the shadow of the mountain peak and walked slowly towards the horsemen, alone. Four riders, in burnished armour and with swords as straight as the road between life and death, rode across the sand to meet him.

Perhaps, thought the pilgrim, they would come and reason together. Perhaps they would accept a drink from his wineskin. He opened his arms wide in a sign of peace.

But the pilgrim was mistaken. The riders cut him to pieces before he could even open his mouth to speak. His staff and his skin fell to the ground and his life drained away, staining the baked earth with water and with blood.

The riders laughed and raised their swords, turned their horses and galloped away.

And the nomads, watching from the barricades of their camp, wept and rent their garments with grief.

For they finally understood the resurrection man.

Day 16 (Final Day)
Windy Gyle to Kirk Yetholm
15 miles

"I felt that I was leaving part of myself behind, and that wherever
I went afterwards I should feel the lack of it,
and search for it hopelessly, as ghosts are said to do."
Evelyn Waugh, Brideshead Revisited

"...nothing irredeemable on either side of the grave."
Rudyard Kipling, The Pilgrim's Way

CHAPTER 33

I WILL DIE ON THIS HILL

This was it.

270 miles. 440 kilometres. 8 counties. 2 countries. 249 stiles. 204 bridges. 4 tubes of Ibuprofen Gel. 2 million cups of coffee. 1 day left.

Morning broke like the bread at the Last Supper, and sunlight, the most precious gold to be found on earth, flooded the world. After 16 days in the wilderness my constant procedure of departure and arrival was coming to an end. I would wake up tomorrow in another world – the old one.

'This is it, old chap,' I said to Alan as I slotted him into his pouch for the final time.

One last hurrah, sire.

I zipped up my pack, pulled on my silicone heels, laced up my boots, and closed the door behind me.

I sat alone at a corner table and ate cereal and fruit for breakfast, no longer needing the calories or the colourful characters from an early-morning meat and greet. The writers were still in bed, heads throbbing in all likelihood, and a lady with her spaniel was the only other walker in the dining room. She barely acknowledged my presence, but she was telling Oli and Laura from the Forest View (who were thinking of getting a dog) that you should always let dogs off their leads in a field full of cows.

'Don't cows try to bully dogs though?' Laura asked her.

'They can do, and that's why you unleash them. A dog can outrun a cow easier than you can. Can't you, Penfold?' she asked her spaniel, who looked so old that he might have viewed a stampede as a merciful death.

Around 8am, Oli barrelled me into his Land Rover and infiltrated me back to Trow's Farm over secret roads and through military firing zones.

'Hope you're not superstitious,' he said cheerily. 'There's a load of red flags dotted about the landscape.'

'I'm not,' I smiled.

There was a miles-away fixedness to my thoughts as I watched the countryside glide by. I was thinking about something Jean-Jacques Rousseau said when he wrote, "I have never thought so much, existed so much, lived so much, been so much myself, as in the journeys which I have made alone and on foot." I hadn't been alone until today really, but the rest of it rang heartily true. I couldn't remember not ever knowing the inner hydraulics of the land, the fierce solace of harsh landscapes. I had been punctured, stalled, run on fumes and seen my engine light come on – but it had been a joyride.

At the end of his book *A Walk in the Woods,* Bill Bryson writes, "I didn't have any feelings…that weren't thoroughly contradictory. I was weary of the trail, but captivated by it; found the endless slog increasingly exhausting but ever invigorating; enjoyed the escape from civilization and ached for its comforts. All of this together, all at once, every moment." *Amen* to that, Bill.

Pulling into Trow's Farm and winching down from the transport, Oli handed me a bonus Mars bar for the journey and offered me his hand.

'Hope to see you again, pal. Give it hell today.'

'Cheers, mate.'

I shook his hand and smiled at the second-to-last face I would see before I reached The Border Hotel in Kirk Yetholm. I am going to make it – just so you know. I watched Oli pothole his way back round the hill, scattering a gang of sheep who were loitering without intent. I took out my phone and made a 'cheery' video of the final start line to send to the girls, which wouldn't win any awards for cinematography but might give me a shot at Best Actor. Then I looked down at my battered Meindl boots, stared up at the mountainous skyline, and started the arduous but necessary process of wedding the two in today's arranged marriage.

"Down to Gehenna, or up to the Throne,
He travels the fastest who travels alone."

I had climbed the equivalent of one and a half Everests over the last fortnight, but climbing a hill never really feels like a pleasure. Today's appetiser was our erstwhile friend 'bonus walking', as I retraced my steps – all steeply uphill, heaving and sweating and blimmin'-bloody-basketing – up from the Coquet valley to the peak of Windy Gyle. For the lymphatic fellow who retched his way up Jacob's Ladder early on the first day, this climb alone would have seemed implausible, a psychological stile too high to cross. But that was 700,000 steps and 5kg ago, and I was good at this now. I passed the time by considering what sort of celebration I might do once I reached the Border Hotel, the unofficial finish line of the Pennine Way. Would I run around the village green with one arm aloft like Alan Shearer, perhaps? One of those head-over-heels flips that American footballers do after a touchdown? Maybe I'd take off all my clothes and do a skeleton dance like a lad at school once did shortly before he was suspended. I was looking forward to finding out.

I reached Windy Gyle's pinnacle and saw the paternal acorn symbol of the Pennine Way on a weather-beaten signpost: "The Schil – 7 miles". Safely back on the official trail then, I turned to the right and pointed myself towards Kirk Yetholm, a place I had tried and hoped and failed to see for 18 years. In *A Philosophy of Walking*, Frederic Gros says, "To arrive on foot at a place whose name one has dreamed of, whose picture has lain for so long in the mind, casts a backwards light over the road. And what was accomplished in fatigue, sometimes boredom, in the face of that absolutely solid presence which justifies it all, is transformed into a series of necessary and joyous moments. Walking makes times reversible."

If I kept up a steady pace I would stamp down the hill to Kirk Yetholm around 3pm – no roaming in the gloaming for this chap. I have to say though, by lunchtime I was not experiencing Day 16 as a "series of necessary and joyous moments." According to the guidebooks, this was supposed to be a "spectacular" day which "you wish would go on forever." Well, it wasn't. It was super hard, with four major peaks to hoist myself up and over and nobody but Alan for company. Windy Gyle, The Cheviot (the second highest point on the whole trail), The Schill and then finally White Law – those four would easily make my list of Top 10 hardest ascents on the entire route. Maybe it was because the commentators all seemed pretty blasé about the whole affair: "You've got this far, just enjoy it," they all said. I didn't. I jolted my ankles, jarred my knees, plunged thigh-deep into a fetid bog. I may not have fallen at the final hurdle, but only because I was hacking through the hurdles with a blunted axe screaming 'Here's Kindy!!' If this was due on paper to be some kind of valedictorian speech, in reality it was more like a dirty protest, and I decided I hated walking. Oh, and sheep – I hated sheep. I have barely mentioned them in this book because I don't like the way they constantly seek the limelight with their bleating and werriting, plus they are just *there* and it would be like describing every blade of grass or air particle. But on any long-distance walk the ovine community is amaranthine and immutable, the Alpha and Omega of the British countryside. And frankly they are idiots.

I trudged on regardless, through bogs lined with great swathes of cloudberry, over duckboards and across stiles, and before midday I reached the peak of The Cheviot, the highest point in the Northumberland National Park. Not technically on the Pennine Way route proper it appears more as a throb than a peak – a slightly underwhelming bulge of unfulfilled potential. It gives its name to this range of hills simply by being the first-born son but, like a lot of older brothers, is more docile and conciliatory than some of its smaller, gnarlier siblings. Nevertheless, reaching its stoutly buttressed trig point felt satisfying. I rested on the flagstone patio and consumed Oli's Mars bar by way of reward, staring passively out over the broad, paludal plateau. In the peat bogs north of the Cheviot's summit lie the remains of a B-17 bomber which went down during the Second World War, and it's chilling that both the opening and closing days of the walk have air crash sites within one's purview. Some people claim you can see Edinburgh from up here in clear weather, but the day was crystalline and I couldn't see Scotland's capital. I could see a load of sheep though, if that's of interest to you? So many flipping sheep.

Half-past 11, my watch said. Eight miles to go. A lone male walker, late teens, was brewing up coffee between two rocks and looking perplexed, an ordnance survey map across his legs like a ridiculous napkin.

'It that Hen Hole?' he asked as I passed him, his words barely clipping me in the wind.

'Is what Hen Hole?'

He was pointing down into a craggy gulley with a watery bottom.

'I have no idea,' I said. 'Sorry.'

'Oh. And do you know what a sike is?'

'Yes, it's a stream. So is a burn. Yorkshire has becks and Derbyshire has cloughs.'

'OK, fantastic! Thanks for your help. I'm walking the Pennine Way – just trying to take it all in.'

'Oh, you are? And how long will that take you?'

'Reckon I can do it in a week or so. Most people take about a fortnight, but they're usually retired and so I reckon I can double the normal speed. I'm in the running club at my school.'

'That's the spirit,' I said.

'You off anywhere nice today?'

'Just walking.'

'Cool. And – aha! – you've got a mascot, too.'

He swivelled his pack and pulled out from its pouch a grey teddy bear in a bowler hat. 'This is Cedric,' he said. 'And I'm Jonty.'

'Nice to meet you, Cedric and Jonty.'

'Have you ever done the Pennine Way,' he asked, 'with all your knowledge of streams and counties?'

I shook my head. 'I have never finished it.'

'Oh, right, well maybe one day.'

'Who knows what the future holds?' I said. 'Enjoy your walk, chap.'

'Thanks so much. You too!'

Well, he's not getting to Edale, is he, sire? Alan said presciently as we strode away.

'Not a chance. Nice lad, though.'

Why didn't you introduce me to Cedric?

'You don't need any more friends, Alan, you've got me. And you'll be back on the mantelpiece this time tomorrow – only seven miles to go.'

Seven miles to go. Which, by my estimation, was also the number of additional miles in bonus walking I had covered along the trail since the beginning. Depending on who you ask, the Pennine Way is calculated at somewhere between 266 and 270 miles – although I would end up at more like 277. A lot of those miles went unnoticed and certainly unwritten about, and of the ones I *have* covered I've tried to be as accurate as possible, using my notes, memory and guidebooks for counsel. Memory is a strange thing though, isn't it? You simply can't remember everything that has happened in your life, and I've noticed as I enter middle age that my mind has started this odd habit of merging certain events into compound memories to save on storage. For instance, when I was about nine years old, Gordon Banks – England's 1966 World Cup winning goalkeeper – came into my Primary school to give a talk and be interviewed (his grandson was a pupil at the school, as I recall). He spoke about life as a professional footballer, lifting the Jules Rimet trophy, and about how it felt to save a shot from Pelé in the 1970 World Cup. He was a tremendous man and it was a memorable occasion.

Later that same year, the Reptile Man came into school, bringing with him a van full of snakes and lizards and inviting some of the more feral children to hang them round their necks *for fun.* Obviously, I stood as far away as possible from anything with more or fewer than two legs and shielded myself with a sickly child from the year below. But here's the point. Even though I know those two events are completely independent of one another – occurring in real time about nine months apart – owing to my mind's incipient need to save on disk space I now remember them as *one,* so that, as I now picture it, at some point in the late 1980s England's greatest ever goalkeeper visited my school and taught me how to feed dead mice to a python. When it comes to accurate reconstructions of events, therefore, you'll have to permit me a little artistic licence is all I'm saying.

Six miles to go.

* * *

The most attractive mountain in the Cheviot Range is The Schil. It is also, to let you in on a little secret, the final climb on the Pennine Way – although I didn't know that quite yet.

The ascent to its summit is steep and unhumorous and the climb towards it hard and wearisome, plus the grudgeful wind was back, too – chewing up the scenery like Olivier and causing me to tilt and titubate all over the place. But the view from the top is fittingly stirring, and a rocky tor fringed with scree blesses the peak with a romantic, handsome quality.

I decided to stop here for my final lunch: a sandwich of leftover burger and a can of pop. I had hardly been deprived of nourishment on this journey, never once feeling a need for food and a lack of it, and people who choose to camp have it much harder in that regard. I bit into cold burger and smiled at the memory of those truffle oil chips from the Greenhead Hotel, at how Chris had looked scandalised at my ordering them for dessert, and how Gordon Banks had turned up unexpectedly and started handing out salamanders.

Beneath the shoulder of the mountain I had passed the refuge hut where Rob had stayed the previous night, and poked my head inside just in case. It was empty – but what was I expecting? He would almost certainly be in the village by now, which was a lovely thought; or else had tumbled fatally into a ravine, which was not. I wondered whether he had found this Grand Guignol of a closing day as angst-ridden as I had, and wondered too what excuse he had devised to give his girlfriend for his shaven head. You lose and gain a lot on pilgrimage, but a full head of hair must surely be a first, and I hoped their joyful reunion wouldn't be tarnished by fears of him turning Neo-Nazi or developing trail-induced alopecia.

Five miles to go. Just a couple more peaks should do it, I thought. I packed up lunch and set off again, seasoned and disciplined and unceremonial. A V-sign of crows cawed above me like an arrowhead, pointing me back towards Byrness in one final red herring – but there would be no wrong turns from here. From the ridge of The Schil I scanned the valleys for a rumour of Kirk Yetholm village, so very close now, hoping for a glimpse of a spire or a chimney or a chequered flag. But it could not be seen – nor would it be until the very end. With directorial flair and a canny grasp of denouement, the village remains completely hidden until the final half mile. The countryside was oddly beaconised now, though: in the valley below, the sun's rays skimmed the surface ripples of sikes and burns and reflected light back up to me as knowing winks.

'You're nearly there, friend,' they said perhaps. 'We see that you are nearly there.'

I *was* nearly there. At the foot of The Schil an acorn signpost sits hospitably with the message, "Kirk Yetholm 4 ½ miles". At this point the path bifurcates and the Pennine Wayfarer has the option of re-entering Scotland via the high road or the low road, "where in soft purple hue, the Highlands we view," as the old song goes.

"And if you take the low road," my guidebook said, "Congratulations! You've just climbed your last hill on the Pennine Way."

The revelation caught me off-guard – I had thought there was more to come. Maybe I just never expected the eucatastrophe of that final hill, for the bell curve to drop off once and for all. But it was true. I had climbed and climbed and climbed and now I didn't need to climb anymore. The giants had all been slain. The snake's head was crushed. It was all downhill from here.

And with that realisation beating in my chest, I turned round and walked slowly back the way I had come, towards the romantic rocky outcrop at the summit of The Schil. There, unbuckling my pack and resting Alan on a slab shaped like an altar, I lowered myself to the ground, and in a gentle voice said:

'My wife has gone and she's never coming back.'

CHAPTER 34

A FAR BORDER TOWN SOMEWHERE

I tell stories for a living. And for a good while now I had been telling one to myself – a bedtime story to get me to sleep each night. And it was a fantasy.

My life over the last two years had been a long tale of terror, and I don't like those stories. I prefer happy endings. I like those stories where the cavalry comes over the hill, or where the church door bursts open and the person you thought dead is standing there, bleeding and alive. I like it when "Reader I married him," when "Aunt Em I'm so glad to be home", when "on top of the forest a little boy and his bear would always be playing". When the hero returns.

That was the story I wanted: one where I would get to the end of the Pennine Way and she'd be waiting. I had persuaded myself that if I just walked over enough horizons, perhaps across the next one I would see her there and we could climb the Hill of Redemption together, hand in hand. And I would say I'm sorry and she would say I forgive you. And she would say I'm sorry and I would say you're forgiven, my love. Because *walking makes time reversible.*

Only it doesn't. And from Derbyshire to Scotland, through Cheshire and Yorkshire and Cumberland and Northumberland, up hill and down dale, across valley floors and mountain peaks, I had been walking on those sodden lumps of fact all along.

In this story, the Wicked Witch didn't melt. The Pevensey children never went back to Narnia. Sauron found the ring. And there was no way now to edit or rewrite it, and no alternative ending possible. And only one thing left for it: to let it end.

"And on reaching those hostile, frozen heights, the pilgrim stops, stretches out the stones like a dying man, and thinks of all those he has failed to love, praying for them, reconciling himself to his past before leaving it for good." (Frederic Gros)

Hope is the killer who keeps you alive. But now, with no more hills and no more risk; with completion assured and victory at hand… I turned my face finally towards death.

I opened the top of my rucksack and pulled out a paper bag containing the three pewter badges that Margot and Geoffrey had bought for my girls. One said 'Gorgeous', one 'Awesome', and the other 'Beloved'. Two of the badges stayed in the bag and were stored in my jacket for a happier day. The third one I held for a while, feeling the cool pewter on my skin and running my finger over its wording. Using my Swiss Army knife I gouged a small hole in the ground, not too deep, but deep enough. The petrichor from the soil filled my nostrils and reminded me of days that had passed and days that never would.

I spoke to her for a while then, under that massive sky and those storied hills, but you won't ever hear what was said, I'm afraid, and nobody keeps secrets better than rocks.

Finally, with my words thoroughly spent on that ancient ground of fossilised hopes, in the presence of God and with Alan as witness, I placed the badge gently into the soil… and laid my Beloved to rest.

I sat motionless for a while, my knees moistening against the earth, my thoughts lapping to stillness. Then, rising to my feet, I removed a handful of items from my bergen – water bottle, wallet, keys and guidebook – and, hoisting my pack for the final time, I wedged it between two rocks and there discarded it. Taking Alan by the hand, and with no more backward glances, I left my burden on that rock and walked down the hill towards the finish line.

But still I didn't cry.

*   *   *

Three miles to go. The last three miles are always the worst, even without a pack.

I was following the fence line along a grassy slope up to White Law, a patchwork of fields down below and with the Eildon Hills in prominent view ahead. It had started to drizzle for some reason, much against the run of play, and the slick grass sponged my trousers with rainy residue. This path found me on the border again, England on my right and Scotland to the left, and with St. Cuthbert's Way branching off charmingly to the North-East. A trio of tiny pilgrims, like finescale figures from a model railway, were bouncing slowly along it with their burdens.

The signpost at the foot of the Schil had given me two options – the high road or the low road. It was hardly Hobson's choice: the low road meant no more hills and a slow deflation into Kirk Yetholm for luncheon. But for some reason that felt too easy – too simple – and so I had dressed to the right and chosen another hill. I had occupied the crease for this long after all, lasting a whole innings, and one more corridor of uncertainty wasn't going to bowl me out. I pursued this final path bent and upright, trying to savour the dull pain in my feet, the strain in my back, the searing burn in my thighs. Trying, finally, to enjoy myself.

Because there was something else beyond saying goodbye. Something more than just dying to the past and laying things to rest. If I was going to die, I had decided, then I would do it standing up and bloody well advancing – like an Englishman. For you have probably heard it said that it's about the journey, not the destination. But I tell you this: bollocks. Not on this occasion it wasn't.

I hadn't been looking to simply go on a journey or *find myself* on the way – I needed to win. I wanted to finish well, to *arrive,* to take back lost ground. To see something end in triumph rather than tragedy.

I had learned to take a beating and now I was determined to give one: to overturn tables laden with caricature and stereotype; to wipe sneers off faces and close flapping mouths. I wanted to channel my wrath into my boots and pound the ground into submission; to raise a banner of Defiance for those friends who stuck around, and two fingers to those who fled the scene. In short, I wanted to march my anger and pain and unforgiveness into the uncaring wilderness, and execute them there amongst those fucking hills.

Kirk Yetholm was never my Neverland. It was always my Colonel Kurtz

Half a mile to go. Right foot then left foot, I crashed down White Law's glistening bank. Without the pack I had carried symbiotically for two weeks my hill legs were suddenly wonky and I slipped over twice, watching Alan gambol down the hill like an idiot. I got to my feet, smarting and exhausted, picked up the fox and tramped across a slope of bracken, passed a tin hut, crossed a footbridge over Halter Burn and found myself on tarmac. Thinking I had done it, I turned to the right… where the road arced horrifyingly upwards between two banks.

'You have got to be joking!' I shouted, stamping the ground with my right foot then my left, right then left and I was back into it. 500,000 steps had got me to this point and not one of them had shirked in their duty, whether blistered steps or fainting steps, hungover steps or hungry steps; through torrential rain and hailstorms, baking heat and spiteful wind; past waterfalls and reservoirs, ancient walls and modern streets; over meadows, into bogs, down that sheep track, up this road. 16 days I'd trekked and yomped… here was the brow of this hill… and plodded and slogged and over it I went… and trudged and trudged and trudged and trudged and….

And there it was. Down there, there it was: the village of Kirk Yetholm. The view I thought I'd never see. The place I thought I'd never reach.

And finally I cried.

Finally I cried, and now I couldn't *stop* crying. Now the only thing I knew how to do was cry. Years of shame and months of grief and weeks of stress and days of hope tumbled from my eyes as I stood above the sight I had imagined since 2003 and could finally picture. I wanted to look at it forever – to never forget this – but I couldn't see through the tears that were rolling down my face and so I started walking again, slowly first, then quicker, quicker still, until suddenly I was running. I was running towards the village and laughing as I did so, and the tears kept coming but they were tears of joy now. And I kept running and shouting, down the metalled road, wiping tears onto the ground, crying and laughing, through the fringe of little cottages and the Scottish flag fluttering and the little lane opening up and there – *there* – was the Border Inn Hotel, the finish line of the Pennine Way.

I had done it.

I had done it.

'Mistah Kurtz, he dead.'

* * *

I stopped and composed myself before walking the final 50 yards of my journey – the easiest 50 yards I have ever walked in my life. I didn't celebrate with shadow-boxing or one of those flips they do after a touchdown. In the end, a single clenched fist was all I felt like summoning.

There was no-one there to cheer me home, no welcoming committee or fanfare. A man walking his labrador across the village green glanced at me as you might a low-flying aircraft, then turned away to scoop up his dog's waste. A row of pebble-dashed houses, some whitewashed, some not, stretched off to my left with cars parked along the road. The Celestial City it was not, but that was OK – I had arrived.

I took Alan out of his pouch and hugged him.

'You're surely the first fox to complete the Pennine Way, Alan' I said.

*I am only an avatar for some of your darker, less redeemed thoughts, sire, as you know. But also, if I may: ******* get in, we did it, ******* come on!!*

I clenched my fist again and gave it a vigorous pump. Nobody else was there. At that moment a hire car driven by a lunatic was crossing the Scottish border to the East and making its faithful way towards me:

'I'm coming, Kindddyyyyy, I'm coming.'

I'd be gone within the hour.

I walked down to the Border Hotel and took several photos of it before going inside. I entered the establishment with low expectations – the guidebooks warn you that they've seen it all before and nobody really cares. I have to say though, that wasn't my experience. The man behind the bar heard the thud of leather boots on porcelain, bid me welcome and reached straight for the beer pump, for since the days of Wainwright a complimentary half-pint has been given to every walker who finishes the Pennine Way. How can you prove it, you might think? It's just dreadfully obvious.

'Congratulations!' he said with a beaming smile. 'How long did it take you?'

'16 days or 18 years depending on how you want to measure it.'

'16 days is good. Well done.'

He handed me the fabled walker's book in which lengthsmen and women have scrawled their epilogues down the years – some nonchalant, some exultant, a few petulant.

"I have done it and I feel like going all the way back and starting again," someone had written a couple of pages prior.

"Really glad to have done this. Can't wait for my hair to grow back," wrote Robert from Nottingham.

I sat there with a packet of crisps and a pen for 10 minutes before realising I had nothing to say. I was thinking about the 22-year-old who didn't get past Malham all those years ago, and wondering what he'd make of the bearded, peat-covered, life-stained 40-year-old with the sun-burnt scalp and fraying knee supports. I slotted a crisp into my mouth and closed my lips around it like a communion wafer.

'40!' I said. That was it. I opened the Bible app on my phone and looked for *Psalm 40,* wondering if something in there would provide a sufficient postscript.

"He lifted me out of the slimy pit,
out of the mud and mire;
he set my feet on a rock
and gave me a firm place to stand."

That would do. I also added, "If you're staying in Hebden Bridge, buy a tent. All the best, Andy Kind."

I bought another pint and went to sit outside on a bench to wait for Vino. I took off my coat and laid it on the chair, then turned to look back at the hills again one final time, along the length of the Pennine Way.

Somewhere back there, between the two points of a distant horizon, through the wastes and at the end of the desert, was my home. I just didn't live there yet. At some point in the future, I would tread upon the soft springy turf of redemption and my strength and joy would be restored – I believed that. And there was only one way to get there: one step at a time, one foot in front of another, right foot then left. I would just have to keep walking. That is, after all, what pilgrims do. Every single one of us.

I sat down onto the chair, onto my discarded raincoat, and heard a gentle, dismal crunch. Standing once more and reaching into my inside pocket, I pulled out a piece of cellophane with pieces of something no longer whole, and watched them fall irretrievably to the patioed ground.

My walnut, I said. *I have broken my lovely walnut.*

And for the second time that day, I began to cry.

The Wayfarers

By Rupert Brook

Is it the hour? We leave this resting-place
Made fair by one another for a while.
Now, for a god-speed, one last mad embrace;
The long road then, unlit by your faint smile.
Ah! the long road! and you so far away!
Oh, I'll remember! but … each crawling day
Will pale a little your scarlet lips, each mile
Dull the dear pain of your remembered face.

…Do you think there's a far border town, somewhere,
The desert's edge, last of the lands we know,
Some gaunt eventual limit of our light,
In which I'll find you waiting; and we'll go
Together, hand in hand again, out there,
Into the waste we know not, into the night?

THE END

AUTHOR'S NOTE

It's a personal proverb of mine that the only thing I've done that was harder than walking the Pennine Way was writing a book about walking the Pennine Way. If you've reached the end, however long it's taken you, I hope that you enjoyed the journey.

As I wrote towards the end of the book, I've endeavored to make *The Wayfarer* as accurate and faithful to the actual events and conversations as possible. Obviously I have used some creative license and tweaked a few things, but I tried to be both confined and freed by the unfolding of the walk as it happened. The book is always emotionally true, and usually factually so.

As is customary, there are people to thank...

Firstly, to Chris, Robert, Ruth and John, Angela, Tony, Phil and Jon for their company on the walk – it wouldn't have been the same without any of you. When can we do it again?

Next, massive thanks to Hannah Jones, Jacob Hussain and Amy Borrell for their work on the book cover through its many drafts. I'm so grateful. Also to Ruth Masters, who did the typesetting at short notice, so well and efficiently, whilst travelling the world.

To Joy and the gang at Broad Place Publishing, for some incredible service – we'll do another book soon!

And the team at St. Andrew's bookshop in Great Missenden, for their promotion and friendship – thank you!

A hearty nod of the cap to Charisa Gunasekera, for all the cheerleading she did for the book, and to James and Rachel Tweats for giving me a room to write in for free.

And I mustn't forget the people who let me read them excerpts as I went along – Tansy and Ross Garrod, Maria and Jon Boston, Tamsin and Chris Gaskell, Nicola Neal, Andrew Cowling, and that couple I stayed with in Dorchester who just wanted to go to bed.

Thanks to Stephen Pile's *The Book of Heroic Failures* for first telling me about Pedro Carolino.

I'm grateful to Alice Hardy, too, who used her Arabic skills to translate *Resurrection Man* for me.

Finally, special thanks to Lorna Farrell for all the help, support, prayer and counsel over the years. You deserved a place in this book, and so here it is!

You can contact me to tell me what you thought of the book: andy@andykind.co.uk. I'm easily found on social media, too. And please, if you *have* enjoyed it, do review it on your preferred reviewing platform – and include Alan in your review! He hasn't had too much to do since we came home.

Books sell through word of mouth, so post your thoughts online, share the story with loved ones, harangue strangers – just have fun with it, basically.

For now, we trudge on.

Andy

Also by the author:

Stand Up and Deliver
The Gig Delusion
The Unfortunate Adventures of Tom Hillingthwaite
Hidden in Plain Sight
Curious Tales of Redemption
A Blanket of Embers

Available on Amazon

Find out more about Andy from his website:
www.andykind.co.uk

9781068257100

BV - #0047 - 230126 - C0 - 211/140/19 - PB - 9781068257100 - Matt Lamination